AF361494

Drawing Back Culture

Drawing Back Culture

The Makah Struggle for Repatriation

ANN M. TWEEDIE

Foreword by Janine Bowechop

A McLellan Book

UNIVERSITY OF WASHINGTON PRESS

Seattle and London

This book is published with the assistance of a grant from the
McLellan Endowed Series Fund, established through the generosity
of Martha McCleary McLellan and Mary McLellan Williams.

Copyright © 2002 by the University of Washington Press

Library of Congress Cataloging-in-Publication Data
Tweedie, Ann M.
Drawing back culture : the Makah struggle for repatriation /
Ann M. Tweedie ; foreword by Janine Bowechop.
p. cm.
"A McLellan book."
Includes bibliographical references and index.
ISBN 0-295-98195-4 (alk. paper)
1. Makah Indians.
2. Makah Indians—Antiquities.
I. Title.
E99.M19T88 2002   979.7004'97—dc21   2001048087

TO MY PARENTS

CONTENTS

FOREWORD

The policy of Indian self-determination was introduced in 1974, but did not encompass Indian control of sacred or religious objects until the passage of the Native American Graves Protection and Repatriation Act (NAGPRA) in 1990. While each tribe will interpret the legislation slightly differently, we are now able to share, via Ann Tweedie's eyes and ears, a uniquely Makah perspective on repatriation. The Makah tribe has had the advantage of extensive experience communicating with museum, agency, and university professionals, as a result of thirty years of involvement with the Ozette excavation and the Makah Cultural and Research Center (MCRC). The Makah have successfully invited and encouraged returns of objects even outside the boundaries of NAGPRA.

The MCRC plans to make the most of the information shared during NAGPRA compliance. Already, the increased communication and interaction with other museums during repatriation consultations have resulted in benefits to the Makah tribe. The benefits cannot simply be measured by the number of artifacts returned to Makah individuals or to the tribe. Makah artists have seen rare photographs of cultural objects made five generations ago. Makah elders have had opportunities to transmit knowledge and information during interviews concerning repatriation. Even our high school students have been exposed to discussions about regaining control of and access to our important cultural objects.

The collecting of Makah material culture has a history strewn with corruption and deceit on the part of collectors. *Drawing Back Culture* gives us a clearer picture of the Makah side of this history. We can now better understand both the cultural and political contexts of early collecting and current Makah repatriation efforts. Ann's work is the first attempt to document a Northwest Coast tribe's current attitudes, perspectives, and activities related to repatriation of material culture. Her research reveals Makah people and customs to be both honorable and fallible. Ann was expected by the MCRC and her colleagues to look hard for the truths, even if these truths are not always flattering. Makah improprieties are not cloaked in rhetoric by the author, although some cultural anthropologists would make a point of excusing the acts of disenfranchised people driven by an oppressive situation. Nor does she feel the need to defend anthropologists and white collectors. Her ability to be objective will ultimately help the Makah people.

Because Ann carefully met the requirements of working through the Makah Cultural and Research Center, she was expected to conduct her research with respect for Makah sovereignty and treaty rights and to be thorough and consistent with her methodology. Ann met and exceeded all of the MCRC's expectations. She supplied the MCRC archives with transcribed copies of her recorded oral history interviews and with references that it had not yet located. The data generated by Ann's project is invaluable to the Makah tribe, and this volume will be available for all Makah tribal members in the MCRC research library. Our plans for future repatriation will be aided by her work.

Although tribal and museum repatriation programs must be developed for specific communities and cultures, other tribes and museums will find much of value in this history and case study, as will all those with an interest in tribal affairs and material culture. It is both a serious and significant work of scholarship and an emotionally engaging success story.

JANINE BOWECHOP
Executive Director
Makah Cultural and Research Center

ACKNOWLEDGMENTS

My appreciation goes first to the people of Neah Bay. I would especially like to thank the elders, heads of families, members of the Tribal Council, and others who participated in my research. The board and staff of the Makah Cultural and Research Center, particularly Janine Bowechop and Greig Arnold, deserve my sincere thanks for guiding me through the intricacies of Makah NAGPRA implementation and supporting this project. Melissa Peterson and Keely Parker served as valuable assistants during fieldwork. To all—*klecko, klecko*!

I greatly appreciate the support my family, friends, and mentors have provided to this endeavor. Thanks go to my parents, Pat and Steve, my brother, David, and to Gretchen Grozier, Sven Haakanson Jr., and Jennifer Sepez for their unfailing confidence and encouragement. Those many others who contributed in small but important ways to the successful completion of this book also have my sincerest gratitude.

I would especially like to recognize the anthropology faculty at Harvard University, notably Rubie Watson, Michael Herzfeld, and Kay Warren, who read many drafts of early versions and made valuable suggestions. The constructive advice of three anonymous reviewers from the University of Washington Press clarified several points and made the manuscript more readable. I am also grateful for the helpful staff at the University of Washington Press, and in particular Jacqueline Ettinger for her masterful editing. None of these individuals is responsible for any interpretations or inaccuracies in this work.

ACKNOWLEDGMENTS

Finally, I must thank my colleagues at Interpretive Solutions, Inc. for providing a supportive atmosphere in which to bring this project to fruition.

Financial support for the research phase of this project was gratefully received from the Wenner-Gren Foundation for Anthropological Research, the Mellon Foundation, and Harvard University.

PREFACE

I t was a warm day in mid-August, and the gathered crowd spilled out the doors of the community hall hoping to catch a breeze; inside it was hot and congested. I had been living on the Makah Reservation for two months when I was invited, along with the rest of the community, to a potlatch. On this occasion, three adolescents from one of the largest and most prominent families of the village were being given Makah names. My parents, who had just arrived for a visit, were thrilled to have an opportunity to attend such a cultural event accompanied by their anthropologist daughter. After exhaustively lecturing them on proper potlatch etiquette, we entered the community hall at the start of the festivities. Following a celebratory midday meal, the tables were cleared from the floor and I secured seats for my guests where they would have a good view of the events to follow. This was not the first such party I had attended; there had been several others since I arrived in the village of Neah Bay. This one, however, had promised to be on a much grander scale. Indeed, the elaborate decorations, the fresh flowers on the dining tables, and the huge attendance seemed to bear this out.

The formal naming ceremony was the first event, followed by dances performed by a series of families to honor the adolescents; the host family would dance last, just prior to passing out their gifts to the community. Returning periodically to explain what I could to my parents about the dances, I circulated around the hall seeking out friends and greeting acquaintances. Then, quite unexpectedly, Greig Arnold, the designated speaker for the evening, called out my parents' names. Their eyes sought mine across the room; this was the one contingency for which I had not thought it necessary to prepare them. It is customary, after each family presents its dances, for them to honor selected attendees with small monetary gifts. The Bowechops, in-laws of Janine Bowechop, director of the Makah Cultural and Research Center (MCRC), had just done this to my parents. Looking quite shocked, but behaving precisely as I would have advised, my father modestly accepted the proffered bills. It was my turn next, and as Greig announced my name, he added for the benefit of the Makah community that I was working at the MCRC and would be in residence in Neah Bay throughout the winter. Later in the evening, Janine's own family, the Markishtums, also acknowledged my parents in this manner. To complete my introduction to the community, and much to the amusement of my parents, I was later forced out onto the floor to participate in one of the social dances.

The events of that day served as my formal introduction to the wider Makah community. My presence was sanctioned through the actions of these two prominent Makah families; in this forum the approval of the MCRC, which oversees all research conducted on the reservation, was communicated. At the time, Greig was the person overseeing implementation of the Native American Graves Protection and Repatriation Act (NAGPRA) at the MCRC, which was my research focus. He had mentioned to me several days prior to this potlatch that people in Neah Bay had seen me around and wondered who I was. I was clearly not a tourist. He had then commented that "everything would be taken care of on Saturday." At the time I was unaware of his meaning, but obviously my introduction in this manner had been planned. In a society where family is so valued, I believe that the presence of my parents at the potlatch lent further evidence that I was a reputable individual.

The setting in which the above events transpired was the Makah Indian Reservation, home to approximately 60 percent of the twenty-two hundred Makahs.[1] It occupies about fifty-five square miles on the tip of Washington State's Olympic Peninsula (fig. 1). Cape Flattery, as the region is known, is bordered on the north by the Strait of Juan de Fuca which separates the United States from Canada's Vancouver Island. On the western side of the reservation are sweeping Pacific Ocean beaches. The reservation and its main village, Neah Bay, are isolated and accessible by land only from the east along a winding road precariously perched between the waters of the strait and the hilly, heavily forested terrain that meets it. The nearest village is Clallam Bay, a thirty-minute drive, where there is a bank and a public library. The nearest town center is Forks, an hour's drive, and the closest commercial center is Port Angeles, an hour and a half to the east.

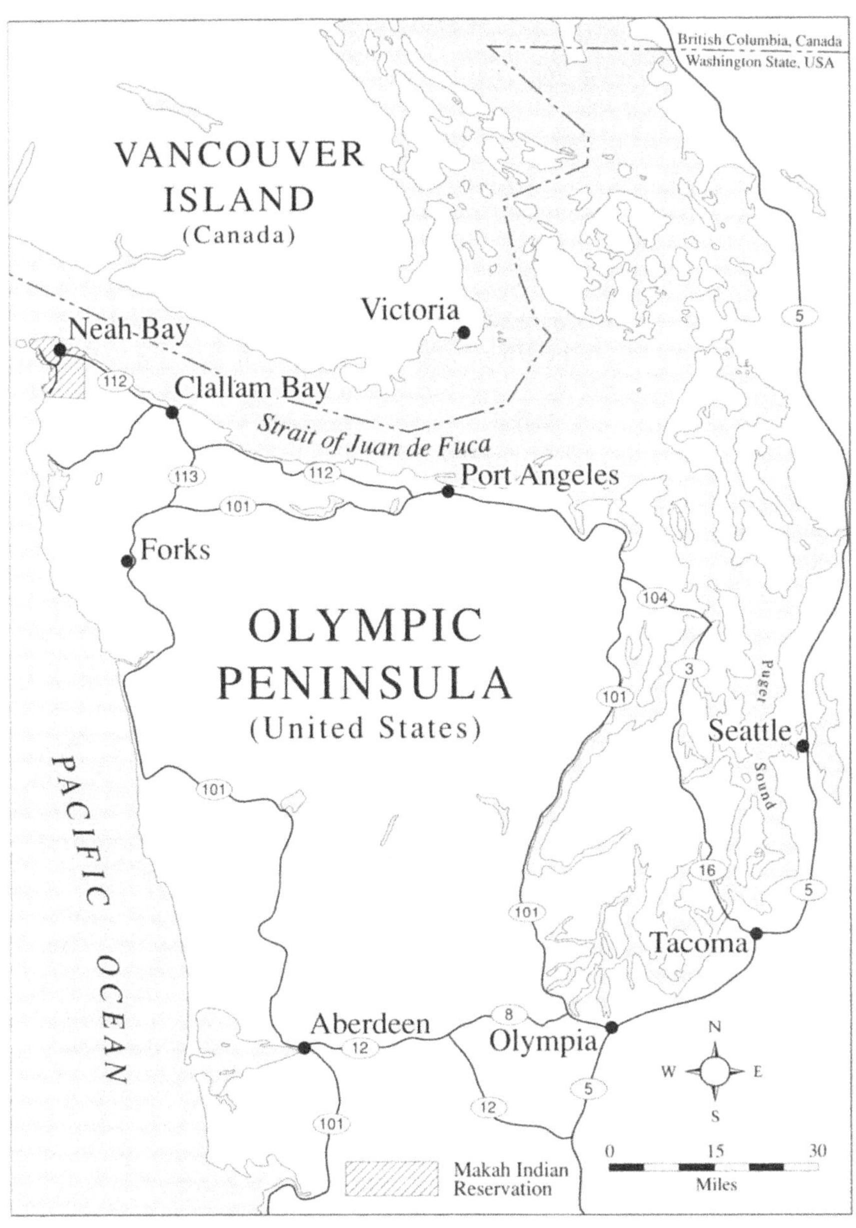

FIG. 1. The Makah Indian Reservation, which occupies about fifty-five square miles at the tip of the Olympic Peninsula, contains the most northwesterly point in the contiguous United States. It takes about five hours by car and ferry to reach Seattle.

On a clear day, the approach to the reservation is breathtaking, with glimpses of the sparkling blue waters of the strait and the green hills of Vancouver Island to the north and rolling hills of forested green (although heavily logged in places) to the south. The first indication a visitor has of the reservation is a large white sign decorated with the Makah crest, a thunderbird with a whale in its talons, marking the reservation's boundary. Soon smaller signs nailed to trees begin to advertise local businesses—craft shops, a pizzeria, and a motel. As the road crests a hill, an area cleared from the surrounding forest marks the active Makah cemetery. A quarter mile farther, a group of buildings can be seen on a small rise to the north along with a large wooden sign that reads "Makah Agency." These buildings formerly housed the Bureau of Indian Affairs and have been remodeled to serve as the headquarters of the Makah Forestry Enterprise, Inc. From here, the road descends into the main village and as it rounds a curve one sees the harbor and buildings which run along the bay.

Like Makah villages in precontact times, Neah Bay is oriented towards the water. The village and the bay after which it is named face the strait in a valley between two hills (fig. 2). While a substantial percentage of the reservation's eighteen hundred residents live in this low-lying area, two large housing developments are located in the hills at each end of town. Front Street is the main thoroughfare and separates the beach from the first row of houses and public buildings. Residential streets along the length of the village run parallel to the beach. There are approximately five hundred homes on the reservation with an average of four members per household.[2] The first public building which greets visitors is the Makah Cultural and Research Center, referred to locally as the museum, which occupies two large modern buildings on the south side of the main road across from an active Coast Guard base.[3] Just past the museum are several large wooden signs which visitors are instructed to stop and read. These discuss the reservation's no alcohol policy, the use of public beaches and natural resources, and other useful information.

As the road continues along the waterfront, it passes a few houses, a small motel, the post office, the Makah Maiden Cafe, Washburn's General Store, the new marina offices, a commercial fishing dock, the Makah business center (which contains a few tourist shops, a pizzeria, the smoke shop, and a small cafe), and Makah Fuel. The remainder of the waterfront is open beach, with private houses on the inland side of the street. On the west side of the bay, the Senior Center is built directly on the beach. Nearby is a large covered fire pit for cooking salmon and several long, narrow canoe sheds.

FIG. 2. The village of Neah Bay looking northeast. Vancouver Island is visible beyond the Strait of Juan de Fuca. Photograph by the author.

Other public buildings in the village include the Indian Health Service clinic, several small churches, the public school campus and athletic fields, a Head Start facility, and the community hall. The Tribe's government offices are located in buildings outside of the village at the site of a former Air Force base.[4]

The overall aspect of Neah Bay is that of a moderately prosperous rural community. Most of the buildings I have described were built or extensively renovated in the last twenty years. Within the village itself, interspersed with settled blocks, are plots of wooded land and empty lots.[5] Along Front Street, there are a number of RV resorts, abandoned when the Tribe did not renew contracts with non-Makah businesses. The 300 non-Indian residents and 350 non-Makah resident Indians are allowed to build houses or commercial establishments on the reservation, but the Tribe retains ownership of the land. Land for residential development is becoming an increasingly pressing issue, as the local population has been steadily growing because of substantial in-migration, mostly by Makahs, and an increased birth rate.[6] Projections indicate that the population of Neah Bay will double between 1992 and 2011 (MEDP 1992).

The majority of the Makah Reservation consists of forested hills which the Tribe utilizes for timber and from which individuals gather wood, basketry materials, and berries and procure fish, elk, deer, and bear (fig. 3).

Aside from the village itself, the only flat lands within the reservation are the floodplains of the Waatch and Tsooes Rivers, which are used for livestock grazing. There is a network of logging roads that were initially built by commercial timber companies and are now utilized and maintained by the Makah Forestry Enterprise. Over one thousand acres of land bordering the Pacific Ocean have been reserved as Makah Wilderness Areas, and the offshore waters are part of the Olympic Coast National Marine Sanctuary.

My arrival and subsequent anthropological investigations in this majestic setting had their inception many years earlier. My first awareness of NAGPRA occurred in 1993, during work at Harvard University's Peabody Museum. I was immediately fascinated by the law's complications and welcomed the intellectual challenges it presented. Even at these early stages of my involvement, I recognized NAGPRA as an arena in which cultural worldviews would conflict, but within which they must also be negotiated. Clifford (1997:188–219), following Pratt (1992), has referred to museums as "contact zones," a concept equally applicable to NAGPRA. As I worked within the NAGPRA framework over the years, first for the Peabody and later with the National Park Service (NPS), my interest in the negotiated aspects of NAGPRA deepened. I had intimately participated in the implementation process from the institutional side. What was going on, I asked myself, at the tribal level? Surely tribes were having to do some negotiating of their own; I had observed some of this in tribal visits to collections at the Peabody. Moreover, I wondered, would NAGPRA do for tribes what it was intended to do?

With these thoughts simmering in my mind, I arrived in the summer of 1997 on the Makah Reservation. My choice of field site was both conscious and fortuitous. I had narrowed potential collaborating tribes to those having a tribal museum or cultural center and therefore an existing institutional framework for implementing the law. Additionally, I targeted tribes that had applied for and received grants through the NPS for NAGPRA implementation. Many tribes at that time, and many still, were not in a position to dedicate the monetary or human resources to deal seriously with NAGPRA. For my research to be most productive, I needed one that was actively involved. The Makah Tribe met these criteria. Moreover, the MCRC Board, to which I formally applied for permission to conduct this research, was open to a researcher exploring this very sensitive topic. This was, in fact, the only tribe I contacted which responded positively to my inquiry. As it turned out, I could not have asked for a better intellectual match, as Makah

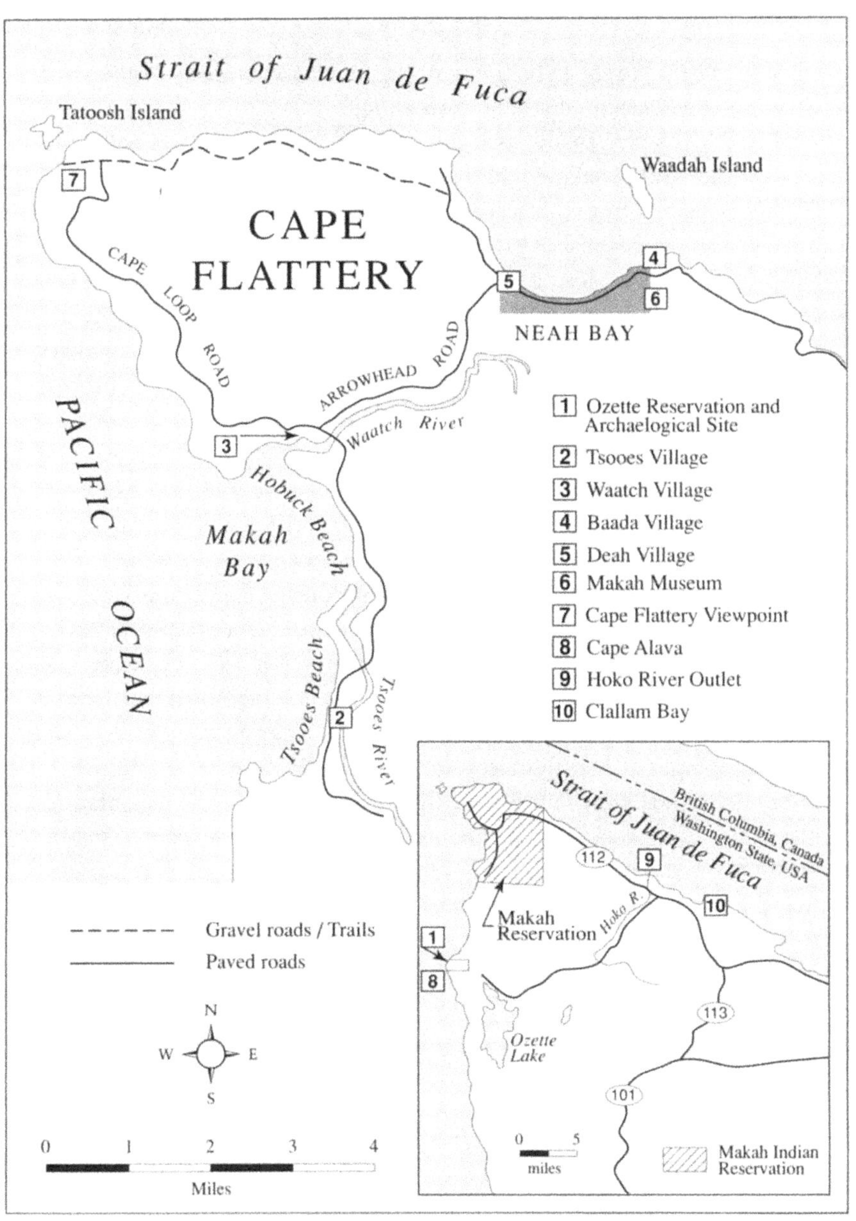

FIG. 3. The Makah Indian Reservation consists mostly of undeveloped land. With the exception of Ozette, residential areas are still clustered around former village sites. (Adapted from the Makah Nation Visitors' Guide.)

tribal members proved to be thoughtfully mulling over many of the same issues that had been on my mind for so long.

One might be led to ask, as I did, why the Makah Tribe was willing to support this work. I believe that there are several reasons. It has a long tradition of collaborating with academic researchers and thus this was a familiar role. It has an established procedure for overseeing and maintaining control over such work. Most importantly, MCRC board members and staff saw an opportunity to gain professional assistance with NAGPRA implementation. One of the criteria a successful proposal must meet is that the project will in some way benefit the Tribe. The tribal implementation process would immediately benefit from my familiarity with the federal NAGPRA universe, my experiences working with the National Park Service, and knowledge of repatriation procedures at Harvard's Peabody Museum. Working with the tribal NAGPRA program was expected of me, but at the same time this philosophy coincided with my personal inclinations.

I performed a number of tasks for the Tribe during the fieldwork period. These included creating an organizational and reference system for NAGPRA inventories and summaries the Tribe had received from museums and federal agencies; reading diaries of an early reservation school teacher and taking notes about his collecting practices; and, on a trip to Cambridge, taking photographs of Makah objects in the Peabody Museum. In addition to these intentional contributions to the Tribe's NAGPRA implementation, interviews conducted with members of the community as part of my research had unexpected benefits. Several MCRC board members recognized that the kinds of questions I was asking tribal members were an excellent means for "taking the pulse of the community" about NAGPRA. They had not anticipated this benefit when approving my project. Thus, interviews conducted for my own research took on the role of a public service, since through them I was educating community members about the law. Findings from these interviews were summarized for MCRC staff members just prior to my departure.

The question must be raised as to what impact my participation had on the very process I set out to explore. From the beginning, I was certainly aware of the difficulties inherent to my situation. However, it is a rare anthropologist these days who does not find herself pondering similar scenarios. My solution was to refrain from actively making suggestions or offering guidance, in an attempt to moderate my influence on the direction or nature of Makah NAGPRA implementation. Instead, I carried out the tasks with which I was specifically asked to assist. I have identified to date two aspects of the Tribe's implementation of NAGPRA that would have been fundamentally different without my presence: my archival reading made this material available slightly earlier in the process and my interviews made more members of the community aware of NAGPRA. The tribal NAGPRA staff's planned research, community interviews, and educational meetings about NAGPRA would have accomplished both of these in time.

Since my departure from Neah Bay, my involvement with Makah NAGPRA implementation has continued. I hosted Greig and Janine when they came to the Peabody Museum in November 1998 on a NAGPRA consultation visit. More recently, at the Tribe's request I drafted a document to assist museums nationwide in identifying Makah and Nuu-chah-nulth objects in collections which might be subject to NAGPRA. (Nuu-chah-nulth or Nootka is the broader cultural group to which the Makah belong.) That document is part of the final report forwarded to the National Park Service at the completion of the Tribe's NAGPRA grant. In the fall of 1999, I helped with the Tribe's application for another NPS grant to further NAGPRA activities at the MCRC.

The reader has thus far received a glimpse of my place within this fieldwork setting, but a few more words on the topic will be informative. The Makah Cultural and Research Center was my primary base of operations. It served as my official affiliation and it was there that I had an office. I spent at least several hours a day at the MCRC and came to know staff members well, many of them both socially and professionally. Through them, I met not only their families, but MCRC board members, elders, artists, and others who were associated with the facility in some capacity. At cultural events, these individuals also took pains to introduce me to a range of tribal members interested in cultural issues, who they thought might be informative interviewees. In addition to the NAGPRA tasks mentioned above, I lent a hand to the overworked staff whenever possible in other ways. Sometimes I drove elders to and from the museum for meetings. On another occasion, I helped to clean tanks where wooden archaeological artifacts were being treated. In addition, I was volunteered to construct the MCRC's entry for the Makah Days parade, a task annually avoided by staff as it comes at the busiest time of year.

I also had a residential base of operations which was as important as, if not more important than, my official one. I rented a room from Marj Chartraw, a Makah woman in her thirties, and her young daughter Lori, and they became my family. They live, like nearly 50 percent of tribal members, in a home owned by the Makah Housing Authority and built with funds from the

U.S. Department of Housing and Urban Development (HUD).[7] Through everyday interactions with my hostess's frequent visitors, I came to know many of her friends and extended family members. I became acquainted with an astonishing number of children through interactions with Lori's playmates. It was rare for me to attend a village event where I was not subsequently accosted by them, much to the confusion of their parents whom I often had not yet met. Marj was exceedingly generous and patiently put up with my frequently antisocial academic habits, incessant questions, and steady flow of out-of-town visitors.

Just as I had physical locations in the field, my research also had a "place," one not always defined by me. Soon after I arrived in Neah Bay, it became clear that there were certain topics that I could not or should not explore with tribal members. As time passed, I noted that my attempts to acquire knowledge about certain subjects were routinely unsatisfactory. My gender limited access to knowledge about whaling, which is a strictly male occupation in Makah culture. Even female tribal members have limited knowledge of many of its aspects. Thus, I did not attempt to directly explore specifics surrounding the contemporary whaling issue. Not being a member of a Makah family meant that I could not obtain specific information regarding spiritual practices or sacred objects. This I had been prepared for and so avoided asking about except in very general ways. While I sought to find out from interviewees what objects they would consider to fit under the NAGPRA definition of a sacred object, for example, I did not press them for information about how such objects were used. Much information of this kind is kept within individual families and would not be shared even with other tribal members. Data of this nature that appear below come from previously published sources.

Not being a tribal member hindered my ability to directly explore questions involving status. While a few interviewees would discuss past status distinctions, virtually none would comment on the present situation. Because this seems to be a critical aspect of NAGPRA implementation on the Makah Reservation, this particular gap in the research is frustrating at best. I had no wish to disrespect my hosts by pressing the issue, and therefore the limited discussions of status in this book are based on information gleaned through that greatest strength of ethnographic research—participant observation. Overall, I do not feel that the delineated "place" my research was given has unduly affected the outcomes or compromised the quality of the ethnography that follows.

Readers will perhaps note in the text a certain ambiguity in my analytical approach. As fieldwork progressed, I quickly became aware of an innate tension between my applied and theoretical interests in NAGPRA. My applied interests grew quite naturally out of my first-hand experience implementing NAGPRA in institutional settings and observing the nuts and bolts of the process at a national level. During fieldwork, these applied interests resulted in a careful documentation of the Makah Tribe's NAGPRA process and discussions with tribal members about priorities and goals. I wanted to know simply whether or not NAGPRA was "working" at the local level. Was it having (or will it have) its intended effect for the Makah Tribe? Will the Tribe be able to accomplish its goals under NAGPRA? What is unique about Makah implementation when compared to other tribes? Finally, what can be learned about tribal implementation of NAGPRA on the Northwest Coast from close examination of the Makah Tribe's process?

On the theoretical side, my deep fascination with the law as an arena of negotiation, required a different set of questions. These I explored through in-depth discussions with individuals directly involved in NAGPRA implementation. Did they perceive a lack of fit between the legislation and Makah material culture? If so, what strategies would they employ to negotiate the incongruity? I believe this tension between applied and theoretical approaches to NAGPRA to be a healthy one, alternately compelling me to remain minutely aware of the actual implementation process and forcing me to take a step back and observe NAGPRA from a wider perspective. As my personal interests, as well as those of my anticipated audience, are divided between these approaches, I have sought in this book to concurrently explore both.

One final note here on a convention I used throughout the text. Readers will notice that tribal members are sometimes not identified by name. In general, I agree with the current attitude among cultural anthropologists that suppressing individual identities of interviewees in ethnographic writing privileges the voice of the ethnographic author and gives the impression that all members of a community are interchangeable. Nevertheless, I also believe that there are some instances in which the practice is justified. This is one of them. There are aspects of NAGPRA which are very contentious within the Makah community. As will be seen, contested ownership among Makah individuals and families over objects is a central issue that must be negotiated and resolved to enable the Tribe to participate productively in implementation. Preserving the anonymity of individuals allowed them to express their concerns and desires without fear of reprisal from other Makahs.

Despite the necessity to conceal individual identities, I have not suppressed individual voices and still make use of extensive quotations. I have made the difficult decision to omit much contextual information about specific interviewees that may have been enlightening to readers. In a small community, such material would make individuals as identifiable as if I had provided names. Even with these precautions, I am under no illusion that this solution will fully prevent tribal members from recognizing each other in this work. While I regret the necessity of such conventions, my intended audience includes members of the Makah Tribe, many of whom will doubtlessly read this book. And it is to them that I owe my greatest debt.

Drawing Back Culture

Introduction

"DRAWING BACK CULTURE"

Now is the future. We keep up the struggle started long ago. We advise our lawyers. We send our children to college. We stock our streams with salmon. We run our own museum. We attempt to strengthen our families with tradition. We continue to live with drums in our hands, with a song on our lips, with our children before us. The desire to hunt whale returns.

—Exhibit text, Makah Cultural and Research Center, 1989

Consider the following hypothetical scenario. A whaling harpoon point collected in 1865 has spent 135 years in a major museum in the eastern United States (fig. 4). From the distinctive markings incised on its bone barbs, it is agreed to have belonged to a Makah ancestor whom many tribal members identify as their great-grandfather. This whaler's descendents now include the heads of three families in Neah Bay as well as prominent members of several others. All agree that the point should be drawn back to the community as a sacred object, for its role in spiritual preparation for whaling, and simply because it belonged to a famous Makah ancestor. Each family head seeks to establish himself as the descendent to whom this harpoon point would have passed if it had not left. Descendents from other families express the concern that they will not have access to it if one of these family heads receives it. Someone suggests that perhaps it should be stored in the MCRC for safekeeping, but this does not address the question of who could use it. One family head, whose son is currently in training for the next whale hunt, would like to see this harpoon point incorporated as a prayer tool in current spiritual preparation, in hopes that the success of this illustrious whaler will positively influence current en-

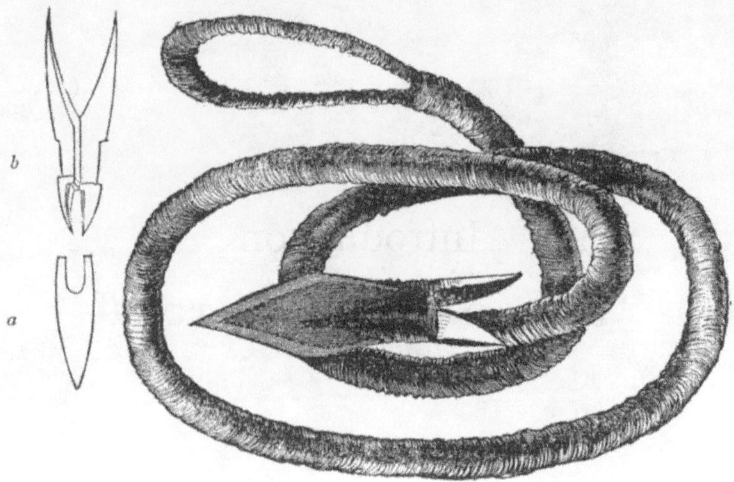

Harpoon point (kwe-kāhptl) and line. *a.* Blade. *b.* Barbs.

FIG. 4. This whaling harpoon point is made of iron or copper, horn, and spruce gum. Originally, points were made of mussel shell. Harpoon points will probably be sought for repatriation by Makah families as sacred objects. Sketch by James Swan, ca. 1870. Courtesy of Manuscripts and Special Collections, University Archives Division, University of Washington Libraries, neg. #UW18702.

deavors. Others disapprove, saying that the object is too fragile to be extensively handled. They suggest that perhaps it could be replicated, but cannot decide who should have the right to do so. Other tribal members, while recognizing the descendents' rights to decide this object's fate, have their own ideas. Some of them feel it should be the focus of educational programs and be shared with the wider Makah community. Some people even feel that it would be appropriate to display it in the MCRC alongside examples of five-hundred-year-old harpoon points excavated at the former Makah village of Ozette, thus educating non-native visitors as well.

NAGPRA was passed by Congress in 1990 to provide a mechanism for tribes to address scenarios such as this. Through NAGPRA, they can reclaim specific objects, such as sacred whaling gear, from museum and federal agency collections nationwide. This is not by any means a straightforward process, as shall be seen, and physically returning objects to the community is often only the first step in the negotiations. This book documents a struggle, to adopt the term from the exhibit text quoted above, to reconcile past practices to contemporary life. Of central concern is the contested ownership and control of cultural goods. By ownership issues in this book I am *not* referring to potential conflicts between the Tribe and institutions over title to specific objects, but to negotiations surrounding the nature of ownership itself.

In precontact Makah culture, the social hierarchy was based on private ownership, not only of objects but also of rights and other intangible property. Ownership was strictly private and jealously guarded. In the above scenario, not only the harpoon point but the distinctive incised markings, the right to hunt whales, and the specific means of spiritual preparations were owned by this tribal ancestor. The property sought for repatriation represents not only an object, but rights to associated practices and status as well.

Today, the negotiations and struggles surrounding ownership are occurring on two separate levels: between tribal members and outside constituents such as museum personnel, and among tribal members themselves. In relationships with outside constituents, the Tribe's struggle is to depict tribal ownership patterns in a manner which allows them to take advantage of the opportunities offered by NAGPRA. Within the Tribe, the innate tension between tribal unity and the autonomy of its constituent extended families is a recurring theme. Once successfully repatriated, how should cultural goods be controlled within the Makah community? This book addresses the major issues in these negotiations from both historical and cultural perspectives. It is an account of a process.

The debates which surface in NAGPRA implementation also underlie other cultural events in the Makah community and thus NAGPRA should not be considered in isolation. Community discussions over issues of ownership and material culture have been spurred in the last three decades by two other key events in the cultural life of the Makah Tribe: a series of archaeological excavations and the Tribe's recent return to whaling.

The Tribe initiated excavations at the former Makah village site of Ozette in 1970 when winter storms began washing artifacts out of an earthen bank. What began as an emergency stabilization project to protect the area from looters evolved into a ten-year excavation which generated 55,000 well-preserved wood, bone, and basketry artifacts dating to around 1500 C.E. (fig. 5). While significant to scientists, the excavations had an even greater impact on the Makah community, spurring them to build a state-of-the-art museum and cultural center. A comprehensive tribal cultural preservation program was subsequently developed. On a cultural level, interest in tribal history and especially artistic traditions intensified. Many tribal members credit the continued strength of such programs to the experiences today's

FIG. 5. A cedar wall panel incised with a thunderbird and a wooden whaling saddle, dating to around 1500 C.E., was excavated during the 1970s at the former Makah village of Ozette. Shown on display in the Makah Cultural and Research Center. Photograph by Yasu Osawa. Courtesy of the MCRC.

leaders had of the Ozette excavations in their youth. I will return to discussions of the cultural impact of Ozette below.

On 17 May 1999, a Makah crew successfully brought in the first gray whale hunted by tribal members in over seventy years. The proposed hunt generated media frenzies and protests by environmentalists even prior to the International Whaling Commission's (IWC) October 1997 ruling that the Makah could proceed. The victorious IWC vote and the successful hunt itself energized the Makah community in a way not seen since Ozette, and with even greater intensity. Whaling is more than mere hunting to Makahs. It is a treaty right that needs protecting at all costs. It is a strong statement of cultural continuity and strength of tradition. Most importantly, it echoes an ancestral way of life in which whaling traditions anchored the spiritual lives and social structure of the entire society. It was, and is, tied up with ownership issues, social hierarchy and status, sacred objects, and other whaling-related material culture.

I conceptually linked Ozette, whaling, and NAGPRA soon after my arrival in the field, both because of shared cultural themes and actual or potential impacts on tribal cultural life. To my surprise and pleasure, I discovered that my interviewees independently made similar connections. Steve Jimmicum, a very thoughtful MCRC board member, succinctly captured these relationships when he described the three activities collectively as opportunities to "draw back culture." In the case of the Ozette excavations and NAGPRA, this drawing back literally means gathering artifacts and expanding the material culture resources of the tribe. Culture, as represented by physical objects, is drawn back through repatriation and excavation. Furthermore, the return of objects encourages the bringing forth of intangible cultural resources that have been dormant. Fostering positive interest in cultural activities such as whaling means that people who know songs and dances, but perhaps have not previously performed or taught them, might be encouraged to bring them out. It is almost as though these songs, stories, and dances are waiting patiently in the background for the right person and the right time to come forth. As George Bowechop, a head of family, explained, "Families have some songs they have not brought out yet. And I don't know if they don't know the words or what it is. But some songs have not come out yet."

Material culture plays a role in this bringing out, as visual images dislodge Makah language terms, oral history stories, and song melodies and words long stored away. A brief illustration from my own experience emphasizes this point. My interviews with elders were designed to elicit stories about specific kinds of cultural objects that they had perhaps seen or used in their youth. I found that few concrete memories were forthcoming until I brought in photographs of masks, headdresses, rattles, and other items. In a similar manner, it is the hope that bringing back objects under NAGPRA will result in more than simply pride of possession. As NAGPRA indeed intends, the potential return of sacred objects will give tribal members further opportunities for drawing back the songs and dances to which these objects belong.

Ozette, whaling, and NAGPRA share another important attribute; all are foci around which other cultural practices can be encouraged and provide the impetus for interest in other aspects of culture. Steve identified these three activities collectively as opportunities to "draw in lots of culture." Further discussions revealed that by this he meant that high-profile events attract the interest of tribal members who might not otherwise be culturally active. For example, many young men who are training as whalers do not regularly participate at potlatches or other community gatherings. Once these individuals are "drawn in," they can be introduced to other related aspects of culture. They might, for example, become interested in learning spiritual practices and Makah songs related to whaling. In this instance, whaling provides both a lure and a window into other aspects of cultural practice for tribal members. On a much grander scale, the same effect happened as a result of the Ozette excavation. The enthusiasm generated by that undertaking eventually resulted in the founding of the MCRC. In the last twenty years, numerous other programs have grown out of this facility, from the Makah Language Program to an ethnobotanical garden.

"Drawing back culture" is clearly another example of the intensified interest and participation in past cultural practices that have occurred in Native American communities in the latter half of the twentieth century. Other scholars have variously discussed similar phenomena as the "reinvention of tradition" (Hobsbawm and Ranger 1983), and "revitalization" or "cultural resurgence" (Clifford 1988; Warren 1998). While it is clear that the artifacts recovered from Ozette, the passage of NAGPRA, and the successful return to whaling each give the Makah Tribe new opportunities for strengthening tribal culture and identity, it is not so clear what terminology is appropriate. Some tribal members would object to the idea of "reinvention" since it implies that contemporary activities differ in significant ways from past practices. Despite the current generation's lack of practical experience in hunting whales, for example, George forcefully told me:

> I think our procedures and preparation and training of Makahs are . . . pretty well set. I think they're going to understand exactly what's required; what their responsibilities [are] in relationship to each other. . . . I think the Makahs pretty well know . . . about whaling. (Interview, 12 March 1998)

In other words, there is no need to "reinvent" practice because it is already known. I choose to employ the terms "resurgence" and "revitalization" when writing of the Makah Tribe, because they imply an intensification of practices that have been (at least sporadically) ongoing. For whaling, "renewal" seems the most appropriate term.

The theme of resurgence or drawing back culture recurs throughout this book in discussions of the MCRC, the effects of the Ozette excavations on the Makah community, and NAGPRA implementation. Whaling is a unique example of renewal among North American tribes, for all other whaling nations have had continuous traditions.[1] It is in a sense most comparable to contemporary interest among Plains groups in reviving buffalo hunts. Any return to past practice engenders controversy, and many Makah tribal members critically evaluate the current phenomenon of resurgence. Some of them feel that returning to whaling is foolhardy, or at best misguided; likewise, others feel that objects subject to NAGPRA "belong on the museum shelf and should stay there" and should not be reincorporated into ongoing ceremonies.

A number of excellent in-depth case studies on NAGPRA implementation at the tribal level have informed the discussions in this book. Notable among them are accounts of the Smithsonian's repatriation of *Ahayu:da* to Zuni Pueblo (Merrill et al. 1993) and human remains to Larsen Bay, Alaska (Bray and Killion 1994), as well as the Peabody Museum's repatriation of a sacred pole to the Omaha (Ridington and Hastings 1997). While my ethnography contributes to this literature by adding a new regional focus, it also departs from the works cited in significant ways. First, to my knowledge it is the only research to date on NAGPRA to result from long-term fieldwork in a native community. Second, while the above works address actual repatriations after their successful completion, I focus on a more preliminary stage of the process and one in which the majority of tribes currently find themselves. This book has also benefited extensively from the numerous treatments of NAGPRA which have appeared in anthropological, museological, and legal journals.[2] With the tenth anniversary of NAGPRA in November 2000, a new crop of publications has focused on evaluating its efficacy to date.[3]

A contemporaneous study by Aldona Jonaitis (1999) with another Nuu-chah-nulth group on a closely related topic conceptually mirrors this one. In 1905, George Hunt purchased a whaling shrine from two Mowachaht chiefs and sent it to the anthropologist Franz Boas at the American Museum of Natural History in New York City. Jonaitis examines the shrine's history from its original context to its contemporary position as a sacred object that the Mowachaht wish to repatriate. (As a Canadian group, the Mowachaht cannot participate in NAGPRA.) Encountering her work after the completion of my own, I found independent corroboration that ownership in Nuu-chah-nulth culture is both central and complex when viewed from the perspective of contemporary repatriation issues. Jonaitis highlights the uncertain historic ownership of the shrine, apparent conflicts between two chiefs over its ownership in 1905, and the implications of this confusion for contemporary Mowachaht. She also discusses the possible fates of these sacred objects if the shrine is eventually repatriated to the community. As in Neah Bay, there appear to be conflicting viewpoints among the Mowachaht. These many common threads render *The Yuquot Whalers' Shrine* an important companion study to this one. To my knowledge, it represents the only other detailed examination of Nuu-chah-nulth material culture that considers ownership in relation to contemporary Native American issues.

In the literature on NAGPRA and repatriation there is an obvious dearth of information about the nuts and bolts of tribal implementation processes. By contrast, there are numerous articles written by museum and federal agency constituents which provide glimpses into the challenges of institutional compliance (Bray and Killion 1994; Isaac 1995; McManamon and Nordby 1992; Merrill et al. 1993; Rosoff 1998; Stoffle and Evans 1994; Tedlock 1995). As Nason writes (1997a:304): "Museum personnel have largely overlooked the impact that NAGPRA has had on tribal communities and tribal museums and centers." Yet this perspective provides a necessary balance to the other two, because after all it is *for tribes* that this legislation was written. This book, therefore, will privilege the tribal perspective with the goal of facilitating an understanding among nontribal participants in NAGPRA about the challenges faced at the tribal level. This is not to downplay, however, the problems that NAGPRA implementation has raised for institutions holding collections. Having extensively worked with NAGPRA in both federal agency and museum settings myself, I am acutely aware of the seriousness of these concerns. I believe that the initial problems with NAGPRA have been voiced by institutional constituents simply because the first activities under NAGPRA were those required of them. This does not mean that NAGPRA presents fewer problems for tribes. In fact, I predict that as greater numbers of tribes initiate NAGPRA programs, their voices will join those of others who complain, often bitterly, about the ambiguities of the legislation.

My discussion focuses on the negotiations behind tribal NAGPRA implementation, specifically those revolving around questions of ownership. Two bodies of theoretical literature I found particularly useful were anthropological writings analyzing the concept of ownership in different cultures and ethnographies on societies exhibiting coexistent pluralistic forms (indigenous and "modern"). Deconstructing the concept of ownership and surveying its cross-cultural variations has occupied many anthropologists. The work of Gluckman (1965), Goodenough (1951), and Barton (1969) are particularly useful for thinking about Makah ownership patterns, past and present, as well as the ownership forms privileged in NAGPRA. The general literature on legal pluralism (Hooker 1975; Merry 1988; Moore 1978; Rouland 1988) helps to articulate why the ownership and control of objects repatriated to the Makah community is such a contentious issue. As discussed at length below, modern and historic forms of ownership coexist (and conflict) in Neah Bay, and make strange bedfellows within the MCRC.

Chapter 1 introduces the complicated terrain of NAGPRA and Makahs' varied reactions to it. I selectively cover the sections of most interest to Makah tribal members and most relevant to my arguments. NAGPRA is a complex law, and a comprehensive overview is beyond the scope of this analysis. For a broader understanding of NAGPRA, including its provisions concerning human remains that I do not explore, readers are encouraged to refer to the complete text in the Appendix and to articles by McManamon and Nordby (1992) and Trope and Echo-Hawk (1992), which provide good overviews. Nason (1997a) furnishes a concise and informative account of the historical factors leading up to the passage of NAGPRA. This chapter also very briefly presents the national context of implementation and some of the challenges faced by museums and federal agencies which will in time impact the Makah process.

Because NAGPRA requires tribes to base their claims for objects on their "traditional"[4] significance, this book too must hark back to Makah culture of the nineteenth century. Chapter 2 provides historical and ethnographic contexts so readers will understand why the objects at issue under NAGPRA continue to be important for Makahs today. After this sketch of precontact[5] Makah lifestyles, which draws primarily on the classic ethnography, I address in Chapter 3 the cultural disruption that the Makahs have experienced over the last 150 years. This disruption presents many difficulties to the repatriation process, especially the lack of firsthand knowledge resulting from the gradual decline of many cultural practices from 1855 to 1934. This chapter closes with a discussion of museum collecting on the Northwest Coast in the late nineteenth century, especially in Makah territories.

Chapter 4 explores Makah history since 1934. During this period, the Tribe has experienced a steady climb towards a cultural resurgence. The awakening of interest in Makah precontact culture on the part of tribal members accelerated with the archaeological excavations at Ozette in the 1970s. This chapter briefly explores the impacts on the community of this excavation and the subsequent founding of the MCRC in 1979. The Tribe's NAGPRA implementation project, described here in detail, is a part of the existing cultural resource management program which actively gathers and circulates cultural knowledge.

Chapter 5 tackles the externally oriented struggle the Tribe faces in NAGPRA implementation. There is considerable circumstantial evidence to suggest that those who drafted NAGPRA assumed that nonsacred objects most significant to tribes were communal, and thus that all tribes had objects that were communally owned. This assumption directly confronts traditionally individualistic ownership patterns in Makah culture. In order to take advantage of the opportunities which NAGPRA offers to the Tribe, its members are being challenged to negotiate a fit between the legislation and their material culture. Makah tribal members are displaying great ingenuity and agency in this endeavor. The negotiation is simultaneously taking two approaches. On the one hand, they are trying to reinterpret NAGPRA definitions to incorporate their significant material culture and intellectual property. On the other, they are presenting alternative readings of past ownership practices to fit Makah objects into NAGPRA definitions. Problematizing the concept of "ownership," as other anthropologists have done, illustrates its malleability and clarifies these re-readings.

The second struggle engendered by implementation, the focus of Chapter 6, is internal to the Tribe. Ongoing discussions over the fate of repatriated objects weigh the rights of individual families to objects (the traditional pattern) against the potential benefits to the entire community through repatriation to curatorial facilities at the MCRC (a modern, institutional form of communal ownership). The problematic site that the MCRC occupies in community life reflects this struggle, as its staff balances the needs of the community as a whole against the desire of families to safeguard their private possessions within its walls. The underlying cause of this internal debate, explored through the structuring framework of legal pluralism, is rooted in the tensions between lingering private ideals of ownership from nineteenth-century practice and a communal form initially introduced with the establishment of the Makah Reservation.

The Afterword addresses more fully what contemporary whaling means to the Makah community as an opportunity to "draw back culture" and the important role of material culture in this endeavor. Particular items of whaling gear are considered sacred by contemporary tribal members, as they were used in ritual preparations prior to a hunt. Much of this material culture currently resides in museum collections and is subject to NAGPRA. Although I had left the field months before the successful hunt in May 1999, I was in residence in October 1997 when the favorable decision came down from the IWC. I knew many of the men directly involved in whaling-related politics and training. Some of them wish to "draw back" as much whaling gear as possible. Material culture is thus integral to the successful renewal of this historic practice.

1 / Makah Perspectives of NAGPRA

It's about time.
Well, sounds like a pretty good law to me.
We shouldn't need a law like this since the stuff is ours.
It's going to be real difficult.
—Reactions of Makah tribal members to NAGPRA

On 13 November 1997, in my windowless but blissfully quiet office in a back hallway of the MCRC, I prepared for the imminent arrival of Glenn Johnson, my next interviewee. Most people opted for the neutral space of the MCRC as a setting for interviews, although I did speak with several elders in their homes. I gathered my paperwork and checked that the thirty-four index cards had been well mixed from the previous interview. On each card was written the name of an object culled from summaries of museum holdings received by the Tribe as a requirement under NAGPRA.

Glenn arrived. Unlike others who tentatively searched for me in this little-used and rarely visited area, Glenn frequently performed odd jobs for the MCRC and thus knew where to find me. The preliminaries dispensed with, I gave him a brief overview of NAGPRA and a more detailed introduction to the definitions of "cultural patrimony" and "sacred object." Then, I produced the index cards and explained what I wanted him to do. Like most people, Glenn had been fairly reserved and a little nervous up to this point. I had quickly discovered that the card-sorting task was more useful for inducing people to talk and relax than for the end result. It served to divert their attention away from the artificiality inherent to formal interview settings. Glenn was no exception.

I asked Glenn to group the index cards into categories that made sense to him. The resulting five piles, he explained, represented whaling-related objects, fishing-related objects, objects that would have been found in a longhouse, objects associated with potlatches, and objects associated with dancing. I shuffled the cards and handed them back to him. "Now," I said, "would you please sort these according to the NAGPRA definitions I went over, with one pile for sacred objects, another for cultural patrimony, a third for objects that qualify as both, and a fourth pile for objects that you think are neither." He did as I asked, and when he finished there were two piles: twenty-three sacred objects and nine objects of cultural patrimony. However, he had defined cultural patrimony as "things everyone owned one of that were used for working." Communal ownership as a criterion, a key component of the definition, had disappeared. As I was to discover during the course of the year, people who classified Makah objects as cultural patrimony during this task had to reinterpret the NAGPRA definition to do so.

My interview with Glenn was in many ways typical, yet it was also exceptional. Looking back at my fieldnotes, it is clear that it represented a turning point in my understanding of NAGPRA from a Makah perspective. It was one of my first interviews with a tribal member who was not intimately connected with the MCRC's daily cultural resource management tasks. This encounter with a person having only limited prior knowledge of the law introduced a fresh viewpoint, which brought the complexities of ownership into sharper focus. Although I had already had some indications, this interview would give rise to the realization of how foreign the concept of cultural patrimony was to Makahs. I began to comprehend the Tribe's impending struggle to implement NAGPRA. Makah frustrations with the lack of fit between the law and their material culture emerged during interviews like Glenn's. The negotiated compromise that is NAGPRA has left no constituent completely satisfied. Let us explore how this situation came to pass.

NAGPRA: A CLEAR INTRODUCTION
WITH GLIMPSES OF COMPLEXITY

Public Law 101–601, the Native American Graves Protection and Repatriation Act, was signed into law by the first President George Bush on 16 November 1990. The law has two main goals, which are to strengthen existing legislation to protect Native American graves and to provide a means through which federally recognized tribes can reclaim ancestral remains and significant cultural objects held in the collections of museums and federal agencies. The law required United States museums receiving federal funds and all federal agencies (e.g., National Park Service, Forest Service) to inventory their museum collections and notify the appropriate tribes of objects in their possession. Notification of unassociated funerary objects, sacred objects, and objects of cultural patrimony was to have occurred by 16 November 1993, and of human remains and associated funerary objects exactly two years later. (Associated funerary objects are those for which the institution also holds the corresponding human remains. Collections of funerary objects alone are unassociated.) Unless they can document right of possession, institutions are required to repatriate the first group of items to tribes who request them. However, the tribes must submit formal claims that show that the objects fit one of these definitions under the law and that the objects are affiliated with their tribe. There is no right of possession clause for human remains and associated funerary objects; institutions must simply return them upon request of the affiliated tribe.

This presentation of NAGPRA's basic elements belies the fact that it is a very complex law. Many Makah tribal members were quick to recognize its inherent complications and identified for me the especially problematic aspects surrounding ownership that are my focus here. My discussions of Makah struggles to implement NAGPRA hinge on close textual examination of its definitions of cultural objects that can qualify for repatriation. These definitions, which are dissected at length as my argument progresses, come from the NAGPRA Regulations, published in the *Federal Register* on 4 December 1995:

> *Sacred objects* means items that are specific ceremonial objects needed by traditional Native American religious leaders for the practice of traditional Native American religions by their present-day adherents. While many items, from ancient pottery shards to arrowheads, might be imbued with sacredness in the eyes of an individual, these regulations are specifically limited to objects that were devoted to a traditional Native American religious ceremony or ritual and which have religious significance or function in the continued observance or renewal of such ceremony.
>
> *Objects of cultural patrimony* means items having ongoing historical, traditional, or cultural importance central to the Indian tribe or Native Hawaiian organization itself, rather than property owned by an individual tribal or organization member. These objects are of such central importance that they

may not be alienated, appropriated, or conveyed by any individual tribal or organization member. Such objects must have been considered inalienable by the culturally affiliated Indian tribe or Native Hawaiian organization at the time the object was separated from the group. Objects of cultural patrimony include items such as Zuni War Gods, the Confederacy Wampum Belts of the Iroquois, and other objects of similar character and significant to the Indian tribe or Native Hawaiian organization as a whole.

The drafters of the legislation, as well as the members of the National Review Committee responsible for the regulations, faced a difficult task. The law had to be specific enough to provide guidance for the tribes and institutions implementing it. At the same time, however, definitions had to be sufficiently broad to address the material cultures of vastly different indigenous groups from Hawaii to Florida. In the words of Suzan Harjo (quoted in AAM 2000:75), it was necessary to "build this door that was big enough to get everyone through."

As a result, the definitions of sacred object and cultural patrimony are paradoxically both very specific and very broad. Consider the definition of sacred object. It narrows the field of objects that qualify for repatriation by specifying that they must have been exclusively devoted to a traditional religious practice and be needed by, specifically, religious leaders in tribal communities today for contemporary practice. This excludes a great range of sacred objects for which the exact manner of traditional use is no longer known, or which had dual ceremonial and utilitarian functions but nonetheless may have powerful religious importance to contemporary cultures. This may be the case with Makah whaling gear. However, certain features of the definition leave room for negotiation: it does not define what constitutes a traditional religion (would indigenous/Christian amalgamations qualify?), it presents a carte blanche for the renewal of traditional ceremonies, and incorporates a rather loose definition of religious leader. McManamon and Nordby (1992:233) point out that certain terms used in NAGPRA definitions such as "religious leaders" and "traditional" will vary among groups and between regions. Most importantly, as Trope and Echo-Hawk point out (1992:66), "the term *sacred* is not defined explicitly in the legislative definition. Rather the definition will vary according to the traditions of the tribe or community." The definition covering cultural patrimony can be dissected in a similar manner to reveal both the strictness and flexibility of the category. Makah negotiations surrounding ownership illustrate this well. Problematizing these definitions is not merely a theoretical exercise. As I will demonstrate clearly for Makah implementation, tribes are taking advantage of these negotiable points and interpreting the definitions to meet their own culturally specific needs and goals.

This rhetoric of negotiation has been part of NAGPRA from the very beginning. Evaluations of the law in its early years stressed the "flexibility . . . needed throughout the implementation of NAGPRA's provisions related to collections" and the necessity to develop "creative . . . solutions to the challenges posed by NAGPRA" (McManamon and Nordby 1992:239, 252). The existence of room to maneuver within the bounds of the law was assumed. Such testing of any law in response to actual situations is a normal part of establishing the full potential and strength of a given piece of legislation. In their attempts to draw back culture, Makah tribal members are participating in a struggle with which all other constituents of NAGPRA are also engaged. That they, when newly introduced to NAGPRA, immediately identified the source of Makah struggles as being rooted in issues of ownership signals the magnitude of the problem.

MAKAH REACTIONS TO NAGPRA: THE STRUGGLE EMERGES

My primary goals during interviews with tribal members were to get their general reactions to the law and, through the card-sorting task, to see what traditional Makah material culture they thought might fit the above definitions. The range of attitudes towards NAGPRA expressed by Makah tribal members is a microcosm of the reactions by native peoples nationwide. Consider, for example, the following four responses to one of my standard interview questions:

ANN: I realize you may not have known a whole lot about this law before today, but I'm going to put you on the spot a little bit and ask you what you think about the law, in terms of what I've told you about it. What are your general reactions to it?

ED CLAPLANHOO: I'm not too happy with it now that I understand it more. I think they're making it more difficult for tribes to get back things that I would be happy to get back. I think that if we can prove that it is ours, [that] it came from here, I think that we should be able to just go and say, "it's ours." If it comes from [a] private collection, then we might have to buy it back. But, I think anything that's in the Smithsonian should be returned to us. Regardless of if it fit any guideline of theirs or not. (Interview, 2 February 1998)

BUCK CLAPLANHOO: There shouldn't have to be a law passed like that. When it's ours to begin with, why should we have to pass a law to get it back? You know, if it belongs here, it belongs here. (Interview, 11 February 1998)

GEORGE BOWECHOP: I have a positive reaction. I think it's a good law. I see a lot of development of relationships between museums across the country. And I think that for Indian Country, it would be real good for them. Where tribes could start talking on a different area instead of all politics or economic development. I think they could share a lot of these items and through the items comes the storyline about what your people are all about. And here's the proof. I think that it could open a whole line of communication between the tribes. And especially those who either have a museum or they're building [one]. . . . I think that to me would be the best thing that would come out of this. (Interview, 12 March 1998)

DONNA WILKIE: Well, my initial reaction is—it is a way that the government is showing the indigenous people of America of respecting our heritage. Protecting our heritage. By passing an Act of this kind is recognizing us as the aboriginal people and that they need to protect those aboriginal rights. And support our aboriginal rights. I see that as a big, positive step in the way the federal government [is] recognizing and respecting those rights. (Interview, 7 May 1998)

While negative sentiments such as those of Ed and his son Buck were common, these were tempered by an acknowledgment that they were glad such a law existed. Donna echoes a reaction seen throughout Indian Country, where NAGPRA was widely hailed as a major victory which signaled a recognition on the part of the U.S. government that tribes' ancestral remains had been unfairly singled out for scientific research.[1] NAGPRA was, in fact, intended as human rights legislation. The passage of NAGPRA was also viewed as a strong statement of commitment to contemporary native cultures, as it was the intent of Congress to "permit traditional Native American religious leaders to obtain such objects as are needed for the renewal of ceremonies" (U.S. House 1990:14).

The particular form of my interview question reflects a situation I was surprised to encounter in Neah Bay when I arrived in 1997: approximately half of tribal members contacted for interviews had not been previously aware of NAGPRA. Those who had heard of it generally knew few specifics. The reality was that few tribal members knew that numerous summaries and inventories from museums and federal agencies had been received at the MCRC and that a tribal research project was under way with a $75,000 grant from the National Park Service. This situation can be explained in part by the fact that the portions of the Tribe's project that involved public meetings and interviewing community members had not yet begun. NAG-PRA implementation prior to my arrival had been strictly an internal MCRC endeavor.

Although initially reluctant to grant an interview on a subject they knew little about, most people were curious enough about how their family might benefit from NAGPRA to want to learn more. Indeed, interviewees were generally pleased to have had the opportunity to find out about the law and seemed to genuinely enjoy our conversations. To MCRC staff initially concerned about my interview goals, this educational aspect was presented as a form of community service. Interviews were structured in such a way as to assume no prior knowledge. People's lack of previous knowledge suited my purpose, as I was interested in initial reactions as well as thoughtful analyses.

Reactions of tribal members to the definitions in the law also initially came as a surprise. The definition of "sacred object" generally made sense to them. When asked to name Makah objects that might qualify, they consistently mentioned masks and rattles. By contrast, the definition of "objects of cultural patrimony" caused considerable confusion. When given lists of objects represented on museums' NAGPRA summaries, ranging from fishing gear to canoe models, most individuals were at a loss to identify any cultural patrimony. Communally owned property was not part of their culture. Moreover, the overwhelming priority for repatriation was whaling-related objects, which did not clearly fit under the law at all.

Reactions to the broader scope of NAGPRA were varied, and concerns were revealed by the questions tribal members asked about it. These questions shed light on their hopes for and apprehensions about repatriation. For example, many people asked whether NAGPRA could be used to bring home objects from museums abroad or from private collections (which it cannot). As is the case with so many tribes, the earliest extant Makah material culture is in Europe, gathered by early explorers and traders. Also, pieces periodically surface at auction houses like Sotheby's, and subsequently disappear again into the world of private collections. Tribal members were naturally disappointed to learn about the law's limitations.

On several occasions it was clear that individuals had a specific object immediately come to mind for repatriation: "If I happened to have seen an item in a museum that I recognized as maybe something that belonged to my family, but I'm not sure, how do I go about making [a] claim?" Many were dismayed at the bureaucratic process necessary to accomplish this. Several questions reflected what I found to be a widespread suspicion that institutions were likely to be dishonest in reporting their holdings. A frequent topic of interest was how disputes between tribes and institutions over objects would be settled.[2] They wanted to know what happens when an institution does not agree that the evidence submitted by a tribe supports repatriation of an object under NAGPRA. In a related concern, Makahs wanted to know about the penalties for noncompliance on the part of agencies and museums. They were pleased to hear about the monetary fines for museums, upset at the lack of accountability for federal agencies, and interested in the convictions under NAGPRA that had already occurred.[3]

TRIBAL IMPLEMENTATION: A BRIEF WORD

Tribal experiences with NAGPRA are the least represented in existing literature. I believe that institutional personnel are often too caught up in their own frustrations with NAGPRA to recognize the complications the law has caused for tribes. Just because tribal peoples are the beneficiaries of the law does not mean the process is any easier for them. The general outline of the tribal process which follows provides both a framework for the Makah situation and a contrasting perspective to that of museums and federal agencies, the most vocal critics of NAGPRA implementation to date.

Tribal implementation begins with the receipt of summaries and inventories from museums and federal agencies; the interpretation of these poses the first challenge. Those received at the MCRC vary drastically in the amount of detailed information they provide. At one end of the spectrum, some museums state only the number of affiliated objects without even specifying the kinds represented. At the other end are museums, usually those with smaller collections, which provide photocopies of catalogue cards, full object descriptions, collection information, and even photographs. For tribes unaccustomed to working with museum collections, the vocabulary used in these NAGPRA documents can be inaccessible to the average reader. Terms such as "accession" (the formal addition of objects to a collection) and "provenance" (the origin or source of such objects) are not part of everyday speech and when abbreviated on catalogue cards are especially confusing. Deciphering the multiple ways in which accession numbers are formed by museums is also a challenge, especially when dealing with different numbering systems concurrently.

While museums and agencies can create a standard form for their NAGPRA summaries and inventories and impose a standard procedure through which they deal with claims, tribal visits, and repatriations, tribes must accommodate themselves to the variations between institutions. While institutions may have collections from hundreds of tribes, it is also necessary to consider how widely the average tribe's material culture is dispersed. Hartmann Lomawaima (quoted in AAM 2000:44) recently summed up the situation at Hopi: "If you go to the repository at Hopi where all these inventories are kept, it's mind-boggling. There are three trailers full of printed material from places that the Hopis had never heard about." Even the Makah Tribe, a small group, received summaries from nearly every state, totaling over 150.

Like institutions, tribes have to set up mechanisms to deal with this volume of incoming data using resources and trained personnel that are often scarce. Many of them have yet to organize NAGPRA implementation in any formal way, especially in the face of other overwhelming tribal economic priorities. Nason (1997a:304) writes: "Logistically, many tribal museums and governments have been very hard-pressed to respond to data summaries issued by museums, much less to actively pursue repatriation actions with a majority of museums." Makah Tribal Council members indicated that while they felt NAGPRA to be important, devoting funds to programs such as unemployment or road construction was more urgent.

It is in the pace of NAGPRA implementation where the differences between tribes and institutions are most marked. NAGPRA implementation by museum and federal agencies, especially for the first five years, was determined by deadlines imposed by the law and was quite rigorous. Many institutions, if not most, scrambled to meet these deadlines because of staffing limitations. Even now, NAGPRA-related work is sped along by ninety-day limits for responding to claims as well as the need to prepare for scheduled consultation visits. The pace of implementation at the tribal level is much slower, in part because there are no deadlines. In my experience, the measured pace being taken by the Makah Tribe and others also reflects the serious manner in which they are considering the consequences of drawing back certain items and the ultimate reincorporation of cultural objects back into their communities. Contrary to initial concerns on the part of many institutions, tribes are not rushing headlong to bring home as much material as possible as quickly as possible.

IMPLEMENTATION: THE SUPRA-TRIBAL CONTEXT

While the national structure of NAGPRA implementation has at the moment little direct relevance for Makah NAGPRA staff and community members, the Tribe's struggle to draw back culture will eventually be played out at this level. The complications being experienced by museums and federal agencies, which have their own quarrels with the law and the process, will in due time impact Makah NAGPRA implementation. A brief introduction to the individuals and bodies with which such exterior negotiations must occur is therefore germane. Some Makah tribal members who are involved with implementing other federal laws expressed interest in these dynamics.

The Secretary of the Interior was charged by Congress with implementing NAGPRA and delegated this responsibility to the National Park Service. Initially overseen by its Archaeological Assistance Division, the National NAGPRA Program is now run by the NPS's Cultural Resources Stewardship and Partnerships Program. As Makah implementation proceeds, the Tribe will be interacting frequently with personnel in this office. National NAG-PRA's responsibilities include facilitating meetings for the NAGPRA Review Committee, reviewing Notices of Intent to Repatriate and Notices of Inventory Completion and publishing them in the *Federal Register*, and providing technical assistance to all parties involved in implementation. It also sponsors NAGPRA training workshops, which Janine and Greig had attended. The Makah Tribe already has had limited dealings with the NPS, which managed its NAGPRA grant.

The Review Committee, consisting of representatives from all constituencies, monitors implementation nationwide and drafts regulations. It serves an important role as an objective sounding-board for difficulties encountered by any constituent and provides a venue in which disputes can be mediated without resorting to lengthy and expensive court proceedings. While its findings and recommendations are not binding or enforceable, the committee's position on a particular case would carry considerable weight in subsequent potential judicial proceedings. Should hearings by the committee fail to produce an agreement, disputing parties can seek resolution through the United States District Court system.[4] Greig and Janine attended a public meeting of the NAGPRA Review Committee in Portland, Oregon, in June 1998. While they were not particularly interested in the primary topic at this meeting, the disposition of unidentifiable human remains, they recognized the importance of becoming familiar with how the committee functions in case they bring disputes before it in the future. In addition, they took advantage of the event to informally network with museum representatives and NPS staff in attendance.

As the Makah Tribe starts making claims and working with museums, it is bound to encounter many of the same frustrations faced by other tribes that have already reached this stage of the process. These frustrations stem in part from delays caused by understaffing at museums. Even when a dedicated NAGPRA staff exists, implementation involves various museum departments, which can cause frustrating delays for tribal constituents. The multitude of duties that fall on staff as a result of NAGPRA can strain resources to the limit and subsequently lead to resentment of the law. Nevertheless, museum staff is also quick to point out the positive benefits to be gained from a more accurate knowledge of Native American holdings and increased cooperation with affiliated tribal groups. While there are those curators and administrators who lament the loss of valuable collections, there is also no shortage of staff members who are fully in agreement with the intent and spirit of NAGPRA. Moreover, many professionals predict that NAGPRA must eventually become a routine aspect of museum practice, especially since a large percentage of tribes are still struggling to get started.

Implementation by federal agencies has its own complications, which can cause additional frustrations for native groups.[5] The logistics of implementation are complicated by the geographical dispersal of collections owned by an agency, frequently to sites that do not have permanent staff familiar with them. Moreover, the common practice of federal agencies depositing collections elsewhere for caretaking has compounded the already complex record keeping and tracking systems over the years. On the positive side, as a general rule federal collections travel less distance from their areas of origin than museum objects, which facilitates consultation with affiliated tribes. Ethnographic and archaeological collections housed at Olympic National Park, for example, are affiliated with the Makah Tribe and other groups inhabiting the immediate area.

Makah reactions to the implementation procedures of museums and federal agencies remain to be fully formed, since they have had little direct experience as yet in claim processes. Nevertheless, a sense of pending complications with the law, specifically with the definition of cultural patrimony, is growing among both Makah NAGPRA staff and the wider reservation community. As the Makah implementation process makes a shift from internal research and organization to increasingly goal-oriented discussions with outside constituents, the extent of the struggle will become more evident. The varied responses of community members to the legislation itself are grounded in individual experiences of Makah history and material culture. Understanding the reasons behind their reactions, suspicions, and concerns requires a deeper knowledge of this background.

2 / "Five Villages, One Heartbeat"

PRECONTACT MAKAH LIFE

There's been a direct disconnect from the authentic way of speaking and singing, but somehow we're able to bridge that gap in a manner that we could declare it Makah. [T]he Makah [Tribe] is really making an effort to bring back all of the authentic, Makah artwork and whatever we have.

—George Bowechop, 12 March 1998

The late twentieth century saw increased activism on the part of Indian peoples to strengthen tribal cultures; NAGPRA is part of this movement. However, these current activities mean little without reference to the historical experiences that preceded them. In the quotation above, George refers to an "authentic," precontact Makah culture. This ethnographic background will provide an understanding of the significance of the objects that the Makah Tribe wishes to draw back under NAGPRA, and the cultural context from which current ownership struggles stem. Many aspects of precontact, "authentic" Makah life as known from early explorer accounts, tribal oral history, and the archaeological record, remain important in Neah Bay today. Whaling, the status system, social organization, ownership of rights and privileges, inheritance patterns, potlatching, and traditional ceremonies are among them. The following narrative weaves back and forth between past and present, linking the typically dry nineteenth-century ethnography to the contemporary problems this book explores. The descriptive information below about material culture and subsistence comes mostly from archaeological analyses of Ozette, and thus depicts Makah village life around 1500.[1] Comments on social structure and cultural practices draw on early explorer accounts dating from the period between 1788 and

1840, writings of Indian agents on the Makah Reservation in the 1850s and 1860s, and formal ethnographic fieldwork done in the 1930s but exploring elders' knowledge of nineteenth-century practices.

There is contradictory evidence as to when Makah ancestors first settled on the Olympic Peninsula. Linguistic research suggests that they migrated to their current location from Vancouver Island (Ruby and Brown 1986:125). This supposition is based on the fact that the Makah culture is the only representative of the Wakashan language family within the boundaries of the United States; all other tribes reside on the west coast of Vancouver Island in British Columbia (fig. 6). A Nuu-chah-nulth elder's story, related by Kirk (1986:23), supports Makah origins on the island. According to this family head, a village on the banks of the Jordan River on Vancouver Island became so crowded that three brothers left. The first founded the Ditidaht lineage at Whyac, the second settled at Clo-oose, while the third crossed the Strait of Juan de Fuca and established Neah Bay.

However, different oral history accounts support a residence in the area of greater antiquity than linguistic evidence indicates. In 1868, Swan recorded in his diary an origin story wherein the Makah people were created on Cape Flattery (Swan Diaries:56). In yet another account, published under the elder's name who related it (Irvine 1921), a tribal member explains that Makahs originally lived in the three villages of Ozette, Waatch, and Tsooes. Then, they took Tatoosh Island and the village of Deah (Neah Bay) from the Nitinats, another Nuu-chah-nulth tribe, who then moved to Vancouver Island.

Archaeological evidence proves that indigenous use of the area dates back much further than five hundred years, but whether or not these early inhabitants were precursors of the Makah Tribe or members of other groups who were later supplanted by them is unclear. A seasonal fishing site at the mouth of the Hoko River, at the edge of Makah traditional territory, has produced one of the oldest Northwest Coast artifacts ever discovered, a mat-creaser dating back three thousand years (Croes and Blinman 1980). An extensive excavation at the precontact Makah village of Ozette revealed evidence of habitation as far back as fifteen hundred to two thousand years ago and a well-established and populous community by ca. 1500 C.E. Artistic motifs from the later community resemble those recorded in the early contact period and even some designs in use today. Another ancestral Makah village site, Waatch, is believed to have been occupied as far back as fifteen hundred years ago (Ruby and Brown 1986:125).

Regardless of such discrepancies, it is clear that there are long-established

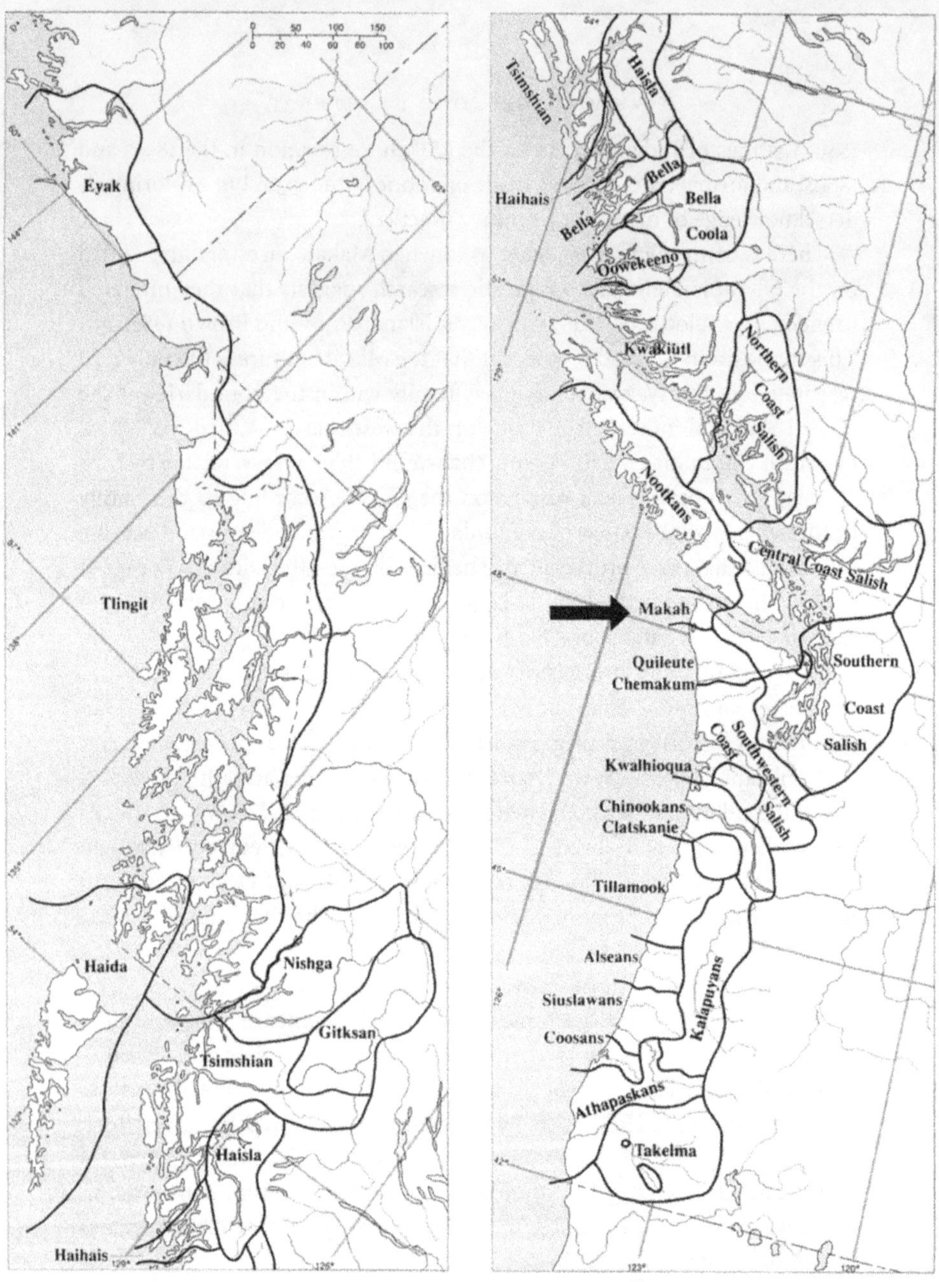

FIG. 6. The simplified ranges shown are generalizations of Northwest Coast tribal territories in the early nineteenth century, with those of the Kwakiutl and Northern Coast Salish for the mid-nineteenth century. The international border is indicated by a dashed line. The Haisla territory is located where the two parts of the map overlap. (Adapted from the *Handbook of North American Indians*. Courtesy of the Smithsonian Institution.)

linguistic, cultural, familial, and social ties across the Strait of Juan de Fuca between Makahs and related groups on Vancouver Island that tribal members do not feel with neighboring tribes in Washington State. This close interaction is still seen today in the frequent summer canoe races, potlatches, and informal visiting which goes on across the United States-Canadian border. There is also a more formal relationship at the political level among these groups. The Nuu-chah-nulth Tribal Council, which represents fourteen Vancouver Island Nuu-chah-nulth groups, gave its full support to the Makah Tribe's NAGPRA documentation project.[2]

The contemporary Makah Reservation encompasses only a small portion of the Tribe's former territory, which extended eastward along the Strait of Juan de Fuca to the Hoko River and southward along the ocean coast beyond Cape Alava. It also included the drainages of the streams flowing into the ocean between these places, offshore islands and reefs, and the ocean out to Swiftsure Bank. Tribes immediately bordering Makah territory were culturally and linguistically distinct, the S'Klallam Tribes to the east belonging to the Salishan language family and the Quileute Tribe to the south belonging to the Chimakuan. The Makah Tribe's five ancestral villages were Ozette, Tsooes, Waatch, Baada, and Deah. With the exception of Ozette, these former village sites are within the boundaries of the current reservation. An additional square mile is owned by the Tribe at Ozette, the site of the archaeological excavation, and managed in cooperation with the National Park Service whose lands surround it.

Before the establishment of the reservation unified them, Makah villages were autonomous rather than unified under an overarching political structure (Colson 1953:76). Each village had its own territory and occasionally warred with its neighbors. Intermarriage was common, but kinship bonds did not override feelings of village independence. Inhabitants of the five villages recognized that they shared similar customs and language (although slight dialectical differences existed) which distinguished them from their other neighbors, but there was no concept that they collectively constituted a "Makah" people. They were known by a common name by other tribes, qʷidicca?a·tx, which simply means "people who live by the rocks and the seagulls." This political structure encompassing both affiliation and autonomy is reflected in the 1997 Makah Days theme, "Five Villages, One Heartbeat." Many tribal members today still identify with the village from which their family came, and extended families remain the primary units of identification as in the past.

Artists' sketches of Northwest Coast Indian villages during the voyages of early explorers differ little from the first photographs captured a century later. These late-eighteenth-century sketches show as many as twenty massive cedar-plank houses clustered close together hugging the beach, weathered to a dull gray. A towering green forest of thick conifers and dense underbrush crowds the steep slope close behind the village. The beach is strewn with canoes in various sizes and stages of production, while others come and go with the tides. In seasonable weather, drying fish were hung on racks or laid out on the roofs of houses. A stream or small river empties into the ocean nearby, providing a source of fresh water. A daytime scene might have encompassed children playing, women near the water's edge cleaning fish, and perhaps men butchering a whale or mending fishing gear.

Unlike more northerly Northwest Coast groups, Nuu-chah-nulth villages were not marked by massive carved poles or house decorations. The ancestors of the Makah Tribe lived in Wakashan style shed-roofed houses as large as thirty feet wide and sixty feet long. These had flat roofs, slightly sloped to aid runoff. The boards overlapped but were not attached, thus allowing them to be easily moved to create smokeholes or let in light. During winter storms, they were secured with heavy rocks. The massive frames of these houses were permanent, with removable boards attached to them with rope. This allowed households to take their valuable boards with them when they moved to summer fishing sites. Inside, the houses were divided into separate living areas for nuclear families by either erecting board partitions or hanging mats from the rafters; each family had its own cooking fire. As many as thirty individuals might live under one roof, usually men related through a common ancestor along with their wives, children, and slaves. This arrangement allowed maximum flexibility for holding large gatherings such as potlatches, when all interior partitions could be removed. Around the walls of the houses were sleeping platforms. Cedarbark mats attached to the walls during the winter kept out drafts and were also used, along with furs and tule reed mats, to cushion sleeping areas. Bladders of whale and seal oil, drying fish, and other household goods hung from the rafters. Houses usually had only one door, which faced the beach.

The climate is mild and extremely wet in this region, which receives an annual rainfall of 90 to 110 inches. The short growing season made the cultivation of plant food difficult enough, but arable soil and flat, clearable land were also scarce. The abundant natural resources of the ocean provided for most of the requirements of daily life. Makah tribal members were (and are) expert fishermen, traveling miles out of sight of land to halibut banks in the open ocean. They also fished for salmon, lingcod, rockfish, and herring. The intertidal resources collected by women provided much of the diet and included octopus and many species of clams, mussels, barnacles, chitons, sea urchins, and limpets. The men also hunted fur seals, sea lions, porpoises, otters, and waterfowl. Marine resources were so abundant that ancestral Makah utilized respectively fewer forest resources. Women gathered berries, various roots and sprouts, and medicinal plants while men occasionally hunted deer, elk, and bear.

Red cedars were the most extensively utilized forest resource, referred to by some scholars as the "tree of life" for Northwest Coast tribes (Stewart 1984). The technology of the Makah ancestors was almost entirely wood-based. Some metal came to the area through trade and was scavenged from shipwrecks; ceramics were unknown despite abundant clay deposits. Cedar has a very even grain that splits easily; large boards were used for houses while smaller ones were fashioned into bentwood storage boxes and cooking containers. The largest of cedars, those used for whaling and war canoes, mostly grew further north on Vancouver Island and were acquired through trade. Local cedars were adequate for most other uses. Cedar bark could be pounded soft enough to make clothing and diapers and strips of it were woven into baskets, hats, sleeping mats, fishing nets, and ropes. In addition to cedar, more durable woods such as yew and alder were used for harpoon shafts, paddles, fishing hooks, arrows, and clubs.

Makah ancestors were part of a vast indigenous trade network even in precontact times, extending from the mouth of the Columbia River to Vancouver Island. Some basketry, shells, and wooden artifacts unearthed at Ozette were of materials and designs indicating origins throughout this range and beyond (MCRC 1979a:16). Swan's (1870:31) observations indicate that at least by the early nineteenth century, Makah tribal members were acting as middlemen in this trade between north and south, largely because southern coastal tribes rarely ventured across the Strait of Juan de Fuca while Vancouver Island groups seldom went south of Cape Flattery. Makahs produced surpluses of dried halibut, blubber, and whale oil as their primary contributions to the trade network. In exchange for these goods they procured sea otter skins, abalone, and vermilion from the south and dentalium, cedar bark, canoes, and dried salmon from the north. They retained a portion of these goods for their own use and traded the rest to other tribes. Slaves also passed between north and south, as slave owners preferred slaves from distant tribes because they could less easily escape and return home. While Makah wealth mainly lay in whale products and dried fish, numerous smaller articles like baskets, mats, and berries accompanied this primary trade.

According to Swan (1870:31), Makah trade with the Chinook on the Columbia River greatly increased when white traders established posts in Chinook territory in the early 1800s. Through Chinook intermediaries, they obtained blankets, beads, brass kettles, and other commodities introduced by whites. When the Hudson's Bay Company opened a post in Victoria, goods were directly obtained by Makah tribal members from there instead. They paid for these commodities largely in dogfish oil, which was acquired from Vancouver Island groups and desired by whites for use in sawmills. During the early reservation period, basketry and carvings produced for the tourist trade also entered this market.

The subsistence pursuit for which ancestral Makah were renowned among Northwest Coast tribes was whaling; thus their particular niche in the trade network. Although other Nuu-chah-nulth groups conducted hunts and most tribes salvaged beached whales, it was near the Makah village of Ozette that the migration route of the gray whale came closest to land (Daugherty and Kirk 1976:69). Each spring and fall, inhabitants could anticipate this migration from summer feeding grounds in the Arctic to winter birthing lagoons off the Baja Peninsula. Excavations at Ozette show that other kinds of whales were also taken, although the gray whale was the most abundant.

Crews consisted of eight men: a family head who served as the harpooner and was the "whaler" proper, and his male relatives. They went out in their sturdy ocean-going canoes and approached close enough to thrust the harpoon into the whale. Blades were made of sharpened mussel shells and attached to the harpoon by antler barbs wrapped with sinew. The sinew was held in place with cherry bark smoothed with spruce pitch. The barbs were incised by their owners with identifying patterns, which also had spiritual significance. Magic "medicine" (plants imbued with spiritual power) was sometimes enclosed in the cedar bark grip of the harpoon shaft (Drucker 1951:28). These points detached from the shaft and remained embedded in the whale. A short rope made of whale sinews, called a lanyard, was attached to the point. The lanyard in turn was attached to a long spruce- or cedar-root rope. Floats made of sealskin secured to these lanyards tired the whale out as it dove. As many points as possible were embedded in the whale to secure it, although the carcass belonged to the whaler who struck first. One member of the crew dove into the water once the exhausted whale surfaced, and thrust a special mussel shell killing-lance into its heart. When it was dead, the whale's mouth was sewn shut so it would not sink.

Once to shore, the entire village helped with the butchering, but there was a strict manner in which the blubber was divided (Waterman 1920:45–46). The choicest parts belonged to the whaler, who gave them away or sold them as he saw fit. Specific portions of the whale belonged to his crew and to that of the canoe to bring the first assistance. Each crew member in turn distributed their shares within their families. Usually a community feast, hosted by the whaler, followed a successful hunt. Whales were important in subsistence; even a few of them taken annually provided a significant proportion of the group's oil (Arima and DeWhirst 1990:395). Makahs cooked extensively with oil and used it to moisten dried fish and other preserved foods while eating.

A critical factor in whaling was the strict observance of certain rituals before, during, and after the hunt. According to Waterman (1920:38), proper spiritual preparation was considered as essential to success as readying the gear. The MCRC's exhibit leaflet points to some aspects of this preparation (MCRC 1979a:3):

> To get ready for a hunt, whalers went off by themselves to pray, fast and bathe ceremonially. Each man had his own place, followed his own ritual, and sought his own power. Weeks or months went into this special preparation, beginning in winter, and whalers devoted their whole lives to spiritual readiness.

Secrecy was crucial to the efficacy of such preparation, which was conducted individually in secluded places in the surrounding streams and forest. Certain of these ceremonies were carefully guarded and passed down in the families of successful whalers. Whaling equipment to be actively used during the hunt was often a part of ritual prayers. While bathing and prayer were most central to spiritual preparation, Waterman (1920:38–39) mentions several other activities. Special whaling shrines are known to have existed deep in the woods and were owned and maintained by individual whalers (Jonaitis 1999:64).

There were also strict taboos for both the whale hunter and his wife. The hunter himself never ate whale meat and avoided intercourse with women during hunting season in case they were ceremonially unclean. For the same reason, women were never allowed to touch whaling gear. During the hunt, the hunter's wife was required to lie still so the whale would be docile and was prevented from combing her hair, because it was thought that breaking any strands would cause the lanyard to snap (Gunther 1942:67–68). The whaling crews sang special songs to flatter the whales into letting themselves be caught and, once the whale had been struck, to encourage it to swim towards shore rather than into the open ocean (fig. 7). When a whale was beached, there were special songs sung to it by the entire community before it was butchered. The whale's dorsal fin, known as the saddle, was decorated with feathers and paint and ceremonially tended for several days before being distributed. A wooden replica of a whale saddle inlaid with six hundred sea otter teeth, unearthed at Ozette, suggests other ceremonial practices surrounding whaling. Current tribal members tell of whaling dances that have not been performed in many years.

The published sources on which this description of whaling is based are currently providing Makah tribal members with material to supplement their own oral history as they prepare a new generation of whalers. While much specific knowledge of hunting techniques, associated spiritual practices, and the processing of whale products has been lost, much has also been passed down through oral history and recorded by early whites in the area.[3] Because of whaling's spiritual aspect, the gear used in this activity is viewed as sacred by the majority of Makah individuals I interviewed, especially those pieces used by whalers during their spiritual preparations. As such, these pieces might qualify for repatriation under NAGPRA as sacred objects, and be incorporated into the Tribe's renewal of whaling traditions.[4]

In the past, whaling was inextricably tied to the social hierarchy of the community. In the ranked social structure, whalers were always heads of powerful families and members of the elite class. There were two reasons for this. First, only heads of large, extended families were in a position to mobilize the extensive economic and human resources required. Second, the right to go whaling was owned by family heads and inherited within elite patrilineages. Whalers enjoyed the most prestige in the community and tribal members today proudly trace the whalers in their families back many generations (Arnold 1994): "My grandfather's father's father's father's father, they were all whalers. So, we know that many back anyway. That we know that they hunted the whale. That they had crews and they had gear and stuff, but it's been a tradition in our family for a long time." Many of the leading (highest status) families in Neah Bay today descend from these famous whaling lineages.

Makah social structure in the precontact period was loosely divided into three classes: elites, commoners, and slaves. The material wealth of the elites

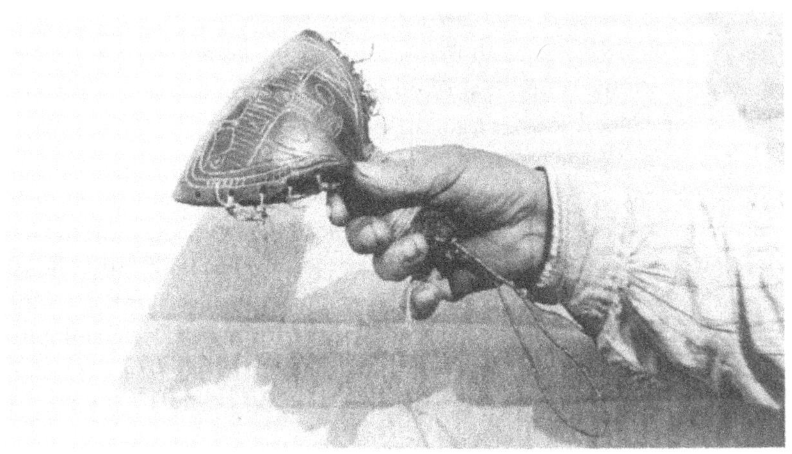

FIG. 7. This Makah whaler's rattle, which belonged to Charles Swan of Neah Bay, was photographed in 1948 in an obviously staged setting. Documentation with the photograph indicates that the rattle was used by Makah whalers to accompany songs to turn a harpooned whale towards the shore. Photograph by Ernest B. Bertelson. Courtesy of Manuscripts and Special Collections, University Archives Division, University of Washington Libraries, neg. #NA795.

was primarily measured in furs (especially sea otter), abalone shells, dentalia ornaments, and later blankets. Elites wore more ornate clothing, owned slaves, engaged in less physical labor, and received the choicest portions of staple foods. The heads of extended families usually had multiple wives, which was an elite privilege. According to Drucker (1951:244), the class system functioned on a gradient and there was no sharp break between elites and commoners. The primary status distinctions were based on ownership of economic rights and ceremonial privileges. The eldest son of a family head inherited his father's position and his family became the highest ranking of the lineage. His younger brothers shared his elite status, but at a slightly lower level. The descendents of younger sons formed a class of subelites. A family head's paternal cousins would have been another step lower. Members of each family were ranked according to their nearness to the direct line of descent from the family ancestor. Thus, a family head's most distant relatives were actually commoners. Women shared the status of their fathers and subsequently of their husbands, but married within their class. Slaves, owned only by family heads, were members of other tribes captured in raids, along with any children born to them after their enslavement. Although the class system and slave ownership were formally abolished at the signing of the Treaty of Neah Bay in 1855, individuals are still keenly aware of status, both theirs and that of others. While it is not openly discussed, having "slave blood" carries a stigma even today.

The status hierarchy was reflected in social organization and the economic system. The family head owned the longhouse and occupied the most comfortable corner with his wives and children. Younger brothers or other male kin occupied the remaining corners of the family head's house. If an extended family was particularly numerous, younger brothers sometimes left to preside over longhouses of their own, which occupied less prestigious sites further from the beach. Commoners lived along the middle walls of the longhouse while slaves were allotted the least desirable quarters near the door.

Upon marriage, a woman transferred her family membership to that of her husband and moved into his longhouse, usually in another village. Although residence was therefore mainly patrilocal, in reality commoners were constantly moving between groups. Family heads sought to attract large households, and thus more laborers, through their generosity. Commoner couples could choose to reside with any family head to whom they were related, even distantly. Relationships with a woman's family were maintained and were considered as additional support in times of economic need. Descent was ambilateral, which allowed individuals to affiliate with more than one local group (Arima and DeWhirst 1990:399). In marriages where the woman's family was of higher status, it benefited the man to make his primary allegiance with his in-laws. Children inherited privileges and names from their maternal relatives as well as their paternal ones. A family head's work force consisted of members of his household, both commoner and slave, and he coordinated their subsistence activities. Family heads themselves did not engage in manual labor as a prerogative of their elite status. Drucker (1951:244) identifies their duties as administrative in nature:

> The activities of [a chief's] people were in his charge: he decided on the time
> of the seasonal movements, directed group enterprises, such as construction
> of large traps and weirs, planned and managed ceremonials, and had the final
> voice in matters of group policy.

Members of his household gathered the resources to which he had rights and were allowed to keep a portion for themselves. If commoners undertook pursuits on their own initiative, they usually donated a portion to their family head.

The term "chief" was applied to heads of extended family households first by early explorers and later by reservation agents. To refer to someone as the "head of the family" more accurately reflects past and present usage in Makah culture and is employed in this book. By "family" in the contemporary context, I refer to a large, extended group of consanguine relatives and adopted members who recognize their relationships to each other. As in the past, families are still the major social and organizational units in community life. Individuals belong to both their mother's and father's families and have a recognized place in the family of their spouse. Although individuals participate in activities with all their family groups, customarily one dominates. For a man this is usually his father's family, unless his father was white. For women this appears to be a personal choice related to whom they get along with. Each family has a recognized head, usually male, who speaks for it on issues and represents its members at potlatches, funerals, and in other community-wide forums. Family meetings occur periodically, usually when an event, like a death, necessitates a coordinated response. A few families that are more organized meet on a regular basis for social evenings, where they may practice songs and dances. The main difference between contemporary family allegiance and its historic form is the participation of women today in activities of both their birth family and their husband's family. In addition, individuals are generally now related to fewer Makah families than in the past, because of intermarriage with whites.

The status system in the nineteenth century was based on the ownership of rights and property, and this remains the case today. The patterns of such ownership are among the most complex aspects of Makah social life. Drucker (1951:247) provides a succinct introduction to precontact practices:

> The head chiefs . . . were those who held the most [rights], the lower chiefs, those who owned less, and commoners were simply people who possessed none at all. The Nootkans carried the concept of ownership to an incredible extreme. Not only rivers and fishing places close at hand, but the waters of the sea for miles offshore, the land, houses, carvings on a house post, the right to marry in a certain way or the right to omit part of an ordinary marriage ceremony, names, songs, dances, medicines, and rituals, all were privately owned property.

Drucker goes on to classify these rights into two types, economic and ceremonial:

By "economic privileges" is meant those associated with shelter, food, and wealth, the ownership of habitations, domains for fishing and hunting, salvage rights, and all the special expressions of such rights. "Ceremonial privileges" included the right to give certain rituals or to perform a certain act in them, the ownership of dances and songs, and the ritual names that went with each privilege of any sort.

Ceremonial rights were collectively referred to by the Makah term *tupa·t*.

Although these systems of rights were intertwined, I will not be focusing on economic rights. Unlike ceremonial rights, precontact ownership patterns of economic rights are no longer practiced by Makah people. Natural resource utilization, both on the reservation and on ancestral lands off the reservation, is governed by tribal, state, and federal laws, notably those regulating fishing. The consolidation of the five ancestral villages and the loss of much ancestral land since 1855 upset the system as it existed prior to that time. While individual families may have preferred places to gather plants and shellfish on the reservation, these areas are now collectively owned and managed by the Tribe for use by all enrolled members. The longhouse as an economic unit was among the first aspects of native lifestyle to come under pressure from government agents, who lobbied for single family households. Many Makah homes today are managed by HUD under federal laws.

By contrast, ceremonial rights remain central to Makah life, and the ongoing ownership debates of NAGPRA implementation revolve around material culture associated with these privileges. The following sketch of the ownership of ceremonial rights comes largely from Drucker's (1951) accounts, based on fieldwork in the 1930s but drawing on elders' memories of nineteenth-century practices. Two aspects of ownership are particularly important for NAGPRA implementation today. The first of these is the overwhelming emphasis on private ownership in Nuu-chah-nulth culture, which causes conflicts with the definition of cultural patrimony in NAGPRA. The second is that ownership was formerly a prerogative of the elite, which means that objects being sought for repatriation by the Makah Tribe now were largely owned by this class. As a result, NAGPRA implementation has the potential to be an activity of the elite, and these families are the ones most likely to benefit from it in Neah Bay.

In nineteenth-century Makah culture, sources of *tupa·t* were supernatural, acquired through direct experience of a family head or one of his ancestors. Such supernatural experiences, and their visual manifestations, were sought because they bestowed spiritual power, wealth, or hunting luck on the recipient. The supernaturals conferred privileges in the form of names, songs, dances, designs, games, and so forth. While commoners could also have such experiences, Drucker (1951:272) indicates that they would give such privileges to their family head, since they did not have the wealth to properly display them.

The right to assume or bestow personal names was one such prerogative of the elite and the names were usually those of ancestors passed down through families. In Nuu-chah-nulth culture, individuals had several different names during their lifetime. Usually, a child would assume a new name at puberty, perhaps at marriage, and on the occasion of other significant events in adulthood. This practice continues today (McCarty 1994):

> When we get a name, we're told to take care of it because for as long as that name was in existence, it's been shined and polished, is what they say. Keep it clean. So, you don't want to have any spots on your name, so it will be bad. So when it comes time to give it to the next one, it's a good name.

Family heads also owned the right to use or give ritual names to slaves, pets, carved house posts or beams, feast dishes, canoes, or other possessions.

In contrast to names, other privileges had visual manifestations. These "display" privileges, as Drucker refers to them, were used at potlatches and included songs, dances, and regalia (masks, headdresses, capes, cedar-bark headbands, skirts, wrist and ankle bands). These often came as bundled sets of privileges.[5] Family heads had rights to use certain artistic motifs, usually representing supernatural beings, on their regalia and personal goods. Today, each family has a recognizable design that functions in analogous fashion to European crests. Other display rights included certain rituals associated with weddings, such as games or contests. Another right, especially important at potlatches, was ranked ceremonial seating. Formal ranked seating is no longer observed at potlatches in Neah Bay, although elders and members of the host family are generally placed in prominent positions in front of the dance screen. The ceremonial privileges involving personal names, songs, dances, and associated regalia are the ones still relevant to Makah life.[6]

It is of critical importance in NAGPRA implementation to understand how inheritance patterns for this regalia worked in earlier periods. By applying these patterns, objects in museum collections theoretically can be traced to contemporary Makah families, and ideally to individuals within those families. (This presumes that the original owner from whom the object was acquired is known.) The central question is this: If a specific object had never left the community, whom would it have come down to in the present day? Our most complete documentation of precontact inheritance practices comes from Drucker (1951) and thus dates from the nineteenth century. While the most characteristic elements of the system seem to be its flexibility and variability, there are nonetheless some dominant patterns. The most important factors in determining who inherited were the relative ages and genders of the children, status, and the type of privilege under consideration.

It generally appears that the eldest son inherited his father's most prestigious rights, both ceremonial and economic. Goodman (1991:232) writes that whistles used in Klukwalle and other secret society ceremonies were usually inherited in this manner. Likewise, the eldest son of a whaler or sealer would be trained in the appropriate prayers and spiritual preparation by his father and inherit this prestigious position. He would also become the owner of the house and natural resources upon which his household depended. Nevertheless, no member of the elite class was entirely without some rights. Younger sons of a family head would inherit minor ceremonial names and display privileges. Some positions, such as speakers and war chiefs, were passed down within this level of lower elites (Drucker 1951:269). A system in which the eldest son was favored preserved a family's most prestigious rights in one bundle and was meant to ensure that the family would retain its status over generations.

Daughters of high-status men also inherited privileges, especially upon their marriage, but the kind of property given to them differed from that given to sons. As Drucker writes (1951:267):

> Ordinarily, a daughter would keep (or a son-in-law be given), only such rights as were transportable (names, songs, dances, etc.), and not such things as seats and fishing rights, unless her husband affiliated himself with her group. It sometimes happened, however, and in recent times with the decrease of population, has become more common, that a woman might retain even such unportables.

By seeking high status or multiple marriages with women who would bring desirable privileges, as a kind of dowry, a family head could expand his wealth. Even if these privileges had been given to the bride by her father in trust for her children, these children would belong to her husband's family. In this manner, property was transferred from one family to another. It was not unusual, if a bride proved barren, for her privileges to revert to her father rather than to her husband.

It is clear from the above sketch that while in theory a family head could manage his property as he pleased, there were actually constraints on who could inherit property and thus to whom heads could give it. These constraints were largely self-interested. It benefited the family head to keep the most prestigious rights within the family to perpetuate its high status. Furthermore, it simply was not practical to give daughters rights to economic resources that they could not utilize when they lived with their husband's family in a distant locale. Commoners rarely were given rights by their distant (high-status) relatives although such cases are known. Usually, this occurred when a commoner performed some extraordinary deed for which his family head wished to reward him. Slaves were never given property of any kind.

In actuality, the inheritance system was much more flexible and complex than I have presented here. It was possible for a specific right to be given to multiple heirs (Drucker 1951:267):

> If the procedure of taking an inheritance [through potlatch] involved considerable formality, the line of descent of rights was singularly unencumbered by rules. A given privilege could be inherited by the eldest son, or shared by several children (all having the right to use it); it could be given to a daughter until her marriage and then bestowed on her brother; it could be given to a son-in-law, who might, as the giver specified, have sole right to it or share it with his wife's brother.

Drucker (1951) explains, however, that the nature of the privilege determined whether or not such an arrangement was feasible. A song or dance, for example, is more easily shared than a potlatch seat.

This characteristic flexibility remains the hallmark of the inheritance system today. Greig Arnold confidently stated to me that if a museum object has a named original owner, he could narrow down to three or four candidates the rightful owner today. When asked if the most significant privileges are still passed down in the eldest son's line, he replied:

> Depends. Depends if there is an eldest son. Depends if this eldest son is in a condition to be holding this material. Depends . . . there is a tremendous amount of variables. And . . . this object can be stored away. These rights can be handed to somebody for them to care for all that the elder has intended for

this family to know, until somebody else in the next generation is ready to receive this stuff. And it could be held by a woman. I know cases here and on the Island [Vancouver] where women hold real important positions. So that until somebody is ready to receive information, then they receive it. (Interview, 2 June 1998)

Therefore, although a strict pattern exists and is preferably followed, the system is still variable enough to address situations where the pattern does not fit. Now, as in the past, inheritance is based on a complex set of variables including the type of privilege under consideration, the number and gender of children in a family, whether or not they are spiritually prepared to receive the rights, if they reside in Neah Bay or not, and if they are or want to be culturally active.

In the past as today, potlatches provided the forum in which ownership of economic and ceremonial rights was transferred to the next generation. When a family head had accumulated enough property to distribute as payments to witnesses, he hosted a potlatch. The occasions for these events included births, puberty ceremonies, marriages, deaths, and small milestones in a child's life such as a first tooth. Rights were transferred as children were growing up, so that by adulthood they would have inherited most of the family's privileges. The entire village was invited to potlatches along with neighboring tribes having kinship connections, however distant, to the hosting family head. The major events during a potlatch were a feast, the ritual display of the privileges to be bestowed, and the distribution of property to those in attendance. The feature of potlatches most familiar to the general American public is the lavish gift giving that occurs as the final event. Among Nuu-chah-nulth groups, this did not have the competitive nature that was typical among the Kwakwaka'wakw (Kwakiutl), Tlingit, and Haida farther north (Bancroft-Hunt and Forman 1988:64).

Parties, the contemporary term for potlatches in Neah Bay, are communal gatherings that commemorate a significant event in a family's collective life. Not all are held explicitly to transfer property. Occasions for parties today include baby showers, namings, weddings, anniversaries, special birthdays, graduations, and as memorials for the dead. The mood of the occasion varies with its purpose; weddings are more formal, namings celebratory, and memorials somber. They are hosted by an extended family group, which initiates planning at least eight months prior to the event. Makah tribal members refer to the serious transactions that take place in the context of parties as "business." There are many different kinds of business that can occur during the course of such parties. The primary business is that for which the host family has held the party—to present children with Indian names, to celebrate a graduate's accomplishments, or to remember the dead. Each of the other families in the village also gets an opportunity to conduct their own business as well. This may include offering public apologies, presenting relatives to the community, transferring the rights to a song or dance, expounding their rights to a particular song or dance by telling when they received it and from whom, or introducing a visiting anthropologist. The length of a party is largely dependent on the number of participating families and the amount of business they have to conduct. At the end of the evening, the actual "potlatch" within a party occurs. At this time, the host family gives presents, mostly small, to everyone in attendance. Among Makah tribal members, this practice is explained as payment to the audience in order that they witness and remember the business that occurs.

Like the potlatch, there were other ceremonies which centrally featured the display of songs and dances and served as "vehicle[s] for conveying hereditary rights" (Drucker 1951:387). Perhaps the best known of these was the Klukwalle, an annual winter ceremony practiced in various forms among most Northwest Coast groups. It is thought to have originated somewhere on Vancouver Island, among Nuu-chah-nulth peoples (Ernst 1952:99–107). The ceremony is known and referred to by many other names in the literature, including Klukwana, "winter ceremonial," the Wolf Ritual, Dukwally/Dukwalli, and "black taman'awas." Individuals could be initiated several times throughout their lives, on each occasion inheriting a different set of privileges. The origin of the Klukwalle is related in a Northwest Coast legend, which has several variants: A young woman admired and subsequently married a wolf chief and went to live with him in the mountains. Years later, she returned to her village and brought a message that people should not harm wolves but instead try to learn qualities of strength and fearlessness from them. She began to teach her people the songs and dances of the Klukwalle, which she had learned from the wolf chief and which were the source of his power.[7] Part of the significance of the wolf in Makah culture was that its cry resembles that of a killer whale; they were thought to be the same animal with one body for land and another for the ocean (Pascua 1991:40). The centrality and importance of whaling in Makah life may also help to explain why the "wolf ritual" or Klukwalle was so important.

The aim of the Klukwalle was to keep people healthy, give them strength, and train them in bravery and endurance in preparation for battle. The ceremony taught children how to mind their elders and not show fear. Alice Ernst (1952:2) has written the most comprehensive ethnographic account of the ceremony as it was practiced by Makah ancestors in the nineteenth century, and describes it this way:

> The core of its movement centers always about the active dramatization of a legend which enacts the capture of a number of people (initiates) by Wolves, their recovery by certain other people already initiated (members of the secret society or fraternity known as Klukwalle) after they have received certain powers or instructions from the Wolves, and the exorcising of the Wolf spirit that possessed them.

The significance of this annual ritual was that village members reconfirmed their collective spiritual link with supernatural helpers, wolves, and introduced new members to them. Even slaves were initiated (Drucker 1951:366, 391; Pascua 1991:48). Through participation, the novice gained the right to participate in tribal dances or ceremonials during the sacred winter season. As Ernst (1952:3) notes:

> All persons, young or old, were expressly forbidden participation in the group performances of the tribe without such initiation, ostensibly by the Wolf spirit. The ceremony was, therefore, fundamental, and marked the induction of the initiate into a substantial body of tribal tradition.

The Klukwalle customarily lasted four or five days, and counted among its most common activities masked processions through the village, singing, dancing, and feasting. The Klukwalle varied slightly between groups and families (Drucker 1951:387):

> [N]umerous details and acts of the ceremonial were privately owned property. Each chief, as representative of his lineage, inherited special songs, dances, display rights, and other performances to be used in the ritual, and sometimes these rights overlapped, that is, two or more chiefs would each own a different procedure for accomplishing the same result.

Throughout the winter season, other performances of this ceremony or similar ones were given as needed or desired. There were other more minor forms of the Klukwalle, including the healing Klukwalle, the Night of Dancing (Kluklukwat'kah or "one-day Klukwalle"), and the Tsa-e'qua-quech.

The latter two were informal, fun occasions where various inherited songs and dances were rehearsed.

According to a contemporary Nuu-chah-nulth spiritual leader, the Klukwalle celebrated the balance and spiritual growth of the mind, body, soul, and spirit and the principle of respect. This man has been at the forefront of renewing Klukwalle ceremonies in Neah Bay, where two have been held in the last few years. The most recent of these was organized with the active involvement of Canadian Nuu-chah-nulth groups among whom the practice has continued. However, community reaction to this renewal is mixed and the most recent Klukwalle initiation was not well attended by Makah tribal members. As one leading family head commented: "Now, there has been some people have come to us and says we need to resurrect the Klukwalle. But, do we know what it is? Do we know what it represents? And if it represents a supernatural thing . . . would we know how to handle it? And could we mess ourselves up?" This reflects a widespread concern among tribal members about drawing back both ceremonies and objects which have power that is not fully understood today.

The regalia associated with the Klukwalle, in addition to that displayed at potlatches, encompassed some of the most elaborate material culture produced by Makahs. Several different kinds of wolf headdresses were central, but facemasks and a multitude of other animals and birds were also represented (figs. 8–10). Most masks were owned by individuals and inherited along with the associated dances and songs by a selected heir. Boas (1890:50) notes that dancers' ornaments were personal property and could not be loaned or borrowed. Masks, however, especially those associated with high-status families, were also symbols of prestige, power, and social recognition in society. Ernst (1952:91) describes the importance of clear inheritance practices for these important items:

> [T]he agents in the secret rites attending this magic transference of being (the mask, the dance, the song) took on enormous importance, both in the life of the individual and in the social fabric of which he was a part. . . . [T]he mask, with its related dance, portraying the chosen spirit protector, became a unique possession, jealously guarded for a lifetime, and relinquished only at death to some duly appointed heir. The individual mask was a single colorful unit in the embracing family legend.

Although masks had this high visibility, rattles and whistles are identified by contemporary Makah tribal members as being the most sacred objects in

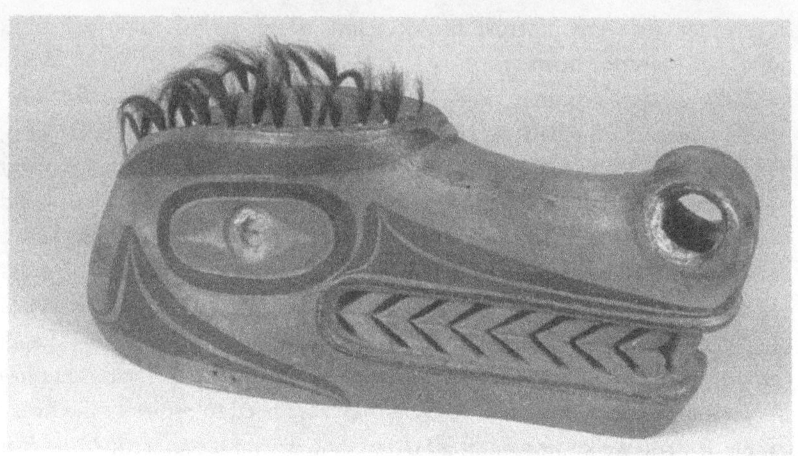

FIG. 8. This Makah wolf headdress dates to the late nineteenth century and is typical of those used in Klukwalle performances. Photograph by Ray Fowler. Courtesy of the Burke Museum of Natural History and Culture, catalog #2.5E1543.

the Klukwalle. Goodman (1991:232) writes that whistles[8] announced the presence of supernatural beings, while I was told during one interview that rattles called the spirits. Whistles could only be handled and blown by properly initiated men and were not to be seen by the general public (Goodman 1991:232). About the bird rattle used in the Klukwalle, Ernst (1952:14) writes:

> The bird rattle (bo-kwitz') used in Klukwalle was always severely plain and undecorated; it was painted in dark colors (black or dark brown), and showed the bird bill. Pebbles inside it gave when shaken the needed audible accompaniment to song. It differed traditionally from rattles used in other dances . . . and offered striking contrast to the brightly painted, intricately carved bird rattles used by shamans, or for other ritual practice among northern tribes. (fig. 11)

One tribal member I interviewed said that all rattles, since they are "prayer tools," should ideally be returned to the reservation.

Most ethnographic sources do not directly address the innately sacred nature of the material culture used in the wolf ritual but tribal members, while not elaborating on it, consistently classified dance regalia under the NAGPRA definition of sacred object. One woman described masks both as having an inherent spirituality and as being alive, like a tree. Ernst (1952:94)

FIG. 9. This Makah facemask dates to the late nineteenth century and was collected on a Field Museum expedition by George Dorsey in 1900. Wright (1991:133) notes its ingenious manufacture: "By manipulating strings behind the mask, at a certain dramatic moment the dancer could make the small human figure at the top pop up, and the corona of sun's rays fan out." Field Museum of Natural History #61927. Photograph by Diane Alexander White. Courtesy of the Field Museum, neg. #A111008.

FIG. 10. This Makah eagle headdress was also collected by George Dorsey and dates to the late 1800s. It is boldly painted in red and black against a natural wood background. Regalia depicting eagles and thunderbirds were worn during Klukwalle ceremonies. Field Museum of Natural History #61904. Photograph by Fleur Hales Testa. Courtesy of the Field Museum, neg. #A108091-3.

does briefly mention that masks belonging to Nuu-chah-nulth groups on Vancouver Island which represent family "guardians" (beings encountered by the family's ancestors) were considered extremely sacred. There seems to be no doubt that the wolf ritual itself was a sacred occasion during which a group's connection to spirit guardians was annually reconfirmed. Greig Arnold (quoted in Rosoff 1998) indicates that masks still play a central role in bridging the human and spirit worlds:

> Once we have a headdress out on the floor and it is being danced, the person with that headdress is supposed to put it on right away and come out—he is that thing, whatever it is that he is doing. If he is wearing a thunderbird or if he is wearing a wolf, he is that on that floor. As soon as that song is over and that energy is gone, he comes off and then transforms. Then he is back to who he is as a person or she is as a person. All that gear is then put away and stored after that, not to be seen until it is danced again.

Ernst (1952:24) also suggests that by putting on an animal mask, participants temporarily gained the animal's powers and exhibited its traits. The masks themselves were the agent of this transformation and thus clearly must have contained some inherent power. When not in use, these masks

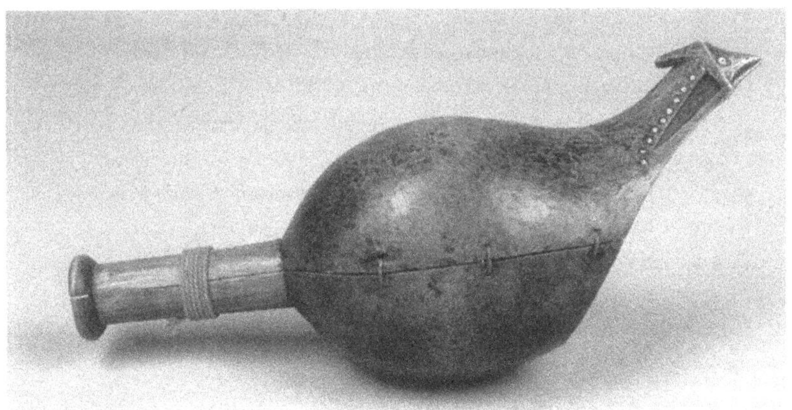

FIG. 11. This Makah grouse rattle dates to the nineteenth century. Rattles figured centrally in both public ceremonies like the Klukwalle and in personal spiritual observance. Photograph by Eduardo Calderón. Courtesy of the Burke Museum of Natural History and Culture, catalog #4857.

and headdresses were kept from public view, either by placing them in a box or wrapping them.

While the Klukwalle and other communal ceremonies were spiritual in nature, most of Makah spiritual life in the past was a very secretive and individual enterprise. Individuals went to their own special places in the woods to bathe and pray. Helen Peterson, a Makah elder, explained it in this way (quoted in Pascua 1991:41): "The Makah knew their lives depended on the Great Spirit Above, and they prayed in secret at sunrise. Each had their own way of praying, of finding a spirit helper. My stepfather held a black rock in his hand, that he would be strong like a rock. You can see the imprint where he held it in his hand." Men hoped to ensure success in fishing and hunting; women prayed for the health and safety of their families and for fertility.

The objects used in these private prayer rituals are not commonly known, for obvious reasons. The Ozette excavations unearthed a number of small, elaborately carved objects thought to have had some spiritual significance (MCRC 1979a:10–11). Many of these on display in the MCRC have holes bored in them which suggest they might have been hung on a string and worn. Subsistence-related objects may also have had spiritual aspects, akin to the carved whaling harpoon barbs. A contemporary spiritual leader in Neah Bay described the use of such items in prayer:

My personal knowledge is that in . . . spiritual cleansing the items were used as an ally. In church, you use the incense thing to swing back and forth. You have a cross or other things you know. And with our people all these items . . . [were sacred] because they used them in their special place of prayer. So they can be good hunters, good whalers, and good fishers. And historically that's where they were at. So whether they went bathing in the river or lake or whether a bathing ritual or a sweat lodge ceremony or going to the mountain, they prayed with these items so that these items would be sacred enough to capture what they wanted to sustain the family and the nation. (Interview, 16 January 1998)

An unusual carved stone effigy in the Peabody Museum collection was identified by Greig as a sinker with magic properties to ensure productive fishing. Although objects in museum collections may be identifiable to tribal members as related to spiritual practices, and therefore sacred, the precise method of use today is often unknown.

Shamans, or doctors in contemporary parlance, also used prayer objects that have ended up in museum collections. Doctors, usually of commoner status, ritually prepared themselves for a supernatural encounter which would endow them with certain powers. Among these powers were the ability to predict the future, affect the weather, and most importantly heal the sick. According to Drucker (1951:181–83), these individuals were treated with great deference in the community; curing rituals were very performative and well attended. He cynically adds that individuals, both men and women, sought to become doctors to gain prestige and wealth, as they were paid for their services. While shamanistic tendencies were not hereditary, certain families encouraged this interest in their children and therefore counted doctors as their members over many generations. The gear doctors used in their curing ceremonies is still thought to be very powerful and dangerous to the uninitiated.

While there are no obvious practitioners in Neah Bay at present, there are individuals who are more prepared and educated in this realm than are others. Helma Swan, an elder employed by the MCRC, speaking about drawing back such material, put it this way: "Lots of times, this shaman's . . . gear might be able to come back. And it only comes back to a person who's going to be brave and sometimes it comes back into a family." She went on to identify one individual who had several immediate ancestors who were respected doctors. Helma thought he had been holding himself back from getting too involved in cultural activities because he was afraid of becoming a doctor, which she believes is his destiny. Overall, while tribal members identified doctor's gear in museums as significant objects, many of them thought it would be too dangerous to bring this material home.

The precontact lifestyle sketched here was irrevocably changed beginning in the 1850s with sustained European-American interaction and the founding of the reservation. Makah tribal members' experiences during this period are similar to those of other tribal peoples throughout the United States. In the late nineteenth and early twentieth centuries, the daily lives of Makah tribal members came under increasing control of government agents and were subject to the influences of this dominant culture.

3 / Makah Culture(s) and
Histories in Flux

[I]f the course and policy I have indicated are honestly and vigorously carried out, the Indians of this Territory [Washington] will be speedily civilized, and they, with their reservations, absorbed into the body-politic of the State; otherwise they will continue as sores and scabs on the body-politic.

—R. H. Milroy, Superintendent of Indian Affairs (Olympia), 1872

It strikes me very forcibly that a tribe of Indians hardy and brave enough to venture 20 and often 30 miles offshore in their frail cedar canoes to engage in such perilous business [whale hunting] that requires undaunted courage, self-possession, and presence of mind, have all the elements of a great people.

—John McGlinn, Neah Bay Agent, Bureau of Indian Affairs, 1891

In the early reservation period, 1855 to 1931, a "disconnect" came about between past and present Makah culture as a result of federal policies and imposed Christianity. This chapter focuses on elements of this upheaval particularly relevant to NAGPRA implementation. How were traditional patterns of ownership altered or abandoned during this period? How did Makah objects come to be in places where they now need to be drawn back to the Tribe? And what were the various means through which cultural objects left tribal hands during this period?

CULTURAL DISRUPTIONS, 1855–1931

The Treaty of Neah Bay in 1855 signaled the beginning of a new era for the Makah people, although changes were not immediately felt. The early reservation period, as I shall refer to it, lasted until 1931 when a road linking Neah Bay to the outside world distinctly changed the character of Makah life yet again. Throughout my account of these years, I pay special attention to the influence of Bureau of Indian Affairs (BIA) agents on tribal members, who responded to reservation life by abandoning or creatively adapting their customary practices.

Although the first recorded European contact with Makah ancestors was in 1788, with initial trading probably somewhat earlier, it was not until the 1850s that significant, sustained contact occurred.[1] Among the first consequences of this prolonged contact was the decimation of the population by diseases, such as smallpox, to which indigenous peoples had no immunity. Such drastic population loss, up to 50 percent by 1860, resulted in the first major disruption to the social system upon which daily life had revolved. Given that identity depended on an individual's place in a ranked status system and membership in a specific family, it is easy to imagine the resulting social chaos. It had especially profound effects on the ownership patterns of cultural goods and ceremonial practices. Drucker (1951:12) notes that the decrease in population following the 1852 smallpox epidemic on Vancouver Island meant that family heads died without heirs in the direct line. Anthropologists working among the Kwakwaka'wakw in the early 1900s noted that there were more named ranks of status than men to fill them (Cole 1985:295). For ceremonies, this population loss had three main impacts. Some ceremonies fell out of practice because there were simply not enough members of a family left to display their privileges. Knowledge of how to perform other dances and songs was lost altogether when current owners died before it was passed on to heirs. Finally, there were objects formerly associated with specific ceremonies that could no longer be used, because survivors either did not know how or did not own the right to use them.

Unlike many intangible properties, objects associated with songs and dances survived the social disruption. Some of them were simply put away and forgotten until decades later when they acquired new value in the cash economy. Cole (1985:295) writes: "The calamitous decline of the native population from contact until the later decades of the nineteenth century . . . must have created a surplus of many objects at precisely the period of most intense organized collecting." Cole also speculates that there may have been more masks for some ceremonies than there were individuals to wear them. The Makah situation was unfortunately similar to that of the Kwakwaka'wakw. An undated BIA record in the MCRC Archives notes: "The Makah population around 1860 was 500–600 people, having lost over half recently to smallpox." By 1852, the Makah village of Baada had been completely abandoned because of disease. Donna Wilkie discussed the effect this had on the ownership of cultural objects:

> A lot of people died of smallpox. And they'd find these objects [that had been put away] and they'd say "Well. Jees." You know. "Nobody owns these. Let's go sell them." And some families . . . entire clans died from the smallpox epidemic so a lot of these objects got to other places and they really had no ownership. It was really hard to tell when you lost all those linkages to the past. (Interview, 7 May 1998)

The lack of obvious owners for such objects benefited the museum collectors. Tribal members had no qualms about alienating these objects and were more than willing to sell them. Unfortunately, this lack of knowledge about the origin and use of objects is reflected in collectors' and museums' records, and makes repatriation today nearly impossible.

The second major assault on ownership patterns for tribal members came with the establishment of the reservation. Treaty negotiations began with tribes on the Olympic Peninsula immediately after the smallpox epidemics of the early 1850s. Representatives from the four surviving Makah villages of Deah, Waatch, Tsooes, and Ozette signed the Treaty of Neah Bay in 1855 with Isaac Stevens, the governor of Washington Territory. The Makah Tribe ceded land in return for education, health care, and rights to fish and whale in "usual and accustomed grounds and stations."[2] Notes on treaty negotiations that have survived clearly indicate that tribal members were more concerned with retaining fishing rights than with losing land (Lane 1972).

The Treaty of Neah Bay was only the first of many government interventions that would change the way land was utilized. The Makah Tribe was fortunate in that all their ancestral village sites, except Ozette, were within the boundaries of the reservation. Therefore, the only forced relocation was of Ozette families required to send their children to school in Neah Bay. Aside from this, the establishment of the reservation did not at first significantly alter either residence patterns or utilization of natural resources. Throughout the late 1800s, however, as more economic opportunities and BIA programs became concentrated in Neah Bay, there was a gradual decline in population at outlying village sites and a corresponding increase in Neah Bay. Isolated families remained in the other villages, but by 1914 Neah Bay had become the primary village of residence and the economic center of the reservation that it is today.

In 1887, Congress passed the Land in Severalty Act, also known as the Dawes Act or the Allotment Act. Its goal was to further the assimilation of Indians by teaching them farming and "the values of individualism and private property ownership" (O'Brien 1989:77), ironically values already more highly developed in Makah culture than in the European-American one in which this act originated. The Dawes Act was not implemented on the Makah Reservation until 1907, when each individual was given a specified number of acres. Allotment destroyed any remaining visages of the former system by which land use areas were controlled by family heads, although families did often receive their allotments in the vicinity of their ancestral villages.[3] By this period as well, the remaining longhouses on the reservation were torn down to force people to live in single family homes (Gillis 1974:112).

On reservations across the country, the BIA had a set of prime objectives aimed at the assimilation of native peoples. In Neah Bay as elsewhere, these focused on farming, the education of children, and the suppression of indigenous ceremonies. The nationwide directive to turn Indian peoples into agriculturists was clearly ridiculous in the Makah Tribe's situation, a point local administrators well recognized (Kendall 1862):

> It will be difficult to induce these Indians to turn their attention to farming. It is essentially a marine tribe, living on and around the water, and obtaining their principal support therefrom. They are experts in all the arts of fishermen, and realize considerable income from the sale of oil obtained annually from various kinds of fish. Not feeling justified in expending public money upon bleak and barren cliffs and unproductive soil, I shall not make any expenditure there until I can make such an examination as will justify me in making some recommendation to the department.

A later agent in his annual report agreed (Hays 1870): "It would be worse than folly to attempt to change these expert fishermen into a tribe of farmers." Repeatedly in correspondence from the late 1800s, Makah Reservation agents stress the lack of suitable land for raising crops and suggest building commercial fisheries instead. In an irony tribal members appreciate, one Makah elder described having used the tines of government-issued pitchforks to fashion hooks for catching halibut (Ides 1994).

Commercial marketing of marine resources met with more success, as Makah traders had been doing this for hundreds of years. Early contacts with Indian peoples on the Northwest coast came about through European-

Americans' desire for otter pelts from about 1780 to 1820, a trade in which Makah tribal members were also active. With a developing market for seal-skins in the 1860s, Makahs began hunting them in great numbers with harpoons and canoes. Starting in the 1880s, however, they began hiring on with white-owned schooners, which often traveled as far away as Japan and the Bering Sea. Sealing was very profitable for many tribal members and by the 1890s, several owned their own sealing schooners and hired white navigators. Overhunting as a result of firearms and, as of 1894, international restrictions on sealing brought this profitable venture to a close by century's end.[4] Another money-generating resource was whale oil, used among other things for greasing logging skids, and dogfish oil, used for machinery.[5] In 1891, Makah tribal members were selling whale oil for one dollar per gallon to other tribes up and down the Northwest coast (McGlinn 1891).

As was the policy in reservation schools across the nation, Neah Bay teachers forbade the use of the native language in order to force children to learn English. Children who experienced these sometimes harsh policies often spared their own children by refusing to teach them Makah; only a handful of elders alive today learned Makah as their first language. In addition to basic subjects like history and math, girls were also taught domestic arts such as cooking and sewing, while boys were taught trades such as raising livestock, farming, and blacksmithing. Both sexes worked in the school gardens. The school at Neah Bay started as a day school in 1863, under the direction of James Swan. By 1874, the school began to board its pupils, reflecting a nationwide policy change aimed at further isolating children from their ancestral lifestyles. In 1868, reservation teacher R. L. Doyle wrote of Makah children in attendance (Doyle 1868):

> I have uniformly found them willing, and rather proud of learning to do and work as white people do, and so far as they can be made to understand the objects and benefit of anything, they take an interest in it as readily as could be expected. These remarks apply to those who are taken away from the Indian families and boarded and lodged at the school-house. I have seen nothing encouraging from those children who come to the school-house for a few hours each day, and the rest of their time are exposed to Indian influence and example. In my opinion, the only way to accomplish any good with them is to take the children who attend school away from their Indian parents, and keep them as much as possible from Indian influence and example, and keep them under the influence of civilized life until they can speak and understand our language and become sufficiently acquainted with the different kinds of

work to enable them to earn a living without resorting to the pursuits of Indian life.

Despite this teacher's recommendation, the boarding school reverted back to a day school in 1896. This schooling succeeded nevertheless in eroding the significance of indigenous practices to the younger generation and accustomed them to the luxuries of white lifestyles to be gained through the cash economy. Many youth who grew up in boarding schools came to view the practices of their elders as backward and even embarrassing, and consequently many of this generation raised their own children without acknowledging their native roots. Schooling thus furthered the disruption of ownership and inheritance of cultural goods that began with population loss, dissuading students from using their native material culture in affiliated ceremonies.

Another early focus of BIA efforts at assimilation of Indian people was the suppression of indigenous ceremonies. In Neah Bay, primary targets were potlatching, the Klukwalle, "gambling" (bone gaming), and traditional healing. The potlatch, in particular, came under pressure. Swan, a sympathetic BIA employee, recorded this incident in his diary entry for 22 May 1880 (Swan Diaries):

> This afternoon Peter [a Makah] came up with David and a large crowd of Indians some 40 in all among which were 4 Nittinats to see about a potlatch. Capt. Willoughby [the Indian agent] met them in the school room and told them that he objects to the Nittinats coming here [Neah Bay] as they bring whiskey and smuggle blankets and it would not be allowed. He wants the Makahs to keep their money and build good houses and buy schooners so they could be independent of the schooners who come here to trade, and not give everything away to the Vancouver Indians.

Agent attitudes towards such activities on the Makah Reservation is further reflected in an 1890 report to the Commissioner of Indian Affairs (McGlinn 1890):

> All heathenish and barbarous practices I have endeavored to stop, and where possible prohibit altogether, such as the "Cloqually dance." This dance, from what I have heard of it, must be a cross between the devil's dance and the can-can. Potlaching (giving away) of all kinds . . . has been carried on here without stay or hindrance, and I have had a great deal of trouble in carrying out the in-

structions of the Indian Department in this matter. I have been successful in a measure, so much so, that it is practically stopped on the reservation, though they now give potlaches on an island near Cape Flattery, in the Pacific Ocean.

Gambling, also known as *slahal* or the bone game, continues to be a favorite pastime of Northwest Coast tribes. Not surprisingly, this was also looked upon unfavorably by Indian agents. In 1929, an agent proudly reported: "There is very little gambling carried on by the Indians. They once in a long time have a secret 'bone game.'" Like potlatching, however, it did not disappear but simply went underground.

Ruth Claplanhoo related to me the following incident, which occurred when she was a young woman and roughly the same year that the agent made the above comment (Interview, 19 February 1998):

[T]his was in the late, late [19]20s I think . . .

Art [Ruth's husband] had a brother that lived in Tsooes and his work was raising cattle. He killed a beef. And he invited a few people from the village. Mostly old people. And it was just a clean fun. There wasn't anything serious. They were just playing that bone game. We stayed overnight because you can't make that trip walking in the daytime. Pretty soon there was a knock on the door. And it was a young man on a horse, he said "I came ahead to warn you that Mr. Dodge [the agent] is sending a policeman and his maintenance man here. He heard that you're having a party here."

I don't know why we got so scared. We weren't doing anything wrong. Of course, we did know that he didn't want us to Indian dance. And when they'd play that bone game, we had no money to bet with. What we betted would be like [a] can of berries or some seafood. Things . . . little things like that.

Well, after this young man warned us, we just scattered. We scattered. Some of us were laying on the floor. Pretty soon, there was knock on the door and it was these two men and the mistake they made was . . . they had guns. They had guns. And Horace told them, Horace was Art's brother, Horace told them, he says "Yeah, we did have a little party, but my guests are mostly old people and having a little party. There's nothing out of the way that we were doing." Well, that broke up the party. It was too good to last.

Next day Art's oldest brother came down and he called Washington, D.C. This Mr. and Mrs. Dodge were part Indians. So, they really, really didn't like us to go back [to] Indian doings. Oh, Jongie came down; he called Washington, D.C. He says "Remove Mr. Dodge at once" and he explained the reason. Just like that, Mr. Dodge was gone.

This story suggests the amount of control exercised by Indian agents over tribal members' lives. It indicates, however, that indigenous practices continued with greater regularity than agency personnel probably realized. The story also sheds some light on the relationships between locals and whites. Ruth speaks about fear of being caught, yet the host of the gathering is anything but intimidated when the policeman shows up. By 1929, tribal members were beginning to be permitted greater decision-making authority on the reservation, presaging the establishment of the tribal council a few years later. In this climate, Makah initiative in successfully speaking out against and subsequently ousting Mr. Dodge is noteworthy. Ruth also told me that after he left, potlatches and "Indian dancing" began again to be more openly conducted.

Healing practices by indigenous doctors were also a target of federal policy. This was part of a wider initiative to improve the health of native peoples by encouraging adoption of European-American standards of personal hygiene, food preparation, and housekeeping. Neah Bay agent Charles Willoughby described his success in his annual report one year, under the heading "Indian Doctors" (Willoughby 1882):

> I am happy to state the pernicious practices of these people are fast becoming a thing of the past. The benefits derived from the agency physician, the efforts of the agent and employees, and the closer intimacy with the manners and customs of the whites all combine to do away with this cruel quackery forever. To destroy their belief in their medicine men, who are ever the enemy of the whites, inasmuch as the presence of the latter is a signal for their overthrow, is to make a huge stride toward civilizing the Indians.

Willoughby's optimism regarding the abandonment of Makah doctoring seems misplaced when contrasted with the situation described by his successor (McGlinn 1890):

> The influence that the native doctor has over them is astonishing; even the young men and women who have had several years' training in school are not free from it. Most of them firmly believe that the medicine men have power to blast their lives or kill them by the power of their magic. You may reason with them, laugh and scoff at their fears, but all is of no avail, their superstition still remains.

Nonetheless, of all the indigenous practices that came under pressure from agency personnel, healing is the one that has least survived into the present day.

The forced confiscation of cultural objects does not seem to have been a tactic of suppression in Neah Bay on the part of missionaries or agents. There was certainly not the same high-profile banning of the potlatch (with associated impounding of objects) seen on Vancouver Island.[6] Makah elders do not recall stories about such confiscation, saying that more often objects no longer being used were put away by their owners. As Donna Wilkie explained, "At the turn of the century when you had people being forbidden to do their traditional practices, then those objects no longer had any value. They were put away in a box and stuck somewhere." Many of these objects were later found and subsequently sold by succeeding generations who either did not know or did not care about their cultural significance. Some items were destroyed, a common practice when an owner died without passing them on, but others were simply carted to the dump. Donna also noted that doctor's gear was more likely to be a focus of confiscation:

> Especially if a missionary felt like a particular person had a lot of control over the community and over the people—control meaning leadership control as a doctor. What modern day society would say "This person is a doctor, this person's a healer." Anybody that had some kind of control over the people and they used certain charms, necklaces, whatever in their ceremony processes. Those things would be confiscated and either destroyed or sent away. (Interview, 7 May 1998)

Doctors were viewed by agents and missionaries as a threat to Christianity, since they functioned as intermediaries to the supernatural. To agents who recorded how fearful tribal members were of a doctor's powers, they also represented a threat to government authority.

Many accounts of the early reservation period stress, as I have, the various efforts agents made to "civilize" the Indians and the impacts this had on cultural practices. With the exception of Erikson (1996), I believe most writers have focused rather less on the strategies used by Northwest Coast tribal peoples to resist such policies of assimilation and preserve traditions under these very oppressive circumstances. Some of the agency documents I have quoted above allude to the resistance encountered from tribal members in response to federal policies. In 1882, one agent penned the following observation: "On my assuming the duties of agent . . . a determined stand against this [the practice of potlatch] was at once taken—and yet withal these people were loyal." Another agent, writing fifty years later, was still encountering the same resistance (Bitney 1931):

> The Indians gamble in the "bone game" also called Sahal, hand game, stick game, bone gamble, etc., to a certain extent. We have stopped this practice on the reservation but they go to Vancouver Island or off the reservation for their games. They also have "Potlatches" or "Indian Give Away" parties, where they give out several dollars worth of merchandise, cash, etc., as well as feed forty or fifty Indians for several days. This is one of the curses of the Coast tribes and should be stopped absolutely. We have curtailed the activity of these potlatches but do not believe it has been stopped. The Indians have enlisted the aid of Indian sentimentalists, politicians, and cheap grafters to be "allowed to carry on their innocent pastimes and exhibit their culture."

This passage describes one of the most common strategies of evasion engaged in by Makah tribal members, which was to hold potlatches outside the boundaries of the reservation, on offshore islands or in Canada, where agents had no jurisdiction. On other occasions, they were simply concealed from the authorities. Like the incident related at length by Ruth, Makah elders' stories are rife with tales of clandestine potlatches and bone games in this period. Potlatches, it is recorded, were also planned to coincide with birthdays or Christmas, when gift giving was encouraged by agents (Kirk 1986:32; MCRC 1987:51). Tribal oral history leads one to question whether the acceptance of agency prohibitions by Makah people was truly as complete as this agent seemed to believe (McGlinn 1890): "My interference in this time-honored and sacred privilege [potlatching] was not well received. There was a howl raised, but they found this only increased my determination, so they finally accepted the situation."

If confiscation of cultural objects as a tool of suppression was not common on the Makah Reservation, they did leave by other means during the early reservation period. Despite frequent lack of cooperation by Makahs, many objects ended up in museums worldwide, where they now await drawing back.

TRADERS, COLLECTORS, AND THIEVES: MARKETING MATERIAL CULTURE

Throughout these years of cultural disruption, many objects that Makah tribal members had used in both their everyday lives and in ceremonies fell into disuse. Some of this material was simply obsolete, replaced by goods readily available at the reservation store. Other objects, associated with practices discouraged by agents, were stored away or sold. Cultural goods left Makah hands during this period in a myriad of ways. Most of these means were legal, some were not. Even when objects were voluntarily parted with, it was often overwhelming economic and social pressures that forced the alienation. My discussion will focus on these issues in the context of historical realities on the Makah Reservation, but also in reference to wider trends in both national and global collecting movements. The bulk of systematic collecting by museums and the development of tourist arts occurred during this early reservation period. However, I have chosen to consider all forms of estrangement here, and some of my illustrative examples date to a later period.

Makah objects first began leaving the reservation in large numbers during the late 1800s, when traders and BIA personnel realized that marketing items such as baskets and small carvings could be a profitable enterprise, both for themselves and for tribal members. Trade in these articles, especially women's basketry, was developed alongside commercial fishing and farming, to encourage incorporation into the cash economy. Throughout the late 1800s and early 1900s, weaving was the primary means through which women participated in the cash economy, thereby providing clothing and staples such as flour for their families (MCRC 1987:41; fig. 12). A more detailed look at the marketing of basketry provides an excellent example of the impact the emerging cash economy had on ancestral forms of material culture.

W. W. Washburn established a trading post in Neah Bay in the late 1800s.[7] In return for being able to lease land on the reservation, Washburn was required by the government to accept local goods from tribal members in return for store credit. These goods consisted primarily of basketry and carvings, although he also purchased halibut. Before tourists came frequently to the reservation, Washburn must have sent these items via steamer to markets in Port Angeles, Port Townsend, and Seattle. Washburn was, in the words of one elder, very particular about the baskets he would purchase. Ed Claplanhoo, whose mother is a weaver, commented:

> The original baskets were symmetrical designs. Everything was done symmetrically. It was only because of W. W. Washburn when he first brought his trading post out here and he told the ladies—if you're going to sell something put objects on it instead of what you're doing. So that's why you'll see piles of older baskets like that being symmetrical, rather than whales, seals, canoes. When my mother first started weaving baskets as a girl everything was symmetrical or geometrical, rather than birds, canoes, seal, whales. See that was made because the demand was for that. (Interview, 2 February 1998)

FIG. 12. By weaving, Makah women were able to provide staples for their families through the cash economy. This photograph, taken around 1900, shows two women at Neah Bay making the characteristic Nuu-chah-nulth style trinket baskets, which are found in museum collections nationwide. Courtesy of the Museum of History and Industry, Seattle, neg. #88.33.52.

Washburn paid set amounts for baskets having specified diameters, as well as carved totem poles or model canoes (made by men) having a specific height or length. This single trader had a profound impact on the forms that are now thought to be particularly characteristic of Makah basketry. In addition to specifying the motifs, Washburn favored baskets that were fully twined with grass, as opposed to more utilitarian (and common) ones made of plaited cedar bark.

In part as a result of Washburn's role, Makah basketry is copiously represented in an astonishingly widespread number of museums. Washburn was a savvy businessman and had various ways of making his basket trade more profitable. Frank Smith Sr., a Makah elder, related this story:

> I was in the back room with Harry Washburn. We was getting some parts for a stove or something and I saw this wall of baskets. You know, shelves. This whole wall—baskets. And the roof was leaking in that spot. [I said] "Jees. Why do you let those baskets get ruined like that?" He said, "Are you kidding?" He says, "Them baskets ain't getting ruined." He says, "That's making them better!" And he had to make them look old, I guess, when he's selling them. (Interview, 9 April 1998)

In the 1930s or 1940s when this incident occurred, it was well known that museums and collectors favored the older, and therefore more "authentic" items. In the early 1930s, the Great Depression brought the basket trade to a close, at least temporarily. In a 1933 report on basketry, Agent Bitney wrote (Bitney 1933):

> Heretofore, the post-trader [Washburn?] has always taken all of them [baskets] in trade for groceries, but had to cease taking them on May 1, 1932 as he had $7,000.00 worth and could take no more under the present economic conditions. He found it impossible to market them as no one would buy them as curios are not in demand at any price.

This presaged a difficult period on the reservation, as elsewhere, during the 1930s.

In order to understand the role of collectors in the flow of Makah objects from tribal members to museums during this period, some historical background is necessary. The most extensive treatment of collecting on the Northwest Coast is, without a doubt, Douglas Cole's *Captured Heritage: The*

Scramble for Northwest Coast Artifacts (1985). The early reservation period I cover in this chapter coincides with the "heyday of anthropological collecting on the Northwest Coast" (Cole 1985:286). This occurred during a time in which museums devoted to the arts, history, and science were rapidly being established in Europe and America. A growing sense of civic pride combined with capitalist philanthropy funded both the building of extensive collections and the institutions to house them. This was not limited to American museums such as the Smithsonian, but also resulted in huge Northwest Coast collections in cities like London, Berlin, and St. Petersburg. Anthropological collecting was particularly competitive and conducted with a great sense of urgency, as civilization was thought to be quickly destroying native lifeways, which included material culture. There was an almost missionary zeal to secure whatever could be had before it disappeared forever.[8] The Northwest Coast was particularly attractive to museums, because the material culture was both abundant and dramatic (Cole 1985:290). Cole (1985:294) notes that "the Northwest Coast was one of the few North American areas of rich and striking material cultures which remained relatively unshattered at the advent of the Museum Age." The beginning of the "Museum Age" coincided with the first long-term intrusions of western culture into native communities in this area.

These trends in collecting have a very intimate and important link to Neah Bay and the Makah Indians. In 1875, the Smithsonian Institution ushered in a new era by becoming the first museum to provide an acquisition budget and place a collector on salary. This collector was James Swan, at the time a schoolteacher in Neah Bay. Swan was also among the first collectors to be employed by the federal government specifically for ethnographic collecting (Cole 1985:22). He was originally from Boston, but in his early thirties left his family to settle in Washington Territory. Swan was regarded as quite a colorful character even within his lifetime. Cole provides a concise sketch of his personality (Cole 1985:15):

> He possessed a sensitivity, rare for the time and place, toward his Indian contemporaries. His sincere and only occasionally supercilious interest in them was reciprocated by an unusual trust and openness. The Makah even named a sealing ship after him. On the other side, he found, as correspondent with the great scientists of Washington . . . and, as a collector for the Smithsonian, a measure of flattering prestige. He could contribute to the universal world of science, be recognized by the best minds of his country, and be honored for his long and intimate knowledge of the Pacific Coast and its native inhabitants.

Swan's enthusiasm for collecting was clearly driven by a desire for fame, recognition, and honor. Smithsonian personnel, for their part, were pleased to have a dedicated correspondent in a region of the country from which little material had yet been obtained.

Swan's association with the Smithsonian began in 1863, when he read a circular from the Institution soliciting volunteers to collect natural history and ethnological specimens. Much can be gleaned about Swan's collecting practices and interactions with native communities from his daily diaries, written over a period of nearly thirty years, and his surviving correspondence with the Smithsonian. His first contributions consisted mostly of natural history specimens; he recruited Makah schoolchildren to bring him shells and birds' eggs. When he turned his attention to ethnographic objects, Swan found that Makah tribal members were great traders and expected to be paid for even the smallest items. Swan kept scrupulous accounts of his expenditures, in hopes of eventual compensation. The Smithsonian wanted a representative sample of Makah manufacture; among the easiest for collectors such as Swan to obtain were household objects that had become obsolete (shell knives, for example) or that were easily replaceable. These included utensils, weapons, tools, bowls, baskets, spoons, knives, and fishhooks.[9] In 1875, Secretary Baird commissioned Swan to collect for the 1876 Centennial Exhibition to be held in Philadelphia. Although Swan himself did not attend the exhibition, his collection, numbering nearly five hundred objects, was the most extensive and valuable yet assembled from the Northwest Coast (Cole 1985:27). One of the collection's signature pieces was an eleven-foot carved Makah figure, purchased for thirty-five dollars.

In 1882, Secretary Baird acquired funds to support collecting for the 1883 International Fisheries Exposition in London. For this, Swan was instructed to focus on fishing, sealing, and whaling gear, much of which he procured from Makah sources. However, he soon found that they were unwilling to part with prized whaling gear (Cole 1985:303). Successful hunts imbued this gear with magic, and tribal members were apparently concerned that if the gear were sold they would not catch any more whales. In order to complete his collections, Swan was forced to commission new, unused gear. For the Cotton Centennial Exposition in New Orleans a year later, Swan purchased a scaled-down Cape Flattery whaling canoe with gear. Although he continued to contribute to the Smithsonian collections until his death in 1900, his last commissioned purchases were for Franz Boas's Northwest Coast display at the Chicago World's Fair (the Columbian Exposition) in 1892 and 1893.

This sketch of Swan's collecting history provides a glimpse into one means by which Makah objects arrived in museum collections. Swan is clearly the best-documented collector to have worked on the Makah Reservation. Yet, since he largely did not record the ownership of objects he purchased, it is unlikely that the Tribe will be able to draw back under NAGPRA much of the material he collected.

Cole takes great pains throughout his discussion to emphasize the fact that for the most part, ethnographic collections were acquired by honest means. Museum personnel generally paid for what they took and many of them were "scrupulous about settling claims to ownership" (Cole 1985:310). He points out that most exchanges of cultural goods were incorporated into established patterns of trade that native peoples had been participating in for a century. He concedes that one can view the relationship between collectors and natives as a product of the colonial encounter where members of the dominant economic system had the advantage. Nevertheless, he prefers to stress the agency of natives in this process (Cole 1985:310):

> Some tourists and visitors were cheated, some natives had to make sales under forced conditions, but the great majority of items changed hands at prices defined by normal market factors. The Northwest Coast Indians were not naïve. They were experienced traders who refused offers as often as they accepted them and who were seldom prepared to part with anything cheaply. They sometimes responded to the demand quickly and adroitly, seeking higher prices in cities when field collectors offered too little and adjusting production to collecting fashion.

Swan observed many of these traits in the tribal members he dealt with. This is not to deny that some material culture may have left the Makah Reservation through theft, pure and simple. When asked about objects being stolen from the reservation by outsiders interested in profit rather than the pursuit of knowledge, elders indicated that they had not heard such stories from their parents or grandparents and explained that this was probably because outsiders would have had to come by canoe. In other words, it would have been very difficult to enter Makah communities unobserved before the road was completed in 1931, at which point the Great Depression was forcing the Museum Age to a close.

Thefts of cultural objects did occur, however. More commonly, they were stolen by tribal, or even family, members. Interviewees indicated that alcohol was often a factor in this kind of alienation, either because people would steal things while they were intoxicated or else steal things in order to get cash to buy alcohol. I was given many specific examples of such incidents from interviewees' own lives. Although this is a sensitive topic and one into which I hesitated to delve, I was told that it was often the younger members of families, who either did not respect the traditions or did not know about them, who stole family gear to sell for profit. Often these items, having been stored away, were not missed until years later:

> I had a dentalium headdress that I owned that my great-grandmother gave me and I left it here at Neah Bay while I went to school in Seattle and I had it put away in the attic in my great-grandmother's home. Well, she died. And people went in there and rifled through her stuff and a relative took the headdress and sold it. Okay. I found it by a miracle. I found it. I saw it somewhere and I said, "That belongs to me." I recognized it. And I went in and I talked to the people and I said "I recognize that as mine. It was given to me." And the lady said, "Well, I got it from this person." And I says, "Well, I want my . . . I'll pay you whatever you paid them. I want the object back." I think it was only sold for twenty dollars, so I did get it back. But see, things like that . . . it's different. And I did know who took it, but it was a family member. But it was a family member that was having a problem with things and knew who it belonged to but they went ahead and did it anyway for money. (Interview, 7 May 1998)

Because collectors did often obtain these objects directly from tribal members, they mistakenly believed that the transaction was legitimate, not realizing that the individual selling the item may not have been the owner. There is a belief on the part of some tribal members that many objects sold to museums were represented by collectors as having been purchased, when in fact they were stolen in this way. It is this group of items that Makah tribal members fear will be the most difficult to draw back, because families would have to prove one of their own members acted wrongly.

In other cases, families are aware that significant objects have gone missing, but do not know exactly when or how this happened. A man from a long line of whale hunters told me:

> I know, probably, my family's whaling gear is somewhere. It probably is in a museum. I wouldn't know where it'd be, where it'd be on show or something. I don't know. Cause we had a harpoon and some sinew lines and cedar bark rope from the harpoon points, to the shaft, to the sinew rope, to the cedar rope. But no floats. But we had that complete set and that was stolen from our house. It's probably out somewhere. It's probably in a museum because it was

all in perfect shape. This was back in the forties, when it was stolen from our house. (Interview, 17 March 1998)

No one really knows how much stolen Makah material is in museums. Some families know that they are missing objects, like the whaling gear mentioned above, but even with NAGPRA face the arduous task of locating it and the difficult prospect of reclaiming it.

In addition to theft, collecting, and legitimate trade, there were other means through which objects, especially archaeological resources, left reservations. Untrained individuals, believing themselves to be amateur archaeologists, would dig at abandoned or temporarily vacated villages or campsites on Indian lands on their own initiative. Many of these individuals were genuinely interested in the history of native peoples. Some items that the Makah Tribe will soon claim under NAGPRA are linked to one such character, by the name of Fred Pennoyer. He lived in Port Angeles but frequently visited a sister who lived in Neah Bay. His attitudes towards his self-proclaimed "fascinating hobby [of archaeology]" are reflected in his writings (Pennoyer[n.d.]d): "Every year more and more of these sites are lost forever through the construction of roads and towns. For this reason I believe it desirable for serious persons to investigate these ancient camps, although they will not be able to record as much information as a trained archaeologist."

Pennoyer made repeated digging trips to sites on Makah lands, probably in the 1940s, including Hoko and Ozette. (Both of these sites were later excavated by professional archaeologists.) One of his finds was a skull he unearthed at the village of Waatch, which he donated to Olympic National Park in 1952. A *Federal Register* notice was published for this skull in August 1996 and the actual repatriation occurred in the fall of 1997. The Burke Museum in Seattle has in its collection a bone comb also dug up by Pennoyer at Waatch, which will be returned to the Tribe as an unassociated funerary object. Pennoyer also engaged in limited collecting, often with unwilling tribal members. In an unpublished account of one of his visits to Neah Bay, he writes of a war club shown to him by an elderly woman (Pennoyer [n.d.]c): "She seemed reluctant to sell it, but when [we] offered to trade a hunting knife, she readily agreed." This leads one to think about how much coercion there may have been in the techniques used by competing collectors on behalf of major American and European museums.

While individuals like Pennoyer attempted to keep professional records of their digs, to follow prescribed archaeological methods, to correspond with professional archaeologists, and even occasionally to publish their finds, others who dug on Indian lands were clearly driven by profit and sought to obtain valuables that could be sold to museums or private collectors. These people worked surreptitiously and took pains not to bring attention to their activities. This was less of a problem on the isolated Makah Reservation than for many other native peoples, but such looting did still occur.

I have traced Makah history from an intact precontact culture through decades of decline in the early reservation period. The population diminished. Cultural practices and goods disappeared from public view. In the twentieth century, the Makah Tribe has gradually rebounded, not only politically but culturally as well. The population has nearly returned to precontact estimates, past practices such as whaling are coming back, and cultural goods have an opportunity to be drawn back with NAGPRA. The struggle to bring these changes about and to "bridge the gap," in George Bowechop's words, is our next focus.

4 / A New Era

TRIBAL POLITICS

AND CULTURAL PROJECTS

We're just lucky that the Tribe has an institution like this [MCRC]. If we carry this whole program out [NAGPRA] in the best interests of the entire tribe it should have some really powerful impacts, because there was so much that was suppressed and that was collected and that was pushed underground. This will really open up a whole new arena of use of objects. It's exciting. It really is.

—Janine Bowechop, 1 December 1997

The establishment of the reservation and the resulting federal policies undeniably curtailed many customary practices, but the daily lifestyle of Makah tribal members remained relatively unchanged throughout the early reservation period. Although new pursuits, such as seasonal agricultural work, gradually came to be a regular part of Makah employment, for the most part tribal members made a living hunting, fishing, and gathering intertidal resources as they always had. However, these subsistence activities were intensified as surplus was sought to permit tribal members to purchase goods in the growing cash economy. Of this period Wray (1997:17) writes, "the remote location of the reservation isolated the Makah from total emergence into European-American culture. It wasn't until 1931 . . . that the Makah were truly absorbed into the acculturation process." Many Makah individuals in their forties and fifties today recall as children visiting or sometimes living with older relatives who did not yet have electricity or indoor plumbing. It is ironic that the long-delayed acquisition of modern conveniences on the reservation coincides with initial efforts to draw back culture.

Around 1930, a confluence of circumstances signal a new era in Makah history and sharply distinguish trends prior to this date from modern events in the twentieth century. In 1931, a road connecting the Makah Reservation to other towns on the Olympic Peninsula was completed, bringing its isolation to an end. It is around 1930, as well, that the most restrictive period of government control over Indian lives was drawing to a close at a national level. In 1924, Indian peoples had been granted full United States citizenship and momentum was building towards the Indian Reorganization Act of 1934, which would establish tribal self-governance. On the Makah Reservation, this increasingly detached attitude on the part of the government encouraged more open participation in activities such as potlatching. The final influencing circumstance at this time was the onset of the Great Depression and the end of the Museum Age.

Below I briefly outline the major events in Makah history during the twentieth century, with special focus on those programs designed by the Tribe to renew interest in cultural activities. While such programs existed from the 1930s onward, the Ozette excavation in the 1960s and 1970s gave them a new energy. These excavations by most accounts marked a turning point and ushered in a new era in cultural resource management at the tribal level, based at the newly founded MCRC. NAGPRA is one of its most recent cultural projects.

There is not as yet a good account of twentieth-century Makah political and economic history, although tribal members are currently writing one. Other scholars also have noted that information about Neah Bay after 1935 is very scarce (Gillis 1974:115). The information that follows has been culled mostly from primary sources and slim mentions in works devoted to Native American issues at the national level during this period. I have also made extensive use of Erikson's (1996) community history to complement gaps in my own research. My interview material, while focused on other subjects, provided additional glimpses into Makah life during the last fifty years. In most cases these are childhood reminiscences of my middle-aged interviewees.

MODERN HISTORY: 1931–1960

The modern political history of the Makah Tribe begins in 1924, when the federal government conferred American citizenship on tribal peoples throughout the United States. Many native communities had been agitating for citizenship since freed slaves were granted the privileges of this status in 1868. After an estimated ten thousand Indian men served in World War I,

Congress rewarded this patriotic contribution by passing the Indian Citizenship Act, which allowed the men to vote in state and national elections (O'Brien 1989:80). In 1934, the Makah Tribe voted to accept the Indian Reorganization Act and two years later adopted a constitution and tribal charter. The vision of John Collier, Commissioner of Indian Affairs from 1933 to 1945, reorganization was intended to re-establish tribal governments and thereby allow tribes nationwide to control their own economic development, education, and social service programs (such as health and welfare). This shift in government policy, according to O'Brien (1989:81–82), reflected an increased sensitivity to the welfare of all peoples during the Great Depression and grew out of the findings of the Meriam Report, published in 1928. This government-sponsored study surveyed conditions on reservations and concluded that existing programs run by the BIA were failing native peoples. In addition, it acknowledged that native peoples were being excluded from managing their own affairs.

Under reorganization, Makah tribal members set up a five-member elected Tribal Council, serving staggered terms. The Makah Tribal Council oversees the administration of numerous tribal departments, including Fisheries, Forestry, and Health Services. The Tribe's initial economic development efforts were focused on commercial fishing, logging, and tourism.[1] One of the primary reasons that tribal members voted to accept reorganization was that it reversed the allotment process implemented in 1907 (Ruby and Brown 1986:126). When Makah tribal members were initially assigned these individual agricultural allotments, there was a trust period during which individual owners could not sell their land. By 1934, the trust period for these allotments had not yet expired, so individual holdings subsequently reverted to tribal control. This timing prevented reservation land from passing out of tribal hands, a process that occurred elsewhere when native owners sold their allotments to non-Indians.

The twentieth century has seen Makah participation in a number of important legal battles re-establishing rights to terrestrial and marine resources. The Makah Tribal Council almost immediately began seeking compensation from the Indian Claims Commission, established in 1946 to hear such cases, for lands ceded under the 1855 treaty as well as for damages for deprivation of hunting and fishing rights. This case dragged on for nearly fifty years; ultimately the Tribe was denied compensation for subsistence pursuits but in May 1984, Waadah and Tatoosh Islands became part of the reservation. (Land surrounding the former village of Ozette had returned to tribal jurisdiction in 1970.) In the 1960s and 1970s, tribes throughout Washington State participated in legal actions to protect their fishing rights. In 1974, the result of the landmark case *U.S. v. Washington,* known as the Boldt decision, affirmed native peoples' rights to half the state's allotted salmon catch. The decision also supported tribal efforts to become active participants in the regulation and management of fishery resources alongside state and federal agencies. The Makah Tribe's Department of Fisheries opened its first salmon hatchery in 1981 and now operates two, on the Hoko and Tsooes Rivers, and has marine biologists permanently on staff. In 1994, the Makah Tribe won a halibut fishing rights case. Whaling and the IWC decision represent the most recent legal battle.

During the twentieth century, a strong military presence on the Makah Reservation shaped the daily experience of an entire generation whose members are now in their forties and fifties, providing not only new economic but social opportunities. Many middle-aged Makah tribal members fondly remember attending dances on the base, going to the bar (the rest of the reservation was and remains "dry"), and bowling at the base's bowling alley. Cape Flattery has always had strategic importance to the military, since it occupies a key geographic location commanding the entrance to the Strait of Juan de Fuca. Since 1857, there has been a lighthouse on Tatoosh Island, directly off the cape, operated by the Coast Guard. It has since been fully automated, but the Coast Guard still maintains an active base in Neah Bay. There is also a U.S. Weather Bureau station located within reservation boundaries.

During World War I, fortifications were begun on the reservation, which were expanded during World War II to include a radar unit and concrete gun emplacements along the coast. In 1950, the Makah Air Force Base was established and, until it closed in 1989, maintained a normal complement of 120 men (Hoonan 1964:25). Most of the reservation's coastal roads were first constructed by the military. In 1942, the Army Corps of Engineers completed construction of a breakwater from Waadah Island, in Neah Bay, to the mainland, that for the first time created a sheltered harbor. The military employed many tribal members during its years of operation and many military men married local Makah women. Nearly every Makah family of my acquaintance has a member who either served or married into the military; many Makah tribal members have thus traveled widely or, in some cases, were even raised abroad. The land that was expropriated for the base has reverted to tribal control and these buildings are now occupied by the tribal government. The former residential area for the base houses Makah families.

The decades from the 1950s through the early 1980s were some of the most prosperous for the Tribe. Good jobs were to be found with the military and in logging, while the Boldt decision provided a boost to the commercial fishing industry. Tourism increased during the 1970s as a result of the publicity surrounding the Ozette excavation. Makah Days, a tribal holiday founded in 1926 to celebrate citizenship, evolved into a celebration of Makah culture and traditions and a major tourist attraction.[2] During these prosperous years, the Tribe devoted energies to both natural and cultural resource management. In 1955, the forest on Cape Flattery was designated by the Tribe as a Makah Wilderness Area and closed to logging and other harvesting; this area was expanded in 1978. In 1994, the Olympic Coast National Marine Sanctuary was established, which incorporates most of the reservation's coastal waters as well as the Flattery Rocks Wildlife Refuge. On the cultural side, the 1950s and 1960s saw the creation of a number of clubs on the reservation, intended to draw back past practices and encourage community events. These included the Makah Club, the Slahal (Bone-Game) Club, and the Makah Arts and Crafts Club, which taught women basketry and shellwork for the tourist trade (Erikson 1996:215). A Warriors' Club organized community gatherings to honor tribal members who served in the World Wars, and later in Korea and Vietnam. Many songs and dances that had not been performed in decades, yet had been preserved within families, came out during this period (Erikson 1996:216).

Cultural programs on the reservation have been possible because of funds provided by the Johnson-O'Malley Act (JOM), passed in 1934. One of the primary purposes of JOM was to provide supplementary funds to states to meet the unique and specialized needs of Indian children attending public schools (BIA 1993). In 1932, Washington State had established a primary and secondary school in Neah Bay. The predominantly native enrollment made the incorporation of Makah cultural activities into the public school curricula a priority for many tribal members, although such programs met with some resistance from the principally white teachers. JOM funds also enabled the creation of extracurricular programs focused on Makah culture. In the 1960s, additional funding was acquired for similar programs from the Office of Economic Opportunity's Community Action Program. In conjunction with classroom education, a more comprehensive summer cultural program was developed that hired elders to teach regalia making, dances and songs, and Makah language (Erikson 1996:226). By the late 1960s, Makah language was being offered as an elective in high school. In recent years, JOM funds have provided incentive awards for children in fifth through tenth grades to attend summer enrichment programs, allowed Head Start to hire a full-time culture coordinator, and sponsored a Summer

Culture Exchange involving youth from Olympic Peninsula tribes. Current activities funded through JOM are language classes from preschool through fifth grade, summer culture programs, and employment of young people to work with these programs. Language and culture programs today are taught largely by MCRC staff, many of whom are associated with the Makah Language Program.

The reservation has experienced an economic downturn since the mid-1980s, partly because two of the reservation's primary employers, the Air Force and Crown Zellerbach Logging Company, ceased operations. Additionally, the Pacific Northwest salmon crisis has led to decreased quotas for treaty salmon fishing and closures of sport-fishing seasons, which have severely affected income from fisheries and tourism. Commercial fishing has become less viable in recent years, with net income to fishermen owning boats dropping from $1.3 million in 1990 to a deficit of $208,000 in 1993 (MEDP 1994). The affect this has had on the local economy is large, as 70 percent of the community relies on fishing for some or all of their income. Although approximately the same number of men fish as in the past, their quotas are so low that they are prevented from catching enough to make a living solely through this means.

The unemployment rate hovers between 50 and 60 percent, and it is estimated that 49 percent of households are below the poverty line (MEDP 1992). Eighty percent of households are in the low to low-moderate income range. The 1995 per capita income was only $4,706. In 1997, there were 103 people on General Assistance and 70 on Aid to Families with Dependent Children and food stamps.[3] The major employers are the Tribe, the public school, the Makah Housing Authority, Washburn's General Store, the Indian Health Services Clinic, and the MCRC. Off reservation, the Clallam County Correctional Facility about twenty miles away employs many tribal members. A number of individuals make a living from making and selling Indian arts such as baskets, carvings, and jewelry. Many people in all the above sectors augment their income with a variety of seasonal work including shake bolting (cutting cedar shakes for roofing), river fishing, seafood gathering, cutting firewood, and gathering mushrooms. There are also a number of cottage industries including catering, massage services, haircutting, and chore services.

THE OZETTE EXCAVATION AND THE FOUNDING OF THE MCRC

I was stunned when I first entered the MCRC, a rather unprepossessing and featureless building from the exterior (fig. 13). As I emerged from the low-

FIG. 13. The Makah Cultural and Research Center is prominently located at the entrance to the village of Neah Bay. The exhibits and research facilities are in the building on the left; the other structure houses collections storage, conservation areas, the curator's office, and a photographic darkroom. Photograph by the author.

ceilinged, narrow passage that serves as the introductory gallery, I was dramatically confronted with a two-story image of a Makah harpooner poised to strike a whale barely visible beside his canoe. This dynamic black-and-white image captured by Asahel Curtis, a late-nineteenth-century photographer of native scenes, dominates the lofty space. The calls of sea lions fill the air from a nearby diorama depicting two realistic (and very large) stuffed specimens. Also in this gallery are two full-sized replicas of sturdy whaling canoes, thirty feet long, carved by tribal members using the same tools their ancestors would have employed. The gear is there as well, and I experimentally hefted a fifteen-foot alder harpoon, wielded a sealing club, and fingered the textures of cedar-bark mats and baskets and a sealskin float. Soon, the skeleton of the whale killed in the Tribe's recent hunt will hang from the ceiling, memorializing the renewal of this proud tradition.

The MCRC exhibit storyline follows the seasonal activities of ancestral Makahs, beginning with whaling and sealing in the spring. The cases display a dazzling assortment of Ozette artifacts of wood, bone, antler, and cedar bark—so well preserved that I found it a challenge to remember that they are over five hundred years old. As I wandered into summer, topics focused on fishing, gathering, and tool making. Another diorama appeared around a bend, with a beautifully executed representation of the beach at Ozette, complete with a sandy shore strewn with whalebones, seaweed, and shells (always a temptation to small children). An inviting ramp of cedar planks leads from this coastal scene to the exhibits depicting the activities of fall and winter. Here, I found cases that discuss basketry, food preparation, toys and miniatures, games, spinning, clothing, and trade. While the dominant colors throughout the museum are natural earth tones, here there are also two eye-catching cases painted in red. While it is not explicitly stated, I learned later that these cases contain the most highly carved artifacts, many of them with whale motifs, which are thought to have had ceremonial or spiritual significance.

Winter is represented by a full-sized cedar longhouse, also constructed by traditional methods, and allowed to weather naturally outdoors prior to being placed in the exhibit (fig. 14). As I penetrated the darkness of the longhouse, one of my first sensations was the smell—real dried salmon were hanging from the rafters. Simulated fires glow in hearths and sleeping-benches materialize in the far recesses of the house. Visitors are free to explore at will and I discovered bearskins and mats that cushion sleeping platforms, cooking boxes, baskets and mats in progress, and a corner with a loom in it. A door at the front of the longhouse faces the "beach" and I peered out to see another diorama replicating the view such a longhouse would have had of the offshore islands at Ozette. Below the house, on the beach, is a canoe in progress with fishing gear strewn about. The sounds of seagulls fill the air and I could almost imagine the fresh sea breeze. It is no wonder that Makah tribal members are so proud of their museum; it has extraordinary exhibits by any measure.

In addition to housing this exceptional display of Ozette materials, the MCRC is an active research facility with a full library and archives, classroom, temporary exhibit gallery, conservation laboratory, and photographic darkroom. Among other ongoing projects, the MCRC is charged with the Tribe's effort to draw back culture under NAGPRA. The path that the Makah Tribe has chosen in implementing the law cannot be fully understood without reference to the active cultural scene that revolves around the MCRC. As previous writers have noted (Broyles 1989; Oxendine 1992), the Ozette excavations, the founding of the MCRC, and subsequently its cultural programming spurred a cultural resurgence within the Tribe that is very much in evidence still today.[4]

Ozette was a well-established and populous community by 1500 C.E., when a mudslide buried a portion of the village and preserved even organic materials. Makah families still lived there until the 1880s, when government

FIG. 14. A replicated traditional longhouse is among the exhibits at the MCRC. It was built outdoors by tribal members using traditional tools and allowed to weather prior to installation. Furnished with household goods, it is used as a setting for hands-on educational programming. Photograph by Yasu Osawa. Courtesy of the MCRC.

schooling policies forced them to move to Neah Bay. The village was occupied seasonally until the 1920s, but even after this date, it was never far from the minds of the Makah community. Living elders still fondly remember trips to Ozette to dig clams and utilize other abundant marine resources.

The recent history of Ozette begins in the early 1960s, when the federal government declared the area around Ozette to be surplus land and notified the Tribe that it intended to turn it over either to the National Park Service as part of Olympic National Seashore or to the jurisdiction of the county. This launched a tribal effort to regain title to the land. Although tribal members could prove that some signers of the Makah Treaty of 1855 were from Ozette, the federal government requested further proof of affiliation. During this time, the Tribe was approached by archaeologist Dr. Richard Daugherty of Washington State University, who wished to conduct surveys of the site. The Tribe granted permission on the condition that he help them utilize archaeological evidence in their land claims case. Daugherty excavated during the summers of 1966 and 1967 and established the extent and antiquity of the site. Through selective excavations on the reservation, Daugherty also established its cultural affiliation as a Makah village. The Tribe was eventually granted ownership of Ozette Reservation by Congress on 21 October 1970.

No further archaeological work was considered until January 1970, when the Makah Tribal Council learned that a storm had washed away part of the bank at Ozette and that pot-hunters were carrying off artifacts. Although some members of the tribe were against any further disturbance of the site, the council decided that a certain amount of excavation was needed to prevent vandalism and stabilize the area. Funding for the project was obtained from the BIA and administered through the National Park Service. With the close oversight and active assistance of the tribal government and community members, Daugherty and a crew from Washington State University began excavations in April 1970. A project begun as a short-term emergency intervention was to continue year round for the next ten years.

The Makah Tribal Council had stipulated in its agreement with Daugherty that none of the artifacts from Ozette would leave the reservation. In 1971, the council therefore donated a building and fifteen thousand dollars to create a lab facility in Neah Bay which could house the thousands of artifacts generated in the first season alone. These artifacts included basketry, mats, household goods such as wooden bowls, tools, gear for whaling and fishing, toys, weaving equipment, and structural elements from the houses themselves. In short, everything used in the Makah ancestors' daily lives was represented. (In all, fifty-five thousand artifacts were eventually recovered from the site.) It quickly became apparent that the Tribe would need to build a museum. Tribal Council members first approached the Economic Development Administration (EDA) for construction funds in 1971, but the EDA was already sponsoring a project on the reservation to build a sewage system that it wanted to finish first. Although the council at this time stated that the museum was a greater priority, the EDA replied that it was already committed for the sewage system. Concurrently with planning the museum, the Tribe was talking with the Burke Museum and the University of Washington about training a handful of tribal members in museology. In 1973, fifty-five thousand dollars to fund this program was obtained from the National Endowment for the Arts. These students eventually participated in exhibit planning and other activities; most are still involved in some capacity with the MCRC today.

The Tribe again approached the EDA in 1974 and was initially told it could expect a maximum of eight hundred thousand dollars, which would cover the shell of the building; other funds would have to be found for exhibit development and installation. A site selection committee at this time settled on the museum's prominent location at the entrance to the village. Throughout 1975, a museum committee coordinated meetings between the EDA, architects, and Tribal Council members in which architectural plans were drawn up. Jean André, a well-known exhibit designer from the Provincial Museum in Victoria, British Columbia, spent six months in Neah Bay developing the exhibit storyline. During this process, it became evident that the original architectural plans were not adequate for the desired exhibit and were discarded. Finally, in 1976, the Tribe received $1.4 million from the EDA and the project broke ground a year later. By 1978, tribal members were installing the exhibits and in June 1979, the Makah Cultural and Research Center opened to the public. Excavations at Ozette concluded in the summer of 1981 for lack of funds.

Throughout the 1970s, the excavations at Ozette captured the interest of the entire Neah Bay community. Many tribal members visited the site and several volunteered to help, especially young people who could obtain high school or college credit. Makah tribal members in their sixties and seventies insisted on walking the four miles to the site; other elders were given rides in National Guard helicopters. Artifacts were taken out of Ozette by Marine Reserve helicopters to the lab in Neah Bay. Many people in the community went to watch the artifacts being unloaded when they heard the helicopters land. Elders worked with archaeologists in the lab to identify artifacts. Word spread quickly throughout the community when important pieces were unearthed. According to Ed Claplanhoo, who was serving as Tribal Council Chairman during this period, it was a very exciting time in the community. Tribal members were proud to be Makah and proud of all that their ancestors had accomplished.

A sense of pride is still evident in the MCRC exhibits which display these "gifts from the past," as one elder described the artifacts. Norma Pendleton, another elder, views the MCRC "like a church" since it contains items that belonged to the ancestors. Greg Colfax, an MCRC board member and artist who got his start during this period, addressed the lasting influence the excavations had on the community (Interview, 20 January 1998):

GREG: But, the huge effect that this museum has had, I think is overshadowed by the effect that open earth with all the things in it had on the people who worked in that place. All of us who are around this building [MCRC] in some kind of capacity—a board member, an archaeologist—there's a lot of folks in the village who worked in that site. All of us were influenced. All of us were somehow shaken or taken by that hole in the ground. And what was going on in there. All of us were affected. And somehow or other ten, twenty years later, I think that effect is still coming off of us. Still influencing those around us.

ANN: So the effect that Ozette had here was largely through the personal experience individuals had with what was going on at the time.

GREG: Yeah. We're just lucky that going into that hole was not a death sentence. We're lucky that what was in that hole provided us with life and not death. Because it could have gone either way. And I think all of us should be thankful for that.

His last comments reflect deep-seated apprehensions about the consequences of disturbing gravesites and the potential calamities that might befall those who do. Mixed feelings towards the excavation were mentioned by several elders, who indicated that they and others were initially uneasy about digging at Ozette. Nevertheless, once objects began coming out and community reaction was enthusiastic, this fear faded. These same individuals even express the opinion that further work should be done at the site, so that the Tribe can ensure that objects remain under its control.

The impact of the Ozette excavations extended far beyond the Neah Bay community. One of the reasons that the Tribe decided to build a museum was that so many outsiders were coming to see the artifacts that the lab space in Neah Bay could not accommodate them. Ozette remains the largest wet-site[5] excavated in North America and the quantity of well-preserved organic artifacts is unparalleled (Kirk 1980:8). The excavation changed the field of wet-site archaeology and scholars came from around the world to study techniques developed there (Kirk 1980:7). In the 1970s and early 1980s, numerous books and dissertations in archaeology were generated about Ozette (Croes 1977; Friedman 1975; Friedman 1976; Gill 1983; Gleeson 1980; Huelsbeck 1983; Mauger 1978; Samuels 1983; Wessen 1982); subsequently, several anthropologists have studied aspects of the MCRC itself (Bates 1987;

Erikson 1996, 1999; Hughes 1978; Oxendine 1992; Tweedie 1999). A series of popular articles and feature stories appeared in publications such as *National Geographic, Smithsonian Magazine*, and national newspapers which brought Ozette to the attention of the general public (Clark 1984; Daugherty and Kirk 1976; Kirk 1974; Kirk 1980; Pascua 1991). Thousands of people a year made the four-mile trek out to the site while excavations were still ongoing and tours were held twice daily during the summer to accommodate them. On one record-setting day over a thousand people visited. Even now, hundreds of people continue to hike there every year.

Visits to the MCRC number over twenty thousand each year, impressive when one considers its isolated location. In 1994, a documentary entitled *A Gift from the Past*, which discusses the excavation and its effect on the community, was aired on the Public Broadcasting Station (PBS). Nevertheless, despite the international and national attention and acclaim, the MCRC fundamentally remains a tribal museum. Tribal cultural projects clearly take precedence over the needs of visitors and outside researchers when allocating staff time or scheduling events in museum spaces. MCRC outreach programs are also almost exclusively geared towards the local community, with fewer resources allocated to advertising to attract tourists or to develop new cultural programs for their benefit. As Erikson (1999) notes, through the MCRC the Tribe challenges the often negative and inaccurate portrayals of Makah culture that the popular media bring to the American public, especially with regard to whaling. This is certainly true. However, I would argue that the MCRC projects this strong, positive image of tribal identity with the primary goal of instilling pride in Makah generations to come.

In June 1999, the MCRC celebrated its twentieth anniversary, making it one of the oldest professionally run tribal museums in the country. Many of the current staff, board members, and other culturally involved individuals were initially drawn into their culture through Ozette. While the excitement generated by the excavations has faded, the MCRC is still a driving force in the life of the community and heads efforts to draw back culture in many different ways. The Makah Language Program (MLP), established in 1978, still teaches Head Start, high school, and adult classes. MLP staff provides assistance and resources for elementary school teachers as well. Additionally, the MLP works with Makah elders to document and thereby preserve what remains of the spoken language. Public school students make frequent trips to the MCRC for educational programs. Adult classes and workshops are offered in crafts such as basketry and carving. During the summer of 1998, the whaling canoe to be used in the Tribe's successful hunt was carved in a re-created outdoor longhouse on the museum grounds. The indoor longhouse described earlier is periodically the site of a storytime in which Makah elders share old stories with a new generation of listeners. Museum staff coordinates and participates in summer children's classes where they teach songs and dances to perform during Makah Days. Community members and outside researchers alike access the MCRC archives for books, manuscripts, and photographs dealing with Makah history and culture.[6] Local artists display their work for sale in the MCRC's craft shop. Janine Bowechop is considering a proposal to build artist studios on the premises for the benefit of both local artists and visitors. An ethnobotanical garden is currently under construction that will grow a wide range of native plants used by Makah tribal members and their ancestors. Accompanying curricula are being developed to teach youth, through the schools, about how such plants were utilized in the past.

Despite the resounding success of the MCRC and its programs in drawing back culture, it is not without its controversial aspects within the Makah community. For example, there are undercurrents of unrest about the ownership and use of archaeological materials unearthed at Ozette. While widely promoted as cultural property of the Makah people as a whole, some individuals whose families are from Ozette have occasionally asserted ownership over Ozette objects, especially those having identifiable artistic motifs. Some of these individuals are upset that a privately owned Makah enterprise in Neah Bay sells T-shirts and other articles with Ozette designs on them. They feel that this is inappropriate, since the proprietor is profiting from designs that she does not own. Many people in the community feel that when ownership of old designs cannot be established (such as those on Ozette artifacts), no one should use them. While it might seem to outsiders preferable to permit the entire community such use in these circumstances, this alternative would virtually ensure that the designs would be used by people whose ancestors were not the original owners. According to some tribal members, it is a worse offense to use designs inappropriately than never to use them again.

Other controversies arise from the MCRC's dual responsibilities to serve the entire community *and* to ensure the privacy of individual families. This dilemma, which I will discuss in detail below, comes to the fore especially in reference to controlling community access to objects and archival material. Tribal members note that parallel issues may arise in reference to objects repatriated to the Tribe under NAGPRA. Although there is no formal policy in place for the Ozette material to serve as a model, the fact that tribal members have been wrestling with these questions for many years has prepared them for some of the major issues they may soon confront in their struggle to draw back culture under NAGPRA.

SHORT TERM GOALS, LONG TERM VISIONS:
THE MAKAH NAGPRA PROJECT

When I picked Janine Bowechop and Greig Arnold up at Boston's Logan Airport one day in November 1998, they looked weary. They had just come from several intensive days in New York City, examining collections at the National Museum of the American Indian (NMAI) and the American Museum of Natural History (fig. 15). Harvard University's Peabody Museum was their last stop before they headed home to Neah Bay.

We arrived at the museum early the following morning and met with Barbara Isaac, Ann-Marie Victor-Howe, and other staff members from the NAGPRA and Collections Departments with whom I had been working for many years. After exchanging introductions, reviewing the schedule for the visit, and completing necessary paperwork, we descended into the storage areas. Staff had conveniently gathered the Makah and Nuu-chah-nulth material in several centralized locations for our examination. Prior to the visit, Janine and Greig had reviewed the NAGPRA summaries sent by the Peabody and indicated items of particular interest. However, since the Peabody's collection of southern Northwest Coast material is not extensive, they had the opportunity to see most of the affiliated holdings.

As we proceeded systematically through the objects, Janine and Greig's personal interests became evident. Janine is a weaver; Greig is a carver. Nonetheless, each object received close attention and was photographed. The photographs would be critical in assisting other Makah tribal members to identify family objects and to gather information about them from tribal elders. The atmosphere was relaxed, and Janine and Greig were clearly enjoying themselves. Museum staff asked questions about specific objects and noted comments and corrections that could be added to the rather sparse museum records. Neither Janine nor Greig took any written notes. The Peabody collection contains a few unique and old Makah pieces and there were excited exclamations as some of these were unwrapped. Some objects were types Greig had never seen before in his long career, while the ubiquitous trinket baskets present in the majority of Northwest Coast collections were certainly familiar.

At the end of the day, everyone felt the consultation visit had gone very

FIG. 15. Janine Bowechop (second from right), MCRC Director, with staff at the American Museum of Natural History, New York. Janine and Greig Arnold made a NAGPRA consultation visit to the collections in November 1998. Photograph by Greig W. Arnold. Courtesy of the MCRC.

well. It had not transpired quite as I expected given other NAGPRA visits I had participated in at the Peabody with other tribes. There were no ceremonies conducted over objects, no contentious debates between staff and visitors, and no intensely emotional scenes. I was relieved at this, although not really that surprised. Perhaps the lack of tension was because there were only a handful of really significant objects that the Makah Tribe might eventually repatriate, and no sensitive human remains or funerary objects. Doubtlessly, my presence also contributed to the genial atmosphere, as I had positive, well-established relationships with both Peabody staff and Janine and Greig. However, I do not believe this to be the sole explanation. It might have had more to do with the relaxed way the Tribe is approaching NAGPRA implementation and their familiarity with museum settings. NAGPRA implementation, like other Makah projects, is being undertaken by seasoned professionals.

Implementing NAGPRA is one of the latest cultural resource management projects taken on by the MCRC. It should not be seen separately, but as part of a continuum of projects to draw back and strengthen Makah culture. It is a new opportunity, but not necessarily of more importance than others in the eyes of community members. The way in which the MCRC has structured implementation incorporates many elements that reflect community values and are hallmarks of numerous projects undertaken by the Tribe. Staff defers to and relies on the superior knowledge of tribal elders. The NAGPRA project emphasizes broad community and particularly family input. There are mechanisms in place to restrict access to sensitive information and ensure family privacy. Finally, there is proactive cooperation with Nuu-chah-nulth groups in Canada. Of these elements, it is the dominant social structure based on strong family identifications that more than any other factor influences the way NAGPRA implementation looks and proceeds for the Makah Tribe.

Tribal members' overall approach to and attitude towards NAGPRA can be characterized as cautious and deliberate. This lack of urgency can be attributed primarily to two factors. First is the absence of large numbers of human remains requiring immediate repatriation. Second, as Janine explained, the Makah Tribe is perhaps not as "desperate" to draw back cultural objects as other tribes since it already has a rich collection of material culture from the Ozette excavations.

Another important point to note about tribal members' attitudes towards NAGPRA is that implementation is viewed as being solely a cultural issue, as opposed to a political or legal one. In some tribes these latter aspects have become dominant, as NAGPRA becomes enmeshed in internal political struggles or land claims cases. The MCRC was established as a tribal entity that cooperates with but is independent from the elected Tribal Council. This was done intentionally to place the cultural activities over which it presides above the realm of tribal politics. (It is therefore slightly inaccurate to refer to it as a tribal "department" as I have done for ease of reference.) Although the Tribe's ideal is to keep NAGPRA out of community politics, members do recognize the potential for this to happen, especially if cases arise in which specific objects are claimed by multiple families. When asked about the legal dimensions of NAGPRA implementation, most of those involved said they did not envision the Tribe's lawyers becoming routinely involved in the claims process, although they also said the Tribe would not hesitate to use them if it became necessary in a dispute. Greig expressed this general attitude: "[T]his Tribe is not afraid to fight with attorneys. But it shouldn't be about attorneys. It should be about culture, and it should be about ceremony, and it should be about people having the heart to understand and explain what it means to be in possession of this particular object."

NAGPRA implementation activities on the Makah Reservation are best discussed as two stages: work conducted prior to the receipt of a National Park Service (NPS) grant in 1996 and activities undertaken as part of the grant, which finished in spring 1999. Soon after NAGPRA was passed, the Makah Tribal Council assigned the responsibility for overseeing implementation to the MCRC, as it does for all projects involving cultural resource issues. Aside from signing any claims, as required by the legislation, and receiving periodic updates from MCRC staff, the Tribal Council will not be an active participant.[7]

Janine took on the Tribe's implementation efforts in 1993, when summaries started arriving from museums. She began with two preliminary tasks. First, she responded to each institution with a standardized letter in which she introduced herself as the official NAGPRA contact. Second, she wrote and submitted a grant to the NPS to fund NAGPRA research on the reservation. The need for such research is reflected in a letter she sent in February 1995 to Patricia Erikson, an anthropologist who had volunteered to photograph objects for the Tribe at the Smithsonian:

> It would be convenient if I could tell you exactly which of these four hundred or so artifacts to photograph, but I can't. We aren't at the stage where we can look at the catalog information and determine which objects would be covered by NAGPRA. I will safely eliminate a number of the objects, but even this will be jumping the gun on research that I have planned.

In 1996, the Tribe was awarded seventy-five thousand dollars. The first hire of project staff under the grant was in January 1997. The duration of the grant was originally to be eighteen months.

The NAGPRA staff was selected from individuals who had been working for the MCRC for many years. Janine, trained in anthropology at Dartmouth College and with six years' experience working with the MCRC collections, served as Project Director. Her attitude towards implementation is reflected in her standard letter to institutions:

> We [the MCRC staff] believe that the best method for accurately identifying the Makah cultural material in the collection held by your museum is to work together. Only then will our institution and yours be working in the true spirit of the NAGPRA legislation.

Janine continues to view NAGPRA as an opportunity for both the Tribe and museums to learn more about objects in which they have a mutual interest, even if they are not subject to repatriation under NAGPRA. Greig has degrees in anthropology and museology and over twenty years' involvement with the Ozette excavations and the MCRC, including service as its founding Director. The grant funded a part-time position for him devoted exclusively to NAGPRA-related activities; he also worked during the grant period as MCRC Curator of Collections. An Assistant Interviewer position was filled by Maria Pascua, who had extensive experience conducting interviews with elders in her duties with the Makah Language Program.[8] Elders in the community acted as consultants to the project. Jeff Mauger, an archaeologist centrally involved in the Ozette excavations who has since worked with the MCRC to develop a computerized collections management system, served as a consultant for designing a NAGPRA database.

The funds provided by the NPS enabled the Tribe to build on pre-grant accomplishments and to participate in the NAGPRA process to a greater extent than would have been otherwise possible. The activities funded by the grant guided and shaped NAGPRA implementation during the period of my fieldwork. The project's overall goal was to gather information and set priorities in preparation for the claims process. To accomplish this, there were five primary objectives stated in the grant proposal: (1) "Identify artifact classes that, according to Makah traditional knowledge, fit NAGPRA guidelines for repatriation"; (2) "Refine and update the MCRC/NAGPRA computer database which manages all the information from the summaries, inventories, photographs, and other documentation provided by museums and federal agencies"; (3) "Through communication with other museums, develop a location inventory of Makah and Nuu-chah-nulth artifacts in other museums that relate to NAGPRA guidelines"; (4) "With two Makah elders, inspect and identify NAGPRA-relevant Makah and Nuu-chah-nulth materials in various museums"; and (5) "Share information and solicit community feedback both during and after the project with the Makah public and the Nuu-chah-nulth Tribal Council on the NAGPRA process and results."

It seemed that every time I entered Greig's office, he had his nose in a book. The sources and exhibit catalogues he was studying were largely the ones I had perused prior to my fieldwork (e.g., Densmore 1939; Drucker 1951; Ernst 1952; Swan 1870; Waterman 1920). This research was important, for artifact classes that fit NAGPRA categories were to be identified through review of such archival documents, exhibit catalogues, and ethnographies as well as oral history interviews. Information about Makah objects and ceremonies that is already in the public domain will be given precedence in drafting claims. Interview data will be used to verify the accuracy of published sources, but will not be divulged unless absolutely necessary. (This issue of controlling sensitive information will be discussed further below.) The other goal of interviews with elders and other culturally knowledgeable individuals was to fill gaps in the written literature. Topics covered during the Tribe's interviews included sacred objects and their former uses; proper treatment and storage procedures for sacred objects, both historically and in curatorial settings; past inheritance patterns; and appropriate reburial procedures for human remains and funerary objects.

Information was also sought which would help establish boundaries for the sharing of information. What knowledge should be kept within specific families or within the Tribe? What information could be shared with outsiders? Interviews were required because, as Maria very perceptively pointed out to me, descriptive ethnographic accounts by early anthropologists such as Drucker are very static. It is only through tribal oral history that inheritance practices, as one example, can be understood through time. Other topics, such as handling restrictions for various types of objects, were not comprehensively treated by ethnographers. However, knowledge of such restrictions (whether based on gender, societal, or family membership) is especially important to ensure that harm does not come to the individual or to the larger community. Some of these are already known and are reflected in MCRC collection management policies.

The creation of a database was the best way to organize information in the summaries and inventories to make them easily accessible. One of the immediate goals was to be able to search by object type and find out where such objects were located. Additionally, having NAGPRA information in a user-friendly database would encourage community members to become part of the NAGPRA process. NAGPRA staff recognizes that active community assistance is crucial to successfully tracing both objects and ownership. Each family has a unique knowledge of objects that belonged to their ancestors, knowledge that they would prefer not to share even with NAGPRA project staff. By necessity, the database has different levels of access to control exposure to certain kinds of information.

Prior to making consultation visits, summaries and inventories were surveyed to identify the institutions having the largest Makah collections. While there were no consultation visits conducted by NAGPRA staff during the period of my fieldwork, Helma Swan and Greig had already seen the collections at the Burke Museum in Seattle. The primary goal of consultations for the Makah Tribe is not explicitly to identify objects to draw back, but to collect information on museum holdings. Photographs of collection material and videotapes of related conversations will be shared with elders and members of the community, and ultimately placed in the MCRC archives as a resource. The grant budget allowed for visits to at least eight institutions, exclusive of the museums of the Smithsonian Institution.[9] In November 1998, Janine and Greig visited collections at the American Museum of Natural History (New York), the University Museum at the University of Pennsylvania (Philadelphia) and the Peabody Museum of Archaeology and Ethnology (Cambridge, Massachusetts) under the NPS grant, and the National Museum of the American Indian (New York) under separate funding. No elders accompanied them on this trip, since it is too difficult for most of them to travel long distances from home. In the spring of 1999, a few MCRC staff members accompanied Janine to the Field Museum in Chicago.[10]

Community feedback was a central aspect of the project, and this grant objective anticipated what I found to be a major concern among tribal members: adequate communication between the MCRC and the community. Feedback was to be solicited primarily through two public meetings advertised through the tribal newsletter and posted announcements. The extent of such communication was perceived as crucial to how NAGPRA is received at the local level. In general, the fact that the Makah community views the MCRC with such pride and expresses such great confidence in the abilities and commitment of the staff favorably influences community opinion towards NAGPRA implementation. In the first of these meetings, Greig intended to do some basic education about the law, talk about collections in various institutions, and perhaps show some slides of objects. After a long enough interim to allow community members a chance to think about the issues and discuss them with their families, a second meeting would be held at which he intended to seek input about NAGPRA and the Tribe's implementation process itself.[11] Community meetings were generally thought to be a good idea, but tribal members believed that many people would be unwilling to address the most sensitive NAGPRA issues in a public forum.

The Makah Tribe will share information acquired from museums with the Nuu-chah-nulth Tribal Council, which represents fourteen First Nations of Canada. These First Nations cannot participate in NAGPRA and therefore do not have the same access to information as the Makah Tribe does about Nuu-chah-nulth objects now held in public collections in the United States. Museums frequently classify objects on Makah summaries as simply "Nuu-chah-nulth," a designation equally applicable to these Vancouver Island groups. A letter dated February 1996 lent Nuu-chah-nulth support to the Makah Tribe's documentation project:

> Our connection with the Makah Tribe has always been strong, and will continue for generations to come. Collaborating on this project will benefit all of the First Nations of the Nuu-chah-nulth, including the Makah, and will aid many U.S. museums as well.
>
> It is fortunate that we have this relationship with the Makah Nation. We are aware that there are thousands of Nuu-chah-nulth cultural objects in the collections of U.S. museums, and now through working with the Makah Tribe and the Makah Cultural and Research Center, we will have access to information on these objects.

The Makah Tribe did not communicate as frequently as planned with the Nuu-chah-nulth, but NAGPRA staff intended to personally deliver copies of relevant NAGPRA summaries and inventories to the Nuu-chah-nulth Tribal Council at the end of the grant period.

In addition to the five project-objectives discussed above, three final reports were to be forwarded to the NPS at the completion of the grant. These were not part of the Tribe's original proposal but were added by the NPS, doubtlessly to document that the project met its stated goals and that therefore the grant money was properly spent. The three documents required were (1) guidelines to help museums determine Makah and Nuu-chah-nulth sacred and funerary objects and cultural patrimony; (2) a care and treatment plan for cultural objects that will remain in museums; and (3) a tribal policy covering the determination of cultural affiliation and repatriation of Makah human remains, sacred and funerary objects, and objects of cultural patrimony. The guidelines consisted of a few pages identifying the general categories of significant objects.[12] By necessity, this information was very general as the claim process usually proceeds on an object-by-object basis. The treatment plan explained traditional handling restrictions and Makah concerns about access, exhibition guidelines, and appropriate conservation. The policy was an internal tribal document to develop standardized repatriation procedures. Ultimately, this will be reviewed by the MCRC Board and the Tribal Council. Such a policy is invaluable should staff turnover at the MCRC or tribal elections result in future NAGPRA implementation being undertaken by people other than those involved in the current project. Together, these three documents establish a stable baseline from which MCRC staff in the future can continue with NAGPRA implementation and benefit from the work conducted under the NPS grant.

Despite the MCRC's predominantly cautious approach and its institutional concern with culturally appropriate ways of implementing NAGPRA, there remain factors not under the staff's direct control which influence the way implementation proceeds. Conversations with Janine in late August and early September 1997 revealed concern about a number of unpredictable factors: NAGPRA staff's working and personal styles with the community and, alternately, the reactions of the community to them; funding; the manner in which NAGPRA-related projects are managed at the tribal level; Tribal Council involvement, financial support, and comprehension of the issues; the extent of open communication with the community; the MCRC's relationships with other museums; and cooperation with other tribes, especially neighboring ones. On a few of these points her concerns appear to be unfounded. In community interviews, a majority of people expressed great respect for and confidence in Greig. They trusted that he had the best interests of the entire tribe in mind. Tribal Council members serving during the fieldwork period were fully behind NAGPRA and the MCRC's efforts. All five council members understood the law and felt that it was important for the Tribe to draw back as much material as possible. Greig is now on the council, so NAGPRA still has strong support from the Tribal government.

MAKAH IMPLEMENTATION IN CONTEXT:
NORTHWEST COAST THEMES

Although certain themes in Makah implementation are shared with other Northwest Coast groups, there are also ones that set the Tribe apart from its neighbors. The combined effect of this confluence of factors is to render NAGPRA implementation simpler for the Makah Tribe in some ways. The first of these is the fact that the current reservation land encompasses the five ancestral Makah village sites. Thus, archaeological and ethnographic objects in museum collections with provenance information from these areas can be culturally affiliated easily to the Makah Tribe.[13] There has been no large displacement of population. This does not rule out complications arising from shared boundaries with neighboring tribes, notably the S'Klallams to the east and the Quileutes to the south, where seasonal fishing camps were shared by families from each group. Nevertheless, when compared to tribes who are far removed in time and space from their original homelands, especially along the eastern seaboard, the Makah situation is relatively uncomplicated.

A second factor that eases NAGPRA implementation for the Makah Tribe is the historical isolation of Neah Bay. While some very early Makah objects found their way into museum collections in Europe through the activities of explorers and traders, the total number of Makah items in museum collections is comparatively small. This is attributable to the inaccessibility of the area, the corresponding lateness of prolonged European contact, and the fact that many American museums bypassed the southern Northwest Coast in favor of the more dramatic material culture found further north among the Kwakwaka'wakw, Haida, and Tlingit. Even Swan, who held Makah culture in high regard, preferred to do his Smithsonian collecting elsewhere, as he thought northern groups to be better carvers (Cole 1985:22). Through the late 1800s, the Makah Reservation was visited only weekly by a mail steamer from Port Townsend. Later, the service was more frequent but the length of the trip, the remoteness of the area, and the frequent storms brought few casual visitors or collectors. By the time the reservation became accessible by road, the Great Depression had curtailed both collecting and tourism. As a result, the Makah Tribe experienced far less removal of objects than tribes in other areas of the country.

Finally, the fact that the Makah Tribe had a well-established cultural resource management program prior to NAGPRA has made the implementation process run more smoothly than it has for other groups. The existence of a facility like the MCRC on the reservation has also meant that some tribal members had been participating in related professional activities and training for nearly fifteen years prior to passage of the law. Janine states that the Makah Tribe's familiarity with the museum world has served them well in NAGPRA implementation, since they are dealing with "colleagues" during consultation, not distant museum professionals with whom they have had no previous contact. MCRC staff knows the culture and language of the museum profession and is comfortable with them. As James Nason at the Burke Museum put it, MCRC staff is "part of the business." He also stated that many Makah tribal members know their own material from a museum perspective. This has allowed them to act on NAGPRA much earlier than other tribes that were less experienced.

If this confluence of factors sets the Makah Tribe apart (to its advantage), a perhaps larger set of concerns links their NAGPRA efforts to those of other groups. A number of common themes emerged in my discussions with a range of tribal representatives and museum professionals. There are undoubtedly other themes, especially in regions outside of the Northwest Coast. In addition to issues of ownership, people expressed concern about priorities for claiming human remains, the weight of tribal oral history versus "scientific" evidence in the claims process, maintaining tribal control over sensitive information, the difficulty of applying NAGPRA definitions of sacred object and cultural patrimony at the local level, and the potential impact of Christianity on the ability to bring home sacred objects. Some of these are shared at a national level among tribes, while others are regional. Not surprisingly, tribes have the greatest misgivings about matters in which the tenets of NAGPRA most conflict with long-established cultural values or procedures.

Although I am not focusing on the portions of NAGPRA that address human remains, this in no way diminishes the fact that recovering remains is the overwhelming priority of Northwest Coast tribes, as it is throughout Indian Country. As a perusal of the NAGPRA *Federal Register* notices shows, tribes in Washington and Oregon have made claims for very few cultural objects to date, as they are devoting NAGPRA resources to human remains.[14] The fact that the return of human remains even has to be negotiated and subjected to strict procedures is offensive to many tribal members. One only has to mention the highest profile NAGPRA case in the country, that of Kennewick Man, to demonstrate how strongly Northwestern tribes feel about this issue.[15] As Janine notes, the Makah Tribe is fortunate because human remains are "not a big issue in quantity," partly since the region's isolation has protected tribal graves from the kind of looting that plagued other areas of the country. It is estimated that there were less than six sets of Makah remains in museum collections. Most tribal members are unaware that half of these have already been returned and represent the only Makah NAGPRA repatriations to date.[16]

While some reburials have been announced to the public through local churches, there have been low levels of participation. Community members do say unequivocally that human remains should be returned and reburied, preferably at the site of the village from which they came when this provenance is known. The small number is one reason why human remains are notably absent from the Tribe's NPS NAGPRA grant. However, there is also nothing in the grant text that would exclude the Tribe from addressing this issue. This was an intentional strategy. At the time the proposal was written, there was already a Reburial Committee associated with the MCRC and a reburial policy, so that establishing new procedures for dealing with human remains under NAGPRA was not necessary. However, human remains were omitted from the grant for another reason as well.

Janine knew that the part of NAGPRA implementation that would be the most likely to upset people would be dealing with human remains. Since she did not want NAGPRA implementation to be perceived in a negative light by the community, especially as human remains were not a primary focus of grant activities, she left it out of the project proposal. She did not want to generate anxiety over NAGPRA by making it too much about human remains. She also wanted to avoid exposing elders to remains during consultation visits.

On one potentially abrasive issue, NAGPRA itself was designed to mediate the differences between tribal and institutional constituents. For many tribal members, the knowledge of elders represents the most authoritative voice on ancestral practices. However, European and American scholars of native cultures have been historically skeptical of the accuracy of such accounts. Even though the text of NAGPRA explicitly states that tribal oral history should carry the same weight as historical, ethnographic, and archaeological evidence in establishing cultural affiliations to objects, tribal members question whether institutions will honor this principle.[17] The theme arose frequently in conversations with tribal members about implementation, as when Ed Claplanhoo offered these observations:

> I think the [challenge] is to take what information we got and try to build on it to say that these different objects meet this criteria [for repatriation]. I think that's a challenge that Greig is facing. He's going to have to go out and talk to what few elders there are. He's going to have to [go] back and look through books, through some of the early work of anthropologists, archaeologists. Even though we didn't really care for them because of what they took away and didn't leave us. But yet, you know, there is enough in those books if we glean it up. Because, our own oral history is not going to be taken as gospel. That what Greig writes down is the truth and nothing but the truth so that we can get that object back to the tribe. What proof? (Interview, 2 February 1998)

A NAGPRA representative from a neighboring tribe said she sends information from European contact-era accounts to museums first because she believes it will be given more credence. She revealingly referred to this as "using their words," by which she meant that the largely white museum community understands the words of Europeans better than those of natives. Greig put it this way: "It seems that our words are not as important as somebody's words who heard our words and wrote those words down with their interpretation, be it a hundred years ago or a hundred and fifty years ago."

Makah tribal members do recognize, however, that when it comes to "scientific" evidence they are much better off than other tribes. As Donna Wilkie pointed out, they can pull out of the MCRC collections five-hundred-year-old objects from Ozette that are similar to ones in museums that they would like to claim:

> 'Course the one thing that helps us here is the fact that the Ozette archaeological site was unveiled and that helps us to identify objects much more clearly. Other tribes don't have that link from the past which is five hundred, a thousand years ago. In that respect we're very, very fortunate to be able to link objects to that era. (Interview, 7 May 1998)

Having the Ozette collection *will* ease the Makah NAGPRA implementation process considerably. This was graphically illustrated during Janine and Greig's NAGPRA consultation visit to the Peabody Museum. Greig carefully unwrapped a miniature whalebone war club, the handle of which was elaborately carved in a design that depicts a thunderbird or eagle. Its resemblance to clubs five times larger unearthed at Ozette was so striking and so unmistakable as to leave no doubt that this was a Makah piece, although the museum's current information listed it as simply "Northwest Coast."[18]

There is another compelling reason for tribal members' emphasis on using published literature as evidence over oral history, and it relates to the strategic control of sensitive information. The framers of NAGPRA assumed that tribes were open to sharing the information necessary to repatriate cultural objects. Many tribal members, as well as museums, do in fact view NAGPRA as a mutually beneficial way to learn more about objects in collections. Other tribal members, however, are threatened by rhetoric that implies a two-way exchange of information. They perceive NAGPRA as yet another vehicle through which predominantly white academic and museum communities can elicit more cultural knowledge from tribes. This unease on the part of Northwest Coast groups is better understood by remembering that knowledge is owned in these cultures and is jealously guarded, shared only with select family members, and inherited by worthy heirs. The free exchange of information for the common good is a cultural value that is not necessarily shared by these tribes. Thus, by first using information already in the public domain, the Makah Tribe (among others) hopes to avoid releasing any additional tribal knowledge about sacred objects and associated ceremonies.

The strength of tribal sentiment on this issue emerged during interviews.

One Northwest NAGPRA representative said it was like giving part of the elders away to share their knowledge outside the community. Greig framed his objection in reference to tribal identity: "How much do we tell them [museums]? You know, this stuff belongs to them but the information belongs to us. Always been us. At what point do we quit being us when we give it to them?" Tribes are crafting some creative solutions to this problem, asserting their right to control dissemination of tribal knowledge. For example, one tribe in Washington worked out a compromise in which their NAGPRA program provides information to museums only if the museums agree not to distribute or copy it and to return the originals at the end of the repatriation process. Their elders feel comfortable with this arrangement and museums seem to accept the restrictions, although the NAGPRA representative pointed out that she is not there to actually see that the tribe's wishes are respected.

A fourth theme that arises often in conversations about NAGPRA implementation concerns not so much a conflict of values between NAGPRA and tribal cultures as a lack of guidance in the law itself. The application of the definition of sacred object, while not as problematic for Northwest Coast groups as that of cultural patrimony, is nonetheless complex. NAGPRA specifies that sacred objects must be "needed by traditional Native American religious leaders for the continued observance or renewal of traditional ceremonies by their present-day adherents." This short phrase raises a number of questions for Makah tribal members: Who were the "traditional" religious leaders? What constitutes a "traditional" ceremony? To what extent can or should sacred objects be used today if they are drawn back? It seems clear that the drafters of the legislation had in mind tribal religious leaders clearly recognizable as such by local communities based on their central role in ceremonial activities. However, ceremonial practices in nineteenth-century Makah society were largely secretive and individualistic. To be sure, each family had a person known to be particularly knowledgeable about the spiritual realm from whom advice was solicited, but these people were not religious leaders in the sense that they organized communal activities. Greig says that although not as numerous, these knowledgeable individuals still exist today and are the most likely candidates to receive sacred objects for the Tribe under the NAGPRA definition.

The case of the Indian Shaker Church problematizes the use of the term "traditional ceremony," not itself defined in the legislation. Not to be confused with the Shakerism of the northeastern United States, Indian Shaker practices are an amalgamation of indigenous and early Christian forms which developed in the 1880s in the Puget Sound region of Washington State (Waterman 1924; Ruby and Brown 1996). Shaker meetings predominantly featured singing, body movements, and bell ringing. Initially focused around curing that involved the active support and participation of the congregation, the church now plays a dominant role in combating alcoholism in Northwest native communities. Thus, there are still active Shakers on the Makah Reservation today, as there are in neighboring tribes. Several Makah community members expressed interest in having rattles used in Shaker ceremonies repatriated.[19] Do such objects qualify for repatriation under NAGPRA? Does the incorporation of Christian elements automatically disqualify Shakerism as an indigenous religion? It will be very interesting to see how Shakerism is defined as Northwest Coast tribes become more active in seeking repatriation of sacred objects. There are broader ramifications of this question, as Christian elements have become part of "traditional" religions throughout Indian Country.

A related problem in Makah implementation concerns the obligatory use of repatriated sacred objects as stipulated by the legislation. The impact of Christianity on the Makah Reservation makes this an issue in Neah Bay, as in other reservation villages in the region. The multiplicity of Makah viewpoints is probably typical of native communities nationwide. There are fundamentalist Christians, who while valuing these objects for their cultural and historical value do not condone the practice or renewal of traditional ceremonies. There are culturally active individuals who see great benefits to the community in renewing ceremonies and strengthening ongoing ones. They advocate the incorporation of repatriated sacred objects into these. There are community members, also culturally active, who are cautious about the use of these objects in ceremonies. They recognize sacred objects as having inherent power, which could be harmful to the community if they are not treated correctly. These individuals are skeptical that the cultural knowledge today is adequate to the task of accurately reconstructing ceremonies, or even accurately using objects in ongoing ceremonies that have changed since these sacred objects left the Tribe.

This cautious stance is reflected in one tribal representative's anecdote about taking an elderly man on a consultation visit to a museum. This elder had been initiated into the Klukwalle as a youth, and therefore had been instructed in the spiritual significance of the ceremony and of the objects used in it. While examining sacred objects during the museum visit, he would nudge them to move them but he refused to pick them up. The woman who related this story to me felt that this incident reflected the caution with which some members of her community approach sacred objects. Finally, there is a small minority of tribal members who see repatriated objects not only being used to revive old ceremonies, but to create new ones. Although culturally conservative community members would certainly shudder at the mere thought, one advocate justified this possibility by saying that traditions are constantly evolving.

The Northwest Coast theme of ownership concerns us for the remainder of the book. Makah tribal members themselves singled out this topic for extensive discussion. These difficult yet critical questions for NAGPRA implementation are the same as those encountered in discussions of both whaling and the artifacts excavated from Ozette. Who will own repatriated objects? Who will be allowed to use Ozette designs? Who will have access to sacred whaling gear to use in prayers? The questions remain the same, the referents are interchangeable.

5 / Reconciling the Spirit
with the Letter of the Law

Ownership, for us, is a critical thing.
—Greig Arnold

NAGPRA implementation in Neah Bay prior to my arrival had been a mostly solitary activity. While Janine had written the application for the NPS grant, Greig alone had been working on implementation. Consequently, regular conversations among MCRC staff about NAGPRA were rare, and structured interactions with community members about it had not yet begun. With my arrival (and persistent questions), the NAGPRA issues that staff had been pondering began to be drawn out. My interviews with Janine, Greig, and others developed as the initial sites in which negotiations surrounding NAGPRA were voiced. Six months after I left the field, a broader community conversation about repatriation was just getting under way. The issues I identify here are now emerging publicly as major concerns.

It became increasingly clear to me as I spoke with tribal members that the Makah Tribe is facing a struggle in order to take fullest advantage of the opportunities to draw back culture presented by the legislation. As Greig's statement above indicates, tribal members themselves recognize ownership as a key factor in successful implementation. NAGPRA requires objects to have been "owned" in a certain way to qualify for repatriation. Nuu-chah-nulth groups, including the Makah Tribe, exhibited forms of ownership that do not fit the generalized notions of ownership patterns written into NAGPRA by legislators. The struggle by Makah tribal members to resolve this problem seems to be simultaneously taking two different approaches. On the one hand, they are presenting alternative readings of past practices to fit their material culture into NAGPRA definitions. On the other, they are trying to reinterpret NAGPRA definitions to incorporate their significant material culture. The first of these solutions works with the definitions as given, and tries to make Makah material culture fit them. The second employs an opposite approach, challenging the boundaries of the definitions to allow material culture to fit into them.

It must be said here that tribal members working with NAGPRA do not pursue these dual strategies in a conscious manner. That is to say, they do not sit down with object lists and the NAGPRA definitions and determine the most plausible means to claim significant pieces. Nevertheless, it is clear from my interviews that these two processes are occurring. My primary goal is to tease out the full complexity of this struggle. After an introductory discussion exploring in detail the source of the problematic aspects of NAGPRA for the Makah Tribe, each of these potential means of resolution will be addressed in turn.

ENGENDERED STRUGGLES: THE NAGPRA DEFINITION OF CULTURAL PATRIMONY

Objects of "cultural patrimony" means cultural items having ongoing historical, traditional, or cultural importance central to the Indian Tribe itself, *rather than property owned by an individual tribal member.* These objects are of such central importance that they may not be alienated, appropriated, or conveyed by any individual tribal member. Such objects must have been considered inalienable by the culturally affiliated Indian tribe at the time the object was separated from the group.
—NAGPRA Regulations, 1997 (emphasis added)

I first began to suspect that the NAGPRA category of cultural patrimony might be a problem when, during interviews with community members, discussions on this topic caused almost uniform confusion. Thus cultural patrimony and especially the communal ownership provision were variously interpreted as "objects everyone in the community owns one of" or "objects that are passed on" (inherited) or even "objects that you would use on a daily basis for economic development." One individual insisted on referring to cultural patrimony simply by the term "cultural" even though it was perfectly clear to me that he understood the communal aspect of the definition. As a result, to his mind nearly all Makah objects fit under the definition as "cultural." This incongruity frustrated my initial attempts to compare responses across the community, since each interviewee was working from a slightly different understanding. However, when I made this confusion itself an object of inquiry by more closely examining its possible sources, some interesting questions arose. At first, I wondered whether the notion of communal ownership was so foreign to Makah culture that individuals were simply unable to grasp the idea. Gradually, however, I came to view a second interpretation as more likely: in order to make the definition sufficiently applicable to enable them to respond to my request for examples of such objects, individuals came up with alternative interpretations of the definition to fit their understandings of Makah traditional culture.

While it seemed that this process was largely unconscious on the part of most tribal members, in some instances this was clearly not the case: "[NAGPRA] will mean a lot when it comes to ceremonial gear. I think that I'm still just really interested in sort of exploring that 'cultural patrimony' and how we might be able to interpret that in a way that will really benefit us." Janine's comments illustrate the strategic fashion in which some individuals are approaching the implementation process. Other tribal members flatly stated that the definition of cultural patrimony did not apply to their material culture. Greig put it this way:

> [T]here are not many objects, and I'm wondering if there are *any* objects, that were communally owned. Because, ownership, for us anyway, is a critical thing. In that you had rights to things and you passed those rights on and on and on and on and on and on and on. That you didn't give them to everybody but you'd give them to who you're passing them to. So, you don't have things that are communally owned. You don't have a totem pole or you don't have a canoe that was owned by everybody. It was *somebody's* stuff. And that's just the way it was. You know, *somebody* claimed it. If it come up on your beach, it was yours. If it come up on somebody else's beach, it was theirs. The harpoons . . . you know, you hear stories about harpoons going in a whale, whale getting loose, the whale washing ashore. The gear comes back to the owner. The whale stays with where the whale come ashore. Or who claimed it. And that's just the way it is. So, the category, you know, doesn't fit well for us. Everything belonged to somebody, not everybody. (Interview, 2 June 1998)

Helma Swan echoed his words, as we sat in her office at the MCRC puzzling out the relationships between objects listed on museums' NAGPRA summaries and the law's definitions:

> Communally owned [objects] . . . I don't think there's any really communally owned. A dance rattle can't be communally owned because only the one that can chant, that has chanting songs, can use the dance rattle. [A] thunderbird headdress has to be owned by one who owns the thunderbird dance. He might not own the thunderbird, but he owns the thunderbird dance. (Interview, 11 December 1997)

Objects could not be communally owned because the rights to *use* them were owned by individuals. Given that this point surfaced repeatedly during interviews, it is not surprising that Makah tribal members came to the conclusion that NAGPRA is biased against their culture and others of the southern Northwest Coast.

This perceived problem with NAGPRA is based on the supposition that Makah ownership patterns in the past were strictly private. This is the dominant contemporary understanding and the image I painted earlier of Makah social structure. However, was private ownership the norm in the past as tribal members today insist? A closer examination of the ethnographic literature reveals that the situation is not quite so clear. Consider this passage from Colson (1953:191), who worked in Neah Bay in the early 1940s:

> Ownership of fishing grounds, berry patches, and stretches of coastline was vested in the kinship group rather than in the individual or in the whole village. Theoretically, control of this property was in the hands of the male head of the house, but all members of the group had access to its resources. The group also owned ceremonial privileges, or *túpatʰ* in the form of personal names, dances, costumes, games, songs, and rôles in the secret societies. These *túpatʰ* could be used only by its members, though in practice the head of the household through whose hands the accumulated wealth of the group passed controlled the uses to which they were put.

Colson clearly suggests that ownership of economic and ceremonial privileges was communally held. What accounts for the contradiction between her writings and contemporary Makah perceptions? Given Makah tribal members' generally critical evaluations of Colson's ethnography, it is likely they would respond that her conclusion on this point is inaccurate. They would also have no difficulty interpreting the above passage as evidence that heads of households were absolute owners of private property, since it was they who controlled it. Another possible reason for the discrepancy is that

Colson read her Makah data in the light of communal ownership patterns known to exist among other Northwest Coast groups, especially the Kwakwaka'wakw, Haida, and Tlingit. There has been much more anthropological treatment of these clan-based cultures than of the Nuu-chah-nulth groups of the southern coast.

When Makah tribal members discuss ownership patterns, a certain ambiguity arises in their speech. Although insisting on private, individual ownership, it is common to hear tribal members say that songs, dances, or designs are owned by certain *families*. This implies the kind of ownership by a kinship group that Colson describes. Based on my discussions with tribal members, I have come to believe that the usage of "family" in this context is a shorthand way of referring to cultural goods that are known to be passed down within a specific family; an individual within that family would still be the true owner. However, I have also been told that songs that have been in families for many generations generally *are* considered the property of an entire family, not just one individual member of it. While reasons for this are unclear, I would suggest that this situation may arise in cases where inheritance patterns are disrupted and the songs, while still known to be associated with a specific family, were not formally passed down to an individual in it. These examples show that there is some variation in ownership patterns, enough to admit the existence of multiple interpretations.

The bulk of the albeit limited ethnographic literature, however, lends support to contemporary Makah readings which emphasize individual ownership. Indeed, Colson's monograph represents the only source identified to date that takes an opposing viewpoint. Drucker (1951), whose 1930s data are based on interviews with Nuu-chah-nulth elders, clearly presents nineteenth-century ownership patterns as private. Likewise, Kirk (1986:43) distinguishes Nuu-chah-nulth ownership patterns from communal forms exhibited by northern Northwest Coast groups with clan property. Nuu-chah-nulth individual family heads directly owned the economic resources and *tupa·t* established by supernatural ancestors, because only family heads claimed ancestral ties to the world as it was before humans came to live in it (Kirk 1986:43). Additionally, Goodman (1991:224) writes: "As the highest-ranking male, a chief owned all of his family's wealth, privileges, and possessions." The interpretation held by contemporary tribal members and supported by these authors is privileged in the discussion that follows. The present generation must deal with NAGPRA, and the fact that they perceive a lack of fit is of utmost importance. However, the absence of consensus on the issue and the existence of ambiguities may potentially benefit the Tribe in repatriation efforts as they create spaces for negotiation in the quest to draw back culture through NAGPRA.

How did this disparity between NAGPRA and the contemporary reading of Makah material culture come to be? As I reflected more deeply on tribal members' comments and returned again and again to the definitions in NAGPRA, I came to recognize that the law assumes that objects most significant to tribes were either sacred or communal (setting aside funerary objects or human remains). This assumption is reflected in a comment by a member of the NPS NAGPRA staff (McManamon and Nordby 1992:233): "The key aspect of this definition [cultural patrimony] is whether the property was of such central importance to the tribe or group that it was owned communally." Is communal ownership a necessary attribute of an object significant to an entire tribe, as his comment implies? It should be obvious that this assumption directly confronts Makah notions of individualistic ownership patterns and severely limits the Tribe's ability to recover culturally significant objects that cannot be considered sacred. One of the few authors who has also noted this problem states: "it is quite possible that cultural items that are not religious in nature may fall through the cracks of NAGPRA" (Byrne 1993:129). I believe the assumption that all tribes possess sacred material is probably true; it is very clear, however, that the same cannot be said of cultural patrimony.

It is tempting to paint this conflict between Makah and NAGPRA notions of ownership as the classic scenario of indigenous forms versus an imposed Euro-American model. However, I believe that the situation is a great deal more complex. This was brought home to me by a thoughtful discussion with Greg Colfax:

> [W]hen I was working at Evergreen State College, we were faced by students who would often say, "Well, tribal people don't feel that they own the earth. They don't own the water. Everything is for sharing." Well, that may be fine. I mean that's extrapolating a certain philosophical idea from a bunch of writings that's been centered on Plains peoples and some groups' philosophies, but it does not apply here. Nor up and down the coast. We owned property. We owned bodies of water. We owned rivers. And the families owned gear— ritual gear. I think [NAGPRA] is flawed in that regard. I think it's flawed because coastal people did not have a say-so in the writing of the law. It sounds clear to me. And we're faced with trouble. (Interview, 20 January 1998)

How did Greg's students come to internalize this perception of what indigenous forms of ownership were like? Macpherson (1962) coined the term "possessive individualism" to illustrate how individuals' identities in Europe came to be shaped by their possessions and the pursuit of them. What one owned came increasingly to define who one was. Ideals of individual ownership were transferred from Europe to the New World and imposed on indigenous peoples, notably through laws like the Dawes Act. However, when the initiatives failed to produce self-sufficient, wealth-accumulating Indians and in fact worsened the economic situations of tribes, steps eventually were taken to reverse these policies.

Commissioner of Indian Affairs John Collier, in addition to promoting tribal self-governance, advocated a "return" to communal governing and utilization of resources. Collier was an idealist and vocally promoted this image of communal living as a balm not only to the problems in Indian Country, but as a worthy model for wider American society. His visions of communal native lifestyles were based on the Pueblo model with which he was most familiar; he did not consider whether this was the norm for Indian Country as a whole (Thomas 2000:191). As one of his biographers notes, his solutions as legislated in the Indian Reorganization Act imposed these communal structures even on tribes whose cultures privileged individual rights, including Northwest Coast Indians (Philp 1977:239). It is this "communal" rhetoric of Collier and those who followed him that we hear expressed in the words of Greg's students and see written into the definitions of NAGPRA. Thus, rather than NAGPRA representing a particularly Euro-American approach to ownership, I would argue that it reflects a stereotypical notion of indigenous ownership. It is ironic that in the case of Northwest Coast tribes, the indigenous understanding that individual status was based on private ownership was similar to ideas of possessive individualism.[1] In fact, it seems that these tribes took the concept of private ownership a step further by applying it to intangible property.

Greg appears to be correct in his assessment that Northwest Coast tribes were not active in the drafting of NAGPRA. Tribes involved in the 1989 Panel of National Dialogue on Museum–Native American Relations, convened to discuss repatriation, and congressional witnesses in pre-legislative hearings represented interior Alaska, Gila River (Arizona), Hawaii, the Northeast (Iroquois), the Southwest (Papago and additional groups), and the Plains (Pawnee, Sioux, and Winnebago). The majority of these native cultures do have traditions involving communal ownership of significant cultural objects. The congressmen who sponsored NAGPRA and related legislation were Daniel Inouye, from Hawaii, and Ben Nighthorse Campbell, an enrolled member of the Northern Cheyenne. One therefore presumes that these congressmen were most familiar with the forms of native ownership in their respective constituencies, which in these states encompassed some communal aspects.

The question must be addressed as to whether the problem outlined above really puts the Makah Tribe at a disadvantage, or whether they can in fact draw back all of their most significant objects under the definition of sacred object. Under this definition, museums and federal agencies against which a claim is made have the ability to resist repatriation if they can show legal title. For tribes, the advantage to claiming objects as cultural patrimony, which makes them inalienable by definition, is that institutions cannot use title as a counterargument. Furthermore, there *are* significant Makah cultural objects that do not qualify as sacred.

For example, while selected items of whaling gear used in prayers probably can be repatriated as sacred, the majority are not likely to qualify under this definition. Whaling gear, as we have seen, was individually owned yet central to collective tribal life and identity. Even those items of whaling gear that tribal members view as sacred may prove difficult to claim successfully, as some institutions are narrowly interpreting the definition of sacred object, emphasizing the phrase "devoted to a ceremony." Whaling gear's dual use, spiritual and utilitarian, may thus disqualify it from repatriation under NAGPRA. Ceremonial regalia constitute another group of objects that are clearly culturally significant, but have an uncertain status under NAGPRA. It is yet unclear whether ceremonial regalia have any inherent sacredness outside the context of potlatches and ceremonies. Today this regalia have more significance in family identity and display of family songs and dances than, I believe, as sacred objects.

A third category of culturally significant Makah objects that slip through the cracks of NAGPRA comprises individually owned sacred objects that were used in private, secret, personal prayer. These objects are seen as "magic," in Greig Arnold's words, and thus are inherently sacred in terms of the NAGPRA definition. However, they too run afoul of the definition when it comes to repatriation. The secretive nature of these prayers means that use of related objects is not known today, in most instances, which inhibits their return to active use. Additionally, the element of secrecy surrounding these objects makes it difficult to identify who the contemporary owners (or "practitioners") might be. Many Makah tribal members, however, feel strongly that objects in this category, which includes doctor's gear, should not be in museum collections because they have an inherent power which may cause harm to individuals who handle them.

These three kinds of Makah objects are excluded from the definition of cultural patrimony on the basis of ownership; nor do they fit well in the category of sacred object. Because they were privately owned, they do not qualify as cultural patrimony. However, because these objects were either not completely devoted to a ceremony or cannot be incorporated back into original practice by descendents of original owners, they do not qualify as sacred objects either. The fact that NAGPRA does not allow for individual ownership of communally significant objects will have very real consequences for Makah implementation. There is no doubt, however, that given the intent of the legislation to renew traditions centrally important to the cultural identity of a people, whaling gear and family potlatch regalia *should* be eligible.

In order for the Makah Tribe to claim significant cultural objects that do not fall under the NAGPRA definition of sacred object, a middle ground concerning ownership must be negotiated between Makah culture and NAGPRA. In the abstract, there are several possible means by which a resolution can be effected; it is yet unclear in the Makah case what the outcome will be. Will the Tribe abandon its attempts to recover nonsacred cultural objects under NAGPRA? Will tribal members present alternative readings of their material culture to bring it in line with the NAGPRA definitions of communal ownership? Or, will the Tribe choose to challenge the boundaries of the definition itself to make it incorporate their significant cultural objects? These latter two may appear at first glance to be the same question, but one implies a certain flexibility in Makah culture while the other implies a certain flexibility in the law.

I believe the first of these alternatives is unlikely for several reasons. As we have seen, there are numerous objects centrally important to Makah culture and identity that do not seem to be sacred or patrimonial as defined by NAGPRA. Most notably, this includes whaling gear and ceremonial regalia. Because of the contemporary whaling issue, I think there will be tremendous pressure on tribal NAGPRA staff to find a way to draw back gear. Furthermore, both staff and community members hold up the MCRC as proof that the Makah Tribe is capable of professionally caring for its own material culture. Some Makahs believe that the Tribe can do so as well as or better than the museums in which these objects currently reside. They point out that they can attend to objects in a culturally appropriate manner and that objects often do not receive the care they should in outdated or overcrowded institutions. These points give tribal members a firm foundation from which to argue for the return of collections. Finally, there are many members of the community who feel strongly that as much material as possible should come back, regardless of NAGPRA categories. Many tribal members assert in no uncertain terms that objects affiliated with the Makah Tribe belong with the Makah Tribe. Period. No restrictions, no questions asked. This group will also undoubtedly place pressure on staff to draw back a variety of objects. Theirs is not the attitude of a Tribe inclined to relinquish their objects to museums without a fight. Although I do not believe that the Tribe will abandon its attempts to bring back nonsacred cultural objects under NAGPRA, I do think they will simultaneously explore other possibilities short of repatriation. Because of the MCRC, the Tribe is in a position to work with museums on long-term loans for objects, an option Janine is already considering as a middle ground.

Within the repatriation framework, the other two approaches are already occurring: the re-reading of Makah material culture to fit NAGPRA and, alternately, the reinterpretation of the NAGPRA definitions to fit Makah culture.

FLEXIBLE READINGS OF THE PAST: SHAPING A CULTURAL PATRIMONY

The first approach to resolving this incompatibility is for Makahs to re-examine past practices regarding material culture to fit it into the definition of cultural patrimony. This NAGPRA definition assumes that communal ownership goes hand in hand with communal benefit and that objects communally significant to a tribe were communally owned. Makah tribal members insist, however, that this is not always the case. Some Makahs are re-reading the standard ethnographic and historical interpretations of their past ownership practices to emphasize communal aspects.

Illustrations of such re-readings are numerous. Cutting to the heart of the problems with NAGPRA, Ed Claplanhoo commented: "I don't think the law is fair enough, 'cause I think there was a lot of objects that were individually owned that are of significant value to the tribe." In addition, many tribal members point out that individually owned regalia have communal significance because they have full meaning only in a community setting. As Steve Jimmicum explains: "[T]he value of [private] objects comes out in public through potlatch." Dances and songs in which ceremonial objects are used are performed during potlatches by various families to honor other members of the community. Unless significant objects are displayed and shared with the wider community in these public events, they are meaningless.

Use of private prayer objects too is subject to a re-reading that encompasses a communal aspect. One Nuu-chah-nulth man particularly knowledgeable about spiritual practices explained:

> So whether they went bathing in the river or lake or whether a bathing ritual or a sweat lodge ceremony or going to the mountain, they prayed with these items so that these items would be sacred enough to capture what they wanted to sustain the family and the nation—the livelihood of the family *and* community. Because they looked after their families, *then* the community. So, it was community that also benefited from all of the things that happened with this. (Interview, 16 January 1998)

While his remarks clearly show the priority family life held during prayers, they also demonstrate a concern with the wider sphere of social life.

These examples demonstrate some instances of re-readings wherein the communal relevance of private goods is emphasized. Northwest Coast ethnographies (Densmore 1939; Drucker 1951; Ernst 1952; Swan 1870) are silent about whether these society-sponsored ceremonies actually had any explicit broader community responsibilities. The Klukwalle, for example, was ostensibly intended for initiates, but in reality, this included the vast majority of tribal members, including slaves. My Makah sources acknowledge that objects used on these occasions were not owned by the secret societies but "go home with someone." However, they also insist, as in the other instances described, that use of these objects benefited more than their owners. A possible precedent for repatriation of this kind has been set by Hopi kiva societies, which have regained objects as both sacred *and* patrimonial on the grounds that the ceremonies they perform are not only for their members but for the good of the community as a whole.[2] It remains to be seen whether this strategic reading of material culture will be ultimately utilized or successful for the Makah Tribe. What is clear is that the combination of values it represents, private ownership and communal benefit, is at odds with ongoing NAGPRA interpretations.

These re-readings of past private ownership practices that emphasize communal aspects may ultimately allow Makah material culture to qualify as cultural patrimony under NAGPRA. On one hand, private ownership is emphasized. On the other, a head of household may initially appear to be an owner but in reality manages (caretakes) property on behalf of a larger group, as Colson (1953) writes. Current tribal understandings thus take a middle ground, arguing for private ownership but communal benefit and transforming the owner into a quasi caretaker with broader community responsibilities. This approach may seem at odds with a culture having such clear notions of private ownership, where we might expect the idea of mere caretaker status to be widely resisted. Strategically, tribal members realize that if a caretaker status can be established, significant objects could be drawn back that would not qualify for repatriation under NAGPRA simply as individual property.

The difference between owners and caretakers of objects is a fine but critically important distinction when it comes to NAGPRA implementation. Objects under caretakership would qualify for repatriation under NAGPRA, because a caretaker has no authority to alienate them from the tribe. Objects under direct ownership might not qualify, since an owner did have the right to alienate. This would mean that most of the time legal title would be held by the Tribe in the first instance and the institution or agency in the second. The argument for repatriation that Makah tribal members are making is that some privately owned cultural objects should qualify as cultural patrimony because they had communal benefit.

A curious result of this slight adjustment to the nature of past ownership practices is to render the Makah system more like that of Tlingit-based clan structures. This connection to Tlingit ownership patterns is important because Tlingit groups are widely accepted to have cultural patrimony under NAGPRA and, moreover, have been successful at getting it repatriated.[3] (This is despite the fact that clans do not coincide with "the tribe as a whole" as specified in NAGPRA, a point I will return to below.) In fact, of all Northwest Coast groups involved with NAGPRA, Tlingit communities are the most active in claiming cultural patrimony.[4] The Central Council of the Tlingit and Haida Tribes of Alaska and the Douglas Indian Association have successfully claimed several objects as cultural patrimony on behalf of Tlingit clan groups. Drawing explicit comparisons between their own material culture and that of Tlingit groups might therefore be a useful approach for the Makah Tribe. Explicating a few points of this comparison is instructive, for it provides another lens through which to view the complexities of Makah ownership and NAGPRA implementation.

I must mention here that these cross-cultural comparisons, like many attempted by ethnographers, hold up only on the most general level. In this specific case, this is because the underlying social structures of Nuu-chah-nulth and Tlingit society were (and are) very different. In both cultures, houses constituted the primary economic units, but here the similarity ends. Tlingit houses (composed of lineages) belonged to clans, the units of ceremonial life, which in turn belonged to one of two exogamous moieties (de Laguna 1990:213). Clans and moieties structured ceremonial life. In Nuu-chah-nulth society, houses (composed of extended families) constituted the only unit of individual identification and were the basic ceremonial units. Each of these social structures supports a different predominant ownership pattern, although the administration of property by leading men in these societies would have differed little in daily operation.

Tupa·t refers broadly to a category of ceremonial rights and privileges, ownership of which was the basis of the Makah status hierarchy. While the head of a family was viewed as the owner of *tupa·t*, with the associated right to alienate *tupa·t* through gift or marriage transactions, other members of his family also had rights to use them. Not all resources owned by a headman were *tupa·t*, but only rights related to ceremonies and their associated objects. In Tlingit society, there is a similar concept attached to spiritual or intangible property, *at.óow*. In Tlingit, this literally means "owned things" (Goldschmidt and Haas 1998:xvii). As in Makah culture, *at.óow* encompasses dances, songs, stories, names, crests, and regalia. In the Makah instance, it seems that all cultural objects used in such ceremonies and owned by headmen were *tupa·t*. By contrast, regalia only become *at.óow* after a ceremonial dedication during a potlatch or other public event. In addition, in the case of *at.óow*, instead of ownership lying with family heads as in the Makah case, the primary ownership group was the clan, and its property was controlled by the clan head. However, *at.óow* belonging to the clan were taken care of by selected members of it residing in its various houses. It is *at.óow* depicting crests that some Tlingit clans have successfully repatriated as cultural patrimony.

The crucial difference between Tlingit and Makah ownership as it relates to NAGPRA is that in one case property was held by the head of a clan, as a caretaker, and in the other by a head of family, as an absolute owner. Most ethnographic literature on Nuu-chah-nulth cultures clearly distinguishes their system of absolute private ownership from native ownership patterns among tribes with moiety and clan social structures. This difference stems from the way in which *tupa·t* and *at.óow* are initially acquired. Nuu-chah-nulth family heads directly owned the economic resources and *tupa·t* established by supernatural ancestors. *At.óow*, by contrast, were most often acquired as a result of an individual's death and were subsequently obtained and owned by his or her descendents (Dauenhauer and Dauenhauer 1994:16):

"Hence, if an animal (or natural object or force) takes the life of a person, its image may be taken by relatives in payment, and the descendants then own this image taken in payment." These authors further explain that while ownership and use are restricted to the deceased individual's clan, "everybody benefits, and the *at.óow* is to be known, appreciated, honored, and respected by other clans as well." Unlike *tupa·t*, *at.óow* come into being for a communal group, the clan, and constitute cultural patrimony in the truest sense.

It may seem that I have painted the ownership of *tupa·t* and *at.óow* as so different that no comparison between the two could benefit Makah NAG- PRA implementation. Yet the administration of property by leading men in these two societies would have differed little in daily operation, making the ownership systems sufficiently alike in actual practice to allow the Makah Tribe to draw some strategically beneficial connections. Both Makah owners *and* Tlingit caretakers had the right to alienate property, despite the fact that other members of their family or clan had proprietary interests in it. My Makah interviewees were adamant about the fact that family heads could do as they pleased with their *tupa·t*, even give them away or sell them. De Laguna (1990:213), speaking of Tlingit *at.óow*, notes that "all clan and lineage property, including territories, songs, crests, or heirlooms are alienable: by sale, as potlatch or marriage gifts, as indemnity for injuries or as part of a peace settlement, or as booty taken in war." In both cultures, social sanctions ensured that family heads or clan caretakers were not irresponsible in their handling of ceremonial property and managed it for the benefit of the larger group. Because of their responsibilities for the welfare of their families, Makah family heads had some characteristics of caretakers. Because they could alienate clan property, Tlingit caretakers had some characteristics of absolute owners. Ownership of *at.óow* and *tupa·t* are therefore not as far apart as they may appear at first glance.

At the base of this discussion of caretakers versus owners of property are questions about the nature of ownership and its variations. Much of the anthropological literature on ownership has focused on land, but nonetheless contributes some useful concepts. Gluckman (1965), for example, notes that among the Barotse a man is spoken of as the owner of a piece of land. However, in reality this does not mean he has absolute control over it, for by virtue of his ownership he has an obligation to let specified others farm it. These individuals own usufructuary rights in the land which the owner must permit or forfeit his right to administer that property. Could this correspond to the Makah case of a family head permitting others access to his economic resources? Gluckman (1965:77) further states that in such situations communal and individual ownership are not contradictory, as both groups and individuals hold different rights simultaneously.

Goodenough (1951:36) speaks of full and divided ownership among the Trukese; however, even full ownership by an individual is subject in part to the interest of his heirs and his lineage corporation. A similar pattern is found among the Ifugao (Barton 1969:32): "Present holders possess only a transient and fleeting possession, or better, occupation, insignificant in duration in comparison with the decades and perhaps centuries that have usually elapsed since the field or heirloom came into the possession of the family." Individuals possess family property as a trust, not as absolute ownership. This resembles Tlingit caretakership, but the Trukese and Ifugao examples are also reminiscent of Makah ownership patterns.

While land may lend itself more easily to multiple ownerships, Gluckman surprisingly makes the same case for objects. His argument is that people do not own the objects themselves but rights to do certain things with or to them. He notes that tribal ownership of movable property is not like absolute ownership in western terms, but can be subject to what he calls "demand-rights" held by others, often relatives (Gluckman 1965:117). Movable property can be subject to a number of these rights held by different people, all of whom are in a sense "owners" of the property. Thus, again, multiple rights of ownership, though of varying kinds, can simultaneously exist. This seems to be the case as it stands for Tlingit clan groups, where a clan leader might have in his possession certain items of regalia, but other clan members own a right to use them.

In many cultures, a senior male who administers property on behalf of the group appears to be an absolute owner. This is rarely the case, however. While retaining veto authority, the head of a Trukese lineage corporation must have the unanimous consent of its adult members to alienate property held by the corporation (Goodenough 1951:36). Among the Ifugao, family property cannot be sold without a special ceremony which requires the participation of a wider group, thus providing a check against an individual alienating property of his family without its knowledge (Barton 1969:32).[5] There were apparently no formal mechanisms through which a Tlingit clan leader was required to gain approval before alienating clan property, but if he made unwise choices in the eyes of his community, repercussions were sure to follow. In each of these cases cited, the head male is more accurately viewed as a "caretaker" on the part of a larger group, despite the temptation to view him as an owner based on his power and authority in community life.

This anthropological literature on ownership clearly indicates the usefulness of the concept of "layers of ownership" for thinking about a particular plot of land, a fishing area, or piece of ceremonial regalia. Despite the differences in ownership patterns between Tlingit caretakers and Makah absolute owners expounded by members of these communities today and described in the ethnographic literature, when analyzed with respect to "layers of ownership" the similarities between the two patterns become more pronounced. Both Tlingit clan leaders and Makah family heads clearly hold possessory rights to *at.óow* and *tupa·t*, although clan property was often given over to the stewardship of specific houses. Clan leaders and Makah family heads owned the right to alienate ceremonial property. In both cultures, members of a larger group, be it a clan or Makah family, owned "demand-rights" (in Gluckman's terminology) to utilize economic resources and *tupa·t* or *at.óow* controlled by their leader. Ownership of rights "to hold," "to alienate," and "to use" exist simultaneously for a single object, thus demonstrating both communal and individual "ownership" at work. I believe the fundamental difference between Tlingit and Makah patterns of ownership is not in actual practice but in how such practice is perceived within each culture. Makah tribal members insist on private ownership while Tlingit culture openly recognizes a communal, clan-based system. Recognition of the nature of this difference is critical to NAGPRA implementation, especially for the Makah Tribe.

It should now be clear why Colson interpreted Makah ownership patterns as she did, and also why Makah tribal members can apply different readings. Ownership is not as simple as communal versus individual. Examining Makah patterns through the lenses of multiple layers of ownership, the interpretations of both Colson and contemporary tribal members can be accommodated. Comparison with Tlingit social structure and ownership patterns demonstrates how the boundaries between individual and communal ownership can be blurred enough to allow Makah tribal members room to negotiate this very critical NAGPRA-related issue of caretakership and cultural patrimony.

CHALLENGING THE BOUNDARIES: CREATING NEW SPACES IN NAGPRA DEFINITIONS

If drawing back culture by reading past ownership patterns as encompassing communal aspects proves to be ineffective, a second solution is concurrently being negotiated. This leaves intact the dominant perception of the way in which objects were owned and attempts to reinterpret the NAGPRA definitions. There are at least two specific ways that these definitions are being challenged. The first seeks to redefine by expansion the "repatriation unit" under NAGPRA while the second seeks to make the NAGPRA definitions fit Makah intellectual as well as material property. This process at work can be explicitly seen in Janine's comments, part of which has already been quoted but merits repeating:

> I'm just really interested in sort of exploring that cultural patrimony and how we might be able to interpret that in a way that will really benefit us. Like, when you think of gaps [in the MCRC collections] that we have like clothing and knowledge about clothing and how abundant it is in some museum collections and how very absent it is from ours. (Interview, 1 December 1997)

Janine's statement clearly illustrates the negotiated aspects of NAGPRA. Such negotiation is necessary so that NAPGRA meets the Tribe's culturally specific needs and goals. One of these is to complement the gaps in the Ozette collections and create a visual link between this archaeological material and contemporary material culture by accessioning objects dating from the historical period. Cedar bark clothing is one such gap; whaling gear is another of importance.

The first of these challenges to the boundaries of the definition of cultural patrimony seeks to redefine the group in which communal ownership must rest in order for an object to qualify for repatriation. Although NAGPRA specifies this "repatriation unit" as the "tribe," Tlingit groups have successfully claimed objects at the level of the "clan." Does this mean that Makah tribal members could conceivably claim objects owned by a "family"? It is interesting to note that the report from the Congressional Panel of National Dialogue on Museum-Native American Relations defines cultural patrimony as "inalienable items owned in common by tribes *or clans* that have historical or governmental importance to present and future generations" (U.S. Senate 1990; emphasis added). Although the phrase "or clans" was dropped from the final NAGPRA definition, its inclusion in this earlier version suggests that a broader application of cultural patrimony was originally intended. One commentator on the proposed NAGPRA regulations recommended broadening this definition to include "any sub-group of an Indian tribe, such as a band, clan, lineage, [or] ceremonial society."[6] If Makah tribal members could illustrate similarities between Tlingit clans and Makah families, then Tlingit successes at claiming subgroup communal property might provide a useful precedent.[7]

In fact, I would suggest that there are sufficient parallels to make a persuasive case for repatriation to Makah families. While NAGPRA's institutional constituents routinely interpret the law to disqualify repatriation to individual families within tribes, the law clearly favors repatriation to tribal subgroups of a corporate nature. Makah extended families or family groups functioned much like Tlingit clan groups. Corporate groups act as a unit in economic and ceremonial activities and often hold some property in common. It is clear that the ways in which Tlingit clans and Makah families owned *at.óow* and *tupa·t* have corporate elements. Furthermore, there is sufficient evidence to suggest that membership in Tlingit clans was on occasion also family-based. Clans are made up of separate but interrelated lineages, or houses, that recognize a common ancestry. De Laguna (1990: 213) notes that some Tlingit lineages grew so large that they became clans; in other cases lineages seem to have been remnants of once independent clans.

The other important consideration under NAGPRA is whether these subgroups, be they clans, lineages, or families, corresponded to village populations. If this can be shown to be the case, then the subgroup would meet the NAGPRA requirement that cultural patrimony must have belonged to the "community as a whole." James Nason (Interview, 6 October 1997) stated that the argument for repatriation of clan objects as cultural patrimony hinged around the fact that entire villages formerly belonged to a single clan. So, clan property was at the same time the property of the entire community and thus communally owned. In fact, it appears that in precontact Tlingit culture, the clan, house, and village were indeed synonymous. Goldschmidt and Haas (1998:11) also note that as a rule clans are associated with one community. Interviews with some Makahs have indicated that smaller, precontact Makah villages also sometimes consisted of just one family, again raising the question of whether claiming property with Tlingit clan crests differs fundamentally from claiming property depicting Makah family designs.

The second way in which the Tribe is seeking to expand the boundaries of the definition of cultural patrimony has perhaps broader ramifications for NAGPRA implementation nationwide. Makah tribal members are wrestling with how (or if) ownership of songs and stories, culturally treated no differently than material property, can be incorporated into the NAGPRA process as "intellectual property." Many individuals I interviewed, when asked for examples of significant items for the Tribe to draw back that did not seem to fit under NAGPRA, responded by asking about recordings of songs, stories, and Makah speech. As among the Trukese studied by Goodenough (1951:52–53), the ownership of knowledge (whether of skills, "lore," or magic) brings prestige and is "carefully guarded as private property." In a similar fashion, Makah concerns about songs and stories arise from the desire of families who own them to control access to and use of these cultural goods. Tribal members are interested in recordings of Makah speech not only to support tribal initiatives to teach native language, but also for the experiential aspect of hearing relatives who have since died. As one man hesitantly confided: "I don't know . . . I don't know how I'd act if I could hear my grandpa's voice again."

Weekly staff meetings at the MCRC were one forum in which issues surrounding intellectual property were discussed. Between cups of coffee and frequently raucous laughter, staff addressed the serious issues raised by activities proposed in researchers' applications. Janine drew on these conversations when she subsequently made recommendations to the MCRC Board, in whose hands the final decisions lay. To say that a new situation arose a couple of times each month is no exaggeration. There was the writer of children's books who wanted to use a Makah legend. While there are a few stories in the Makah public domain (not family owned) that could be used, staff hesitated because there was no evidence in the author's previous books that she had actively collaborated with the respective native communities. In addition, since no royalties were mentioned by the author, staff wondered how the Tribe would benefit from this project. The general consensus was that a Makah person should be the one to write such a book.

Then there was the archaeologist who, without consulting the Tribe, had published on the Internet photographs of artifacts excavated from a Makah site outside the reservation. While the question of who held official copyright to these images was unclear (Was it the archaeologist? His university? His granting agency? The Tribe?), his failure to even consider the Tribe's position was indicative of his established pattern of not treating it as an equal partner in cultural resource management. There was the linguist who had denied outright repeated requests from Makah tribal members to have some level of access to twenty years of interview tapes housed in a California university archive. These tapes contained material in Makah from some of the last fluent speakers, and thus were invaluable to the Tribe's own language preservation efforts. The linguist's request to do further research was denied by the MCRC Board pending his agreement to hand over duplicates; he eventually agreed. The list could go on. As these examples show, to many tribal members NAGPRA represents a further means through which to gain access to and control over intellectual property.

Discussions of indigenous efforts to regain control of intellectual property, and the ethical issues these efforts raise for anthropologists and other researchers, have become increasingly common in the professional literature. Some scholars believe such pressures to be a threat to the dissemination of knowledge, while others recognize them as a justified reaction by indigenous peoples to an enduring power struggle throughout which they have been too long on the weaker side. In one of his latest articles on the topic, Seeger (1997) takes the reader on an instructive journey detailing the ethical issues an ethnomusicologist faces from his initial recordings of songs in the field to their eventual "publication" under United States copyright law. His reflective discussion of how to involve native composers and owners of music at each stage of the process is particularly laudable.

Coombe (1997), in a more academic treatment, tackles the complex issues surrounding Canadian First Nations' efforts to gain recognition that theirs is the authoritative voice for representing their own history, stories, and artistic traditions. She argues (Coombe 1997:86) that neither existing intellectual property law (copyright law) nor cultural property law adequately addresses indigenous peoples' accusations of cultural appropriation against dominant Canadian society:

> The appeals made here cannot be reduced to a purely monetary claim for the royalties due to individuals, because they encompass an insistence upon the respect due to peoples, their histories, and their collective self-determination. Nor is the assertion of cultural presence made in the name of an ahistorical collective essence, but in the name of living, changing, creative peoples engaged in a very concrete contemporary political struggle.(Coombe 1997:88)

Coombe (1997:92–93) concludes by arguing that trying to force native concepts of ownership into these existing Canadian laws is yet another instance of colonization. I have been making a parallel argument about the application of NAGPRA to Makah traditional culture.

Several authors have directly addressed the intellectual property aspects of NAGPRA. For example, Nason (1997b:241–242) writes:

> These definitions [in NAGPRA] have been widely assumed to refer strictly to tangible objects, as tangible sacred and patrimonial objects which were the focus of attention in the first instance. For example, a sacred object might

refer to a mask or rattle or pipe but not, from this perspective, to a song or chant. Similarly, cultural patrimony would also be objects but not oral literature. In other words, our usual understanding of the provisions contained in NAGPRA would not lead us to believe that it also encompasses intellectual property in the form of songs, chants, visual arts and motifs, oral literature of all kinds, or the recorded versions of any of these in drawings, paintings, photographs, film, or sound recordings.

However, he points out that many tribal cultures do not make a distinction between the objects themselves and information about these objects that may be contained in archival or collections records in museums. He argues that NAGPRA sets the stage for tribes to "extend the object-based intentions and definitions in NAGPRA to include intellectual property" (Nason 1997b:249). It does this by recognizing tribal governments as sovereign entities with special powers of ownership and control over certain types of cultural property, defined as that which is inalienable and corporate in nature (Nason 1997b:242). Farrer(1994) provides a concrete example in her convincing argument that the *words* used in Mescalero Apache ceremonial songs, some recordings of which reside in the Library of Congress as part of the Federal Cylinder Project, are repatriatable under the NAGPRA definition of cultural patrimony. She explains that Mescalero Apaches consider the words of songs to be in the same category as tangible objects. They are not individually owned, but held in trust by a person on behalf of the tribe; they cannot be alienated and should not be transcribed. Brown (1998:194) agrees with Nason that the presence of NAGPRA provides tacit support for "comprehensive assertions of control over cultural records currently excluded from consideration." His self-avowed "contrarian arguments," followed by comments from some dozen social scientists, raise a host of complex issues indicating the far-reaching implications of this law when it comes to intellectual property.

I have sought to address in this chapter two primary approaches through which Makah tribal members are struggling to make NAGPRA fit with their understandings of material culture and past ownership practices. Embedded in the above discussion is also a policy critique of the law itself, which contains underlying assumptions about ownership that place some Northwest Coast tribes at a distinct disadvantage in NAGPRA implementation. NAGPRA as written does not allow for individual ownership of communally significant objects (Byrne 1993:128–29). The fact that one of NAGPRA's major categories is not relevant limits opportunities for the Makah Tribe to draw back culturally significant objects. The spirit of the law is to enable tribes to reclaim objects that are significant to the collective tribal membership. NAGPRA, in essence, will *not* work for the Makah Tribe in this respect without extensive re-readings of material culture and negotiations of NAGPRA definitions.

6 / Unresolved Ownership

FATES OF REPATRIATED OBJECTS

[A repatriated object] should come to the museum [MCRC] and be part of the museum. And stay here. It shouldn't be handed out around. Unless it's privately owned, I guess. Then it's probably up to the individual. But, I think it should all be returned to the museum where it can be taken care of. And everybody should be able to see it and admire it. I think people should honor it, you know. Unless it's mine. [Laughter]
—Makah Family Head, 10 March 1998

While the previous chapter explored one struggle unfolding as tribal members seek to draw back culture through NAGPRA, this chapter outlines another—an internal one. Ongoing debates over ownership within the Makah community take on new dimensions with the potential repatriation of objects. Repatriations of cultural objects have yet to happen in Neah Bay, so it is still unclear exactly how these issues will play out when repatriations eventually occur. The undercurrents of debate that surfaced in my interviews, and inform my discussions below, are bound to intensify as NAGPRA implementation proceeds.

In the absence of actual case studies, I explored through interviews the range of possible ownership fates awaiting repatriated objects. I found that the opinions of tribal members on this issue were remarkably consistent, but also inherently contradictory. The struggle between private ownership and communal benefit was thus played out even at the individual level. The following passage represents a very typical interview exchange on this topic and introduces a number of key points:

ANN: Under the law, the Tribe has complete control over what happens to objects once they're repatriated here. Do you have any opinions or suggestions about what should happen to objects that come back?

FEMALE INTERVIEWEE: Well, I think they should be kept in a safe place where people can observe them. Maybe be able to replicate for their own personal whatever. But certainly not should be in a person's personal property where other tribal members wouldn't be able to see or experience some of these objects. A tribal public place, like the museum, the schools. Put them on display at the school. That type of thing.

ANN: That's one of the main issues is that, you know, I think that the state of the museum records is really so poor that there's going to be very few instances where a particular object could be linked to an . . .

FEMALE INTERVIEWEE: . . . individual.

ANN: Yeah, or even family. But the question is in cases where that can be done, you know . . .

FEMALE INTERVIEWEE: Oh, they definitely should go back to the family, unless they want to put it on display. But if something belongs to a certain family, it should go to them. I mean that's their right and it shouldn't be anybody's right to say because it's being repatriated that it goes to a museum in that community. If it belongs to an individual, I would . . .

ANN: So in cases where the ownership, then, is unclear is when it should go to a . . .

FEMALE INTERVIEWEE: Definitely.

ANN: . . . public place for everybody to benefit from.

FEMALE INTERVIEWEE: If somebody can prove that that object belongs to them and they show clear title to it in some form, maybe they have something that matches it or . . . it's really hard to do that anymore, though. It's very unlikely that anybody would be able to claim something as theirs even if the design was in that particular family. It's very hard to claim that. (Interview, 7 May 1998)

A concern with the safety of returned objects, their wider educational value, the absolute right of families to decide what to do with their objects, the difficulty of establishing personal links to this historical material, and the undercurrent of distrust all have bearing on the ultimate disposition of repatriated objects.

I was led to a deeper understanding of this internal struggle through exposure to readings in legal pluralism. Viewing the situation in this framework revealed that the emerging tensions stem in part from the pluralistic forms of ownership currently operating on the reservation. This struggle can thus be broadly depicted as a conflict between two outcomes: objects return to some form of communal ownership at the MCRC (a modern form) or return to control of families or individuals within them (the traditional pattern). At the nexus of this debate are concerns about how strictly and to what ends traditional ownership patterns can, or should, be practiced in contemporary tribal life.

Readers should bear in mind that the struggles depicted in this chapter exclusively concern sacred objects. Most tribal members hold to the ideal that these objects should return to families, and that ownership by the MCRC would be undesirable and inappropriate. The MCRC, as an institution for the entire Tribe, logically would be the depository for objects of cultural patrimony should any be found to exist. Most Makah tribal members would agree to this. However, as we have seen, this definition is likely to result in few, if any, actual repatriations.

PRIVATE DESIRES, PUBLIC BENEFITS: THE STRUGGLE
TO MANAGE SACRED OBJECTS

While the ideal scenario from the tribal point of view is a strict adherence to traditional patterns of ownership, this is clearly problematic and in many ways unrealistic. At issue is the appropriate application of these traditional patterns and the potential for disputes between Makah families over objects when conflicting interpretations of the system are called upon. What is particularly intriguing is a willingness to resort to modern forms of ownership, as represented by repatriation to the MCRC, when traditional forms prove inadequate or unsatisfactory. Many tribal members do advocate such a move in cases when ownership is unclear or disputed.

Perusal of the general literature on legal pluralism (Hooker 1975; Merry 1988; Moore 1978; Rouland 1988) has helped me both recognize and articulate why the ownership and control of objects repatriated to the Makah community is such a contentious issue. When viewed through this lens, the internal struggle over ownership becomes clearer. One of the fundamental tenets of legal pluralism is that multiple systems coexist within societies for governing basic aspects of human existence. The way in which multiple systems come about differs between cultures, the most common being voluntary adoption for political reform or forced imposition in colonial situations. While the incorporation of outside laws is thus a shared experience across many cultures, the ways in which a coexistence is reached in each is unique. Still, there are some interesting cross-cultural similarities. For example, both theorists and fieldworkers examining this question have noted that in many cases the outside legal forms come to dominate realms such as business, finance, and development while indigenous forms persist in the realm of family relationships (Rouland 1988:298). This persistence of indigenous practices in the personal realm often continues despite outside laws designed to specifically eradicate it. This happened with the dowry in Greece and India, where despite official abolition of the practice, it is still the norm in rural areas of these countries (du Boulay 1983; Hirschon 1984; Sharma 1984). For the Makah Tribe, questions of ownership are characterized by a duality between outside law, dominating areas of life that most resemble those outside of the Tribe, and indigenous law still governing internal, solely tribal activities.

Viewing contemporary Makah ownership practices through the lens of legal pluralism, two coexisting systems of property ownership are brought sharply into focus. As discussed earlier, the management of land and natural resources no longer follows indigenous patterns; the establishment of the reservation and the resulting "democratization" of resource use destroyed the status-based system. Reservation land is now controlled by the Tribe in accordance with federal regulations for the benefit of all members. There are exceptions for allotments assigned to individuals, but ownership is not absolute for they are forbidden to sell to non-Makahs. Many tribal members live in HUD housing and these houses are managed according to federal rules. In addition, of course, whaling and fishing are heavily monitored by both federal and international agencies.

In contrast to the above property rights, indigenous patterns still dominate when it comes to *tupa·t*. The utilization and inheritance of songs, dances, stories, artistic designs, and regalia are still governed by nineteenth century cultural norms. As Greig explained, "[there] still is a system. And there are still people who abide by the system." Ownership of cultural goods remains completely and absolutely in the hands of individual families. These cultural norms have, of course, adapted and changed over the course of the last 150 years. Potential complications in NAGPRA implementation arise from varied interpretations and applications of these indigenous forms of ownership, as well as from the conflicting mentalities behind these two coexisting ownership systems.

As we can see, there exists in Neah Bay ownership of property that is influenced by outside forces (land, natural resources, houses) and ownership of property that is not (*tupa·t*). To put it another way, some forms of ownership are mediated by the federal government (HUD, BIA) and others are still purely in tribal hands. With this dichotomy in mind, we must address the question of where the MCRC fits as an institution and what kind of ownership it represents. It is indeed an anomaly from the tribal perspective, as a nonnative, modern institutional form charged with caring for traditional cultural objects. It is communal but holds objects that belonged to individuals. Other anthropologists writing about the MCRC have noted its dual functions as a depository for private possessions and as an educational facility serving the local public, but have not addressed the inherent contradictions and repercussions of these functions (see Broyles 1989; Erikson 1996:241; Oxendine 1992). As the former MCRC curator pointed out:

> [A]lthough everything here belongs to everybody, the material really belongs to somebody. So you really have a conflict within itself. Because the objects that come from Ozette are objects of people and whether those people have ancestors within this village or have connection to this village [or not], it still belongs to them. Them personally. Not us *as a people* here today. (Interview, 27 May 1998; emphasis added)

At the institutional level, the MCRC encompasses conflicting ownership responsibilities: as a caretaker in a modern sense to the whole community and in a traditional sense to individual families. Colson (1953:196) noted that this tension between family and communal responsibilities affected the operation of many organizations in Neah Bay:

> Kinship solidarity is thus a factor that interferes with the functioning of the tribe as a unit. Any organization within the Makah group is faced with this same obstacle to the development of full participation and co-operation of all members. Kinship solidarity usually proves a stumbling block over which all organizations topple.

Although Colson is discussing social clubs in the 1950s, this could equally apply to the MCRC today, although the situation is certainly not so dire. The MCRC is thriving, despite the pluralistic forms of ownership within this single institution.

The MCRC's lack of obvious affiliation with one type of ownership or another is not simply of theoretical interest, but has tangible consequences for what staff and community expect of the institution. The MCRC is caught between those individuals who are ardently protective of Makah culture and those willing to share to a greater extent with wider audiences. The former in Neah Bay identify more with the MCRC as a caretaker of individually owned objects while the latter are more likely to stress the communal benefit and responsibilities of the institution. The extent to which individuals align themselves with one set of views or the other influences their opinions on a wide range of cultural resource management issues. Let us look more closely at how these tensions play out in relation to one key problem.

The tensions inherent in these two contradictory missions are voiced in almost daily conversations among MCRC staff, especially in regards to access. On the one hand, as a tribal facility, the collections and archival material should in theory be accessible to all enrolled tribal members. On the other hand, the MCRC has an equal responsibility to protect and preserve knowledge belonging to limited segments of the community. For example, many oral history tapes and transcriptions are restricted to members of families associated with the material. One woman said that the MCRC access policy must protect the privacy of families but not leave in the hands of these individuals exclusive control over how objects and information are accessed.

Archival collections are not the only resources caught in the middle of this debate. Although all community members and approved outside researchers are permitted to view Ozette artifacts in storage, few Makah tribal members avail themselves of the opportunity and the MCRC makes little attempt to actively promote such community interest and use. It seems that this position stems in part from feelings of some staff that since family affiliation is unknown for these artifacts, no one should be permitted to view them lest design elements or other knowledge be utilized by inappropriate individuals. The MCRC as an institution must walk a fine line between service to the entire community and adherence to traditional patterns of ownership, control of personal objects, and private knowledge. Just as staff members differ in their commitment to one mission or the other, so too do community members have differing expectations of the MCRC. The extent to which they see their favored ownership pattern adhered to by the MCRC influences their feelings on whether objects drawn back through NAGPRA should be housed there.

Predictably, there are different interpretations of what NAGPRA says about repatriating sacred objects to modern facilities such as the MCRC. NAGPRA purportedly leaves the decision of what to do with repatriated objects in the hands of native communities. Nevertheless, as Greig notes:

The way the law is written, it's written specifically for material to go back to the individuals who use them in the practice of ceremonies. And that this [the

MCRC] is not an individual and it doesn't practice ceremonies ... [laughs] So, then it becomes a place of storage. And is that what the law is intended? I don't know. I think those things will have to be posed as we go through the process. [T]hese facilities are fairly new within Indian Country and they're fairly new within the United States as a profession. You know, a hundred years or so is not very long in terms of the span of human history, or thirty years for tribal facilities. [T]his law wasn't meant for these things to come into these facilities. It was meant to go back to the practitioners of these ceremonies so that they exist. (Interview, 2 June 1998)

He believes that the provision of the law that mandates that sacred objects return to religious practitioners prevents the MCRC, as an institution, from drawing back such objects on behalf of the Tribe. In essence, this practitioner clause limits repatriatable sacred objects to those that can be linked to contemporary Makah families, whose individual members would be the practitioners. Makah sacred objects that lacked adequate documentation to link them to specific families (which is the case with most Makah objects in museum holdings) could not be claimed.

Janine, while acknowledging the oddity of a museum-to-museum repatriation, views this issue differently than Greig:

[I]f you just think about it in general terms, it's a step up. I mean, we're better equipped to care for these pieces both spiritually and physically, when it comes right down to it than [non-tribal curatorial facilities] and tribes have gone out of their way to develop institutions like this [the MCRC], you know, for those reasons. And that NAGPRA would sort of overlook that kind of is hard to believe. That the law would intend to overlook, you know, communally owned centers as repositories that tribes have created. (Interview, 15 July 1998)

Indeed, many tribes built such facilities in anticipation that someday they would be able to house repatriated items in them, or at the very least mount exhibits with objects on loan from museums. In fact, an argument made by mainstream museums against repatriation was that tribes did not have what they considered proper facilities to curate sensitive collections; the implication was that should tribes develop such facilities, repatriation would be looked upon more favorably (AAM 2000:49). Regardless, the juxtaposed perspectives of Janine and Greig serve to highlight the fact that there are negotiated aspects of NAGPRA that are not the obvious ones over the objects themselves. The basic question, in this instance, is whether sacred objects have to be repatriated to families and thus return to their control, or whether objects can be repatriated under a more general interpretation and return to the entire Tribe in the ownership of the MCRC.

When asked during interviews whether repatriated objects should go to families or to the MCRC, people had uniformly the same response. If an object could be traced beyond a doubt to a specific family, then it should be repatriated to the family. However, if family ownership was not clear objects should come to the MCRC for the benefit of the entire community. Community benefit is always secondary to private ownership and control. Problems arise when a family feels that their ownership of an object is clear but other families do not agree. Potential ownership disputes over repatriated objects were often mentioned as the community's greatest obstacle to NAGPRA implementation. While interviews revealed multiple sources of such conflict, I believe they all stem from basic disagreements about the application of traditional ownership patterns.

Ownership of cultural material is linked to the status hierarchy among Makah tribal members, both in the past and, to a lesser extent perhaps, now. For this reason Makahs do not seem inclined to come together as a community to ease repatriation rather than arguing over objects as they appear poised to do. Asserting ownership of material culture, especially dance regalia and selected sacred objects such as masks and rattles, also asserts ownership of the rights to songs and dances associated with them. That community members are concerned with the "right" families gaining objects or the "right" families having access to objects repatriated to the MCRC is partly a status competition. One would expect to find, in this atmosphere, elements of mutual suspicion. An MCRC board member implied this when he said that there needs to be some protection for community members to ensure that their family objects are not being claimed by others. As one elder commented, some families will be truthful in the NAGPRA claim process and others not. Another elder, when asked about where he thought objects should go, expressed one more oft heard sentiment:

> I believe that they [objects] should come to the museum. I know they [families] claim songs, names, even things. People don't know anymore. They claim to know but they don't. That's one of the things that I wouldn't want to just stand up and say. I've been carving since 1939 and even today, I hear people say, our people, say "That old guy don't know nothing about what he's doing. And he doesn't know what it means." That's an attitude. (Interview, 9 April 1998)

Other community elders also observe that members of the younger generation sometimes express more confidence in their cultural knowledge than is warranted.

The basis for family claims of ownership of specific objects is likely to rest on two kinds of evidence: genealogical and artistic. The first involves establishing consanguine relationships to original named owners of objects in the rare instances when museums know this information. Making a connection from an individual in a contemporary family to a named ancestor means tracking, according to traditional inheritance patterns, to whom a specific object would have come down if it had never left the tribe. Although many families do have detailed oral histories documenting ancestry, the tracing of inheritance down through the generations is complicated by the historical realities of population loss and intermarriage (both between formerly distinct Makah families and with whites). Past and present ways of thinking about family relationships also conflict, adding further difficulties. Makah tribal members today, unless one parent was white, generally identify with both paternal and maternal families. Thus by today's standards, an individual could express legitimate interest in cultural objects from either side. However, in the past, status and family membership for men came exclusively from the paternal side. Women joined their husband's family at marriage, but returned to their father's family in cases of divorce or widowhood. Family affiliation in Nuu-chah-nulth culture, however, has always had a strategic element to it. Individuals, especially commoners, could choose to reside in any house to which they had some affiliation and there were obvious advantages to affiliating with the highest ranking one (Drucker 1951: 278–79). Makah individuals today could conceivably make strategic choices about asserting membership in extended families for purposes of NAGPRA.

Another example of the strategic application of indigenous patterns concerns how marriage with non-Indians has disrupted the system. If indigenous patterns were strictly followed, Makah tribal members today who have non-Makah fathers would not be considered tribal members and would have no status. I have heard some individuals deride the cultural status of others in the community on this basis. Nevertheless, it is ironic that some of the most adamantly expressed opinions about the necessity to strictly follow Makah inheritance patterns come from individuals whose fathers were white. They utilize the indigenous system to disqualify others while at the same time ignoring its application to themselves.

To prevent conflicts arising from such fluidity, one young man made the following proposal on how to ease NAGPRA implementation in relation to genealogical evidence:

> [F]irst of all, back here in Neah Bay, tell exactly whose family's is whose. So, by the time any artifacts get back here, if and when they get back here, then there would be no dispute as to the ownership of it. So, define the families, and which family you've come from. Before it gets here. And that way there will be less, you know, less arguments. And there will be. There will be arguments. (Interview, 19 April 1998)

It is yet unclear how realistic it is to sort out genealogical histories prior to repatriation, as this man suggests. An often heard comment in Neah Bay is that now Makah families are "all mixed up." In early contact times, a high percentage of marriages occurred outside the immediate village, and therefore Makah families stayed relatively distinct from each other. That is no longer the situation, and disputes are likely to arise in cases where the original named owner of an object is an ancestor to multiple contemporary Makah extended families.

The second kind of evidence upon which ownership claims are likely to rest is family-owned design elements that appear on objects. This knowledge has also been lost over time and it is more than likely that design ownership will be disputed between families. I asked Greg Colfax, who has extensively studied objects in collections nationwide and is the Makah Tribe's best-known contemporary carver, what percentage of the masks he has seen in museums could conceivably be traced to specific families based on style and design elements. He replied that while carvers traditionally knew the ownership histories, stories, and dances of each mask they carved and that contemporary carvers still do, this knowledge today does not extend to the older material. There are so few elders left to rely on that he feels skeptical that associations could be made to specific families by merely viewing objects in collections.

Nonetheless, designs remain important for the relationships they signify. One man told me that "an item could tie a family together." He illustrated this through reference to his sister's wedding, when his family made special handkerchiefs to give away: "[Everyone] got a red handkerchief with the design on it. You look at this red handkerchief and it's got this design that my grandpa made. That ties me to my brother." He concluded his story by explaining that by giving these handkerchiefs to others, it made them friends. Through use of design elements on objects, an individual could strategically display his place in the network of relationships within the community. I was told that upon marriage, a nuclear family intending to start their own house would combine design elements from the crest of both the bride's and the groom's families so that over generations complex designs developed that were akin to family trees.

As if the preceding issues did not present enough obstacles to establishing affiliation, there is a wild card: gifting. Because of the frequent giving of potlatch and marriage gifts across families, a specific family's design on an object does not necessarily mean it was owned by this family at the time that the object left the tribe. As Donna Wilkie explained: "Well, it might have been something that [one family] had given to someone else, to another family. For we were very giving, sharing people. We gave a lot of stuff back and forth. So it's really hard to pinpoint, even if [the object] is signed." Because of gifting, ultimately there is no way to know with certainty which families objects currently in institutional collections belonged to at the time they left tribal hands. Therefore, disputes will no doubt be common and dispute resolution a routine aspect of NAGPRA implementation in Neah Bay.

ENABLING NAGPRA: RESOLVING THE STRUGGLE

What are the possible dispute resolution procedures in situations where there are multiple claims on objects? Although a tribal court system exists in Neah Bay, it is clear that Makah tribal members feel that cultural matters should not be resolved in this venue. Drucker (1951:311–18), in his discussion of Nuu-chah-nulth dissension and social control, depicts a society where fighting was very uncommon, since the predominant social attitude was that violence was unseemly. Disputes primarily took the forms of verbal engagement and witchcraft, the latter of which Drucker identifies as the major crime problem in nineteenth-century Nuu-chah-nulth culture. There was no formal "machinery" for punishing those who disregarded norms of good behavior. He gives no examples in his text of instances where families argued over property. One might suggest that such disputes were a rarer occurrence in the past, when traditional inheritance patterns were pervasive, than they are now. However, in his summary statements on this topic, Drucker does make some comments relevant to the contemporary situation. He says that the most common means of control was for an individual's own family to give him advice, especially his elders. They frequently appealed to his loyalty to the family and prevailed upon him not to dishonor the family name. In extreme cases, an elderly relative would shame the wayward individual in a public forum, such as a feast. In general, these measures sufficed; and if not, the life of the individual was made so unpleasant that he voluntarily chose to leave the community.

There is not, as yet, a formal mechanism in Neah Bay for resolving disputes over cultural goods. However, as the following excerpt from an interview with Janine shows, many aspects of the traditional patterns remain the ideal:

ANN: I want to go back, for a minute, to something you said about the disputes between families. What mechanisms could be developed to resolve [situations] like that?

JANINE: Well, we've got generally accepted lists and just knowledge of who in what family takes responsibility for family matters. And, in other cases, like song disputes (we've never really implemented it to my knowledge) we've talked about getting a group of family heads together and putting this problem in their hands. 'Cause I can see a dispute being because of the split in families. I mean, four generations ago Mr. X would have been the one who was clearly owner of this piece. It was sort of scammed away from him in whatever kind of deal and now his family has grown and splintered off. Where his two sons or two grandsons clearly established very different families, which of course happens over the generations. I think that, like our archival department, would be able to provide whatever supporting evidence either family would ask them for. And then, kind of throw it in the hands of community members, 'cause I think that's something that the [MCRC] Board would really hate to be involved with. They'd say, "Go ahead and provide the framework for these disputes to be worked out." I mean, some [of] them as family heads might be involved in this decision-making, but I think they would make every effort for it not to be a decision that the MCRC Board, per se, would have to . . .

ANN: The board would not be put in a position where they would rule on where the [object goes].

JANINE: Right. As far as I can tell, considering how they operate. So . . .

ANN: Well, and what about, though, would it ever end up in the hands of the Tribal Council? Ruling one way or the other?

JANINE: Probably not at this point. From what I can tell over the last number of years, the Tribal Council has relied pretty heavily on the MCRC to provide input on these types of matters. And the charter does really say, and the mission, that that's what we're to do for the Tribe. But I think it would only get to their table if for some reason a dispute resolution process didn't work with us. So, I would think, though, that they would try to have the MCRC sort of set up a structure that would allow for that decision to be made before they would see it. And if they still had to see it, they'd probably stick with the recommendation that came from what the MCRC set up. But, that's hard to predict too. I mean, in a couple of years we could have an entirely different council that loved to deal with this kind of mess. [Laughter]

ANN: 'Cause some of the scenarios I was putting forth, I mean, sort of worst cases, that you would have a dispute that couldn't get resolved and it would go to the Tribal Council just 'cause they would have to sign off on one or the other to submit a claim. And then you'd get . . .

JANINE: You'd get the political . . .

ANN: And the family pressure. It could be just a big mess.

JANINE: Oh, yeah. If it were a big family that made the claim and it were a smaller, but very legitimate family, that countered it, it could come down to votes for the next election. Which is the sickest thing in the world to think about. So, I would think most people would rather have it resolved in a less political fashion than that. I couldn't say apolitical, 'cause nothing's apolitical [laughter]. So these will work themselves out. (Interview, 15 July 1998)

The aspect of Janine's comments that forcefully stands out is still the ideal of letting families and community members work out solutions, as opposed to establishing a more formal, institutional mechanism to accomplish this. She presumes that the MCRC would organize a committee of family heads that was broadly representative of all Makah families. Elders would probably be included, for theirs are the most authoritative voices on cultural matters. They are highly regarded and, as in the past, their recommendations are the most likely to be respected and followed by disputing parties. Then, such disputes would be brought before this committee for a decision. It would jeopardize the neutrality of the MCRC if its board became involved in this process, although Janine acknowledges that as members of the community some board members might become involved on behalf of their own families.

In the end, I believe there is a range of possible ownership scenarios for repatriated objects. One is the direct return of sacred objects to their families of origin. Exclusive rights to control access and use would lie completely with the family. This is the community ideal, although it is acknowledged that the state of documentation in institutional collections is such that direct family associations will be rare. Some members of the community see a drawback to this scenario, in that families might so closely guard the objects that there would be no wider community benefit. One young man commenting on this possibility vehemently stated:

I'd almost say for them to maintain ownership of that mask, they have to know the song or a song to go with it. Because you can't just have it there to just say "It's mine and it's been in my family for years." Well, use it! If you have it, use it. Learn the song or try and find out which song goes to that mask or whatever. (Interview, 19 April 1998)

While all acknowledge the individual family's right to decide whether to share the object for educational purposes (such as through display at potlatches), many tribal members feel that because of the rarity and historical value of some of these pieces that families should be encouraged to do so.

A second scenario is direct control and ownership of repatriated objects by the MCRC on behalf of the entire Makah community. This situation would support the creation of a Makah cultural patrimony, of which the Ozette artifacts represent the first such objects in the history of the Makah people. The struggle to have objects returned to the facility under NAGPRA is only one possible challenge to this scenario. Another concerns the amount of storage space remaining in current buildings and whether funds could be located for a planned expansion of the facility to incorporate new material. There are also some concerns about an institution, rather than a family or an individual, being gatekeeper for sacred objects. One man was worried that if numerous sacred objects were housed together, the resulting high concentration of power might be dangerous to employees. While some tribal members feel that repatriating objects to the MCRC would prevent contentious disputes between families, others feel that its neutrality would be challenged since the facility would be required to cede to families' wishes regarding care and treatment of their objects. To enable the MCRC to continue to serve the entire Makah community equally, these people believe that families should get objects whenever possible. The suggestion that all repatriated objects automatically go to the museum regardless of whether or not named individuals are associated with them also goes against the dominant ownership ethic in Makah culture.

In reality, it is probably a third scenario that will dominate for recovered objects, a hybrid of the above two. Community members recognize that old and fragile historical objects require special care which the MCRC can best provide. Families are concerned with security for such objects, but also know the benefits of humidity control, regulated lighting, strict handling procedures, and other standard museum storage practices. While some families will doubtlessly want to be in physical possession of their objects, the vast majority of individuals I spoke with thought that their families would approve of storing objects in the museum for safekeeping, as long as their ownership and complete authority over them were unquestioned.

FAMILY HEAD 1: Well, I mean speaking for my own family, you know, I wouldn't mind sharing anything with anyone. I mean, it'd be taken care of probably better here [MCRC] than families. *I wouldn't mind sharing things as long as it's known who the family, who it belonged to.* So, speaking for our family, I would say I'd keep it here. (Interview, 11 February 1998; emphasis added)

FAMILY HEAD 2: I think if the items are old, preserving it's probably number one. I bet most families would want it preserved and taken care of. Which probably the museum [MCRC] has better access to those technologies and, *as long as the families get credit for the object* . . . (Interview, 18 February 1998; emphasis added)

In fact, there is precedent for such an arrangement between community members and the MCRC, which does care for some objects that are "on deposit" from individuals. The MCRC cannot permit access, display, or otherwise make decisions about deposited material without the consent of the owner. The MCRC has a good reputation in the community for safeguarding the privacy of family-specific knowledge and objects. Thus, I believe that some permutation of this third scenario, involving MCRC housing of objects but family ownership and control, will become the norm for repatriated objects in Neah Bay.

CONCLUDING COMMENTS

I have sought to examine the implementation of NAGPRA at the local level, from the perspective of one tribe actively involved in drawing back significant material culture. For the Makah Tribe, this process has given rise to two distinct struggles, linked by the shared theme of ownership. The first requires tribal members to reconcile the conflicting forms of ownership in NAGPRA definitions with those expressed in Makah culture in order to take advantage of the law. The second is internal, as the community deliberates on where ownership of repatriated objects should lie.

Based on this close examination of Makah implementation, we can draw some tentative conclusions about tribal implementation in general. First, because NAGPRA definitions were intended for widespread adaptability, each tribe will have to negotiate a fit between these definitions and their own material culture. Whether it is the notion of communal ownership or another key aspect that proves problematic, most tribal groups will be forced to engage in this struggle. Second, the broad range of viewpoints within any given tribal community, whether these are based on religious attitudes or other factors, means that internal negotiations over NAGPRA are also inevitable.

I have also sought to evaluate NAGPRA from a more applied perspective as a piece of legislation and ask if it is "working" at the tribal level. It is too early in the Makah implementation process to offer more than a partial answer to this question. However, it is clear that the definitions in NAGPRA, while intentionally drafted for broad applicability, nonetheless cause problems for the Makah Tribe and others of the southern Northwest Coast. Tribal members are displaying great ingenuity and agency as they strive to make the legislation meet their culturally specific needs and goals. Until the MCRC, through the Makah Tribal Council, has submitted claims for cultural objects in museum and federal agency collections, the success of the struggle will remain unknown.

For anthropologists, my research contributes new perspectives on a number of additional topics having widespread interest. First, it highlights the central role of material culture in indigenous cultural revitalization movements. Makah tribal members themselves point to how the drawing back of significant objects under NAGPRA could potentially bring out intangible aspects of culture—dances, songs, stories—thus giving deeper meanings to those objects. Indeed, this phenomenon was previously observed in the community when artifacts were unearthed at Ozette. While it is tempting to view repatriations of objects to native communities as the end of a long process of struggle and negotiation, it is clear from this project that it is rather a beginning.

Second, my discussions provide a requisite counterbalance to previous depictions of indigenous ownership patterns on the Northwest Coast. These depictions tend to classify coastal peoples in a like manner as having communal ownership based on clan or household units, largely dismissing the private ownership insisted upon by Nuu-chah-nulth peoples. By drawing out the communal aspects of private systems and the private aspects of communal systems, I have dissected this dichotomy and shown its constituent parts to have more similarity than perhaps formerly appreciated. My goal was to problematize the concept of ownership; further research is clearly essential to an accurate understanding of the complexities of ownership in this region.

Finally, a number of themes explored here emerge in similar situations among indigenous peoples in other parts of the world. I believe that most cultural revitalization efforts to an extent force native peoples into new readings of their past to capitalize on opportunities in the present. These opportunities may be legislation like NAGPRA, favorable climates for pursuing land claims, or tourism. In participating in such activities, native peoples frequently confront issues concerning intellectual property, self-representation, and the maintenance of continuity in the face of rapid change. We also see played out in the Makah situation a growing trend towards professional indigenous cultural resource management in the late twentieth century. The thoughtful comments by Makah tribal members cited here reflect the cautious approach to these endeavors seen in many indigenous communities.

Despite the struggles faced by the Makah Tribe in this process of drawing back culture through NAGPRA, tribal members remain optimistic. Many community members identify this as a pivotal time in the tribe's collective cultural life. As Greig stated:

> It's an interesting journey that's about to be taken. I always thought that this time in our lives is like real, real, real critical. That we're an hourglass and the sand's running out. We're at the very end of our hourglass from the real old times. And that we're pulling now the last of the sand through. And whatever it is that we get, once the last [native Makah] speaker's gone, that we then turn it over again and start. I think you're probably here at the most critical time of all. (Interview, 27 May 1998)

This metaphor of an hourglass with the sand of knowledge about to run out is an apt one. When the last elder with knowledge of nineteenth-century life acquired from his or her parents' direct experience passes on, the hourglass must be turned over. The cultural resurgence will continue, but can be based only on the knowledge which has been "pulled through" from previous periods. An hourglass of sorts has turned over in the museum world as well, signaling a new beginning. As Nason writes (1997a:308): "As perhaps the most important single example of cultural policy legislation in the history of the United States, NAGPRA has permanently changed the way in which museums can operate." It will be fascinating to continue this journey and see where it takes both native communities and the museum profession in the new century.

7 / Afterword

What the buffalo is to the Indians on the plains, the whale is to the Makah.
—Henry A. Webster, Neah Bay Agent, 1865

[W]hale is the sacrament in our communion with the sea.
—Makah Tribal Member, 1997

Glenn walked through the lobby of the MCRC twitching violently, but with a huge grin on his face. An inveterate joker, he proclaimed to anyone who would listen that the atmosphere was so charged that the very air was shocking him. This image stands out in my mind as one of the most vivid moments of one of the most historic days in the life of the Makah Tribe, 23 October 1997. In distant Monaco, the tribal delegation learned that the IWC had granted their request to harvest four gray whales a year for subsistence and ceremonial purposes. Indeed, the excitement throughout the village caused by this victory was palpable. Phones in Neah Bay had begun ringing about 6 A.M. as the news spread like wildfire. It was greeted with relief, joy, laughter, tears, singing, and dancing. The MCRC exploded into a hub of activity which lasted for most of the day.[1] Members of the Makah whaling commission, representing all former whaling families, and other interested people began to gather early to revel in the moment and peruse the media reports that were already arriving by fax and being downloaded from the Internet. A constant stream of reporters from Seattle and environs arrived via helicopter, float plane, and automobile. MCRC phones were uncharacteristically busy, as staff fielded calls from media around the world.

Later in the morning, plans for celebration were initiated. All tribal employees were given a half-day holiday, and an impromptu parade at noon saw thirty vehicles, some of them appropriately decorated, driving the main streets of the village with horns blaring. It seemed that the entire village lined the parade route. Tribal singers consulted the MCRC archivist to get audio recordings of victory songs in Makah, which they began practicing that very night. These songs would be sung in the community hall at a party held the following week to honor the returning Monaco delegation. At the elementary school, where 95 percent of the children are Makah, students were hastily assembled for the last fifteen minutes of the day so the importance of the IWC ruling could be explained to them.

This ruling represented the culmination of many years of hard work by both the Tribe and the United States government on its behalf.[2] It had been necessary to develop compelling arguments on a number of key issues in order to convince IWC members that whaling was crucial to the survival of a distinct Makah people and culture.[3] The Tribe fought an uphill battle, but was persuasive enough to influence the conservation-oriented IWC to make a landmark decision: the Makah Tribe is the only group in the history of the organization to be permitted to *reinstitute* whaling. In the end, the Makah proposal succeeded only through the active support and assistance of native subsistence whalers from Alaska and Russia, who volunteered to reduce their quotas of gray whales so that despite the number requested by the Makah Tribe, the worldwide quota would be less than in previous years. In explaining why the Tribe took on the IWC, tribal members said they were fighting not so much for the opportunity to hunt whales as to preserve the *right* to do so—a right that their ancestors had insisted on in treaty negotiations in the 1850s. The excitement generated by the IWC decision was due in part to the Tribe's success in upholding its treaty rights for future generations.

The exhilaration demonstrated by Makah tribal members on this day can only be understood with reference to Makah history and traditional culture. Whaling was a spiritual as well as subsistence activity and permeated many aspects of community life. Several seasons of the year included references to whales, such as "the season for preparing to go whaling." In a social structure historically divided into elite, commoner, and slave families, the elite were always the whaling families. The descendents of these whaling families are recognized as the leading Makah families today. Of the seven or eight secret societies which formerly dominated the spiritual life of the community, the whaling society was arguably the most important and prestigious. Preparation for whale hunting went well beyond the individual men involved, as their wives also observed strict taboos during hunting season and other family members helped in the preparation of whaling gear and canoes. The entire community benefited when a whale was killed, since each family was entitled to a specific portion of the blubber. In a culture dependent almost entirely on the sea, the whale held a special place.

Makah people and their ancestors have been whalers for hundreds of years, as evidenced by archaeological materials and tribal oral history. They were renowned at least by the early contact period among other Northwest Coast groups for their skill in this pursuit. It remains a central aspect of their identity today. Until late 1998, Makah men had not actively whaled for about seventy years, since they voluntarily abstained when the gray whale became endangered as a result of overhunting by nonnatives. Nonetheless, tribal members' collective identity as whalers never dwindled. During these years, interest in whaling was sustained through oral history and by archaeological excavations at Ozette, which unearthed a longhouse belonging to a whaler. These artifacts of whaling gear served as powerful catalysts for unlocking tribal elders' remembered stories of the last great whalers of the late nineteenth and early twentieth centuries. As tribal members examined this whaling gear and marveled at its ingenious techniques of manufacture, a sense of communal pride in the remarkable feats of their ancestral whalers grew. The multitude of objects with whale motifs indicate whaling's centrality to life in that era; the M C R C logo today depicts two whales, a design element copied from carved house boards excavated at Ozette.

There are further indicators of the importance of whaling in the cultural identity of contemporary tribal members. The official crest of the Makah Indian Nation depicts a thunderbird with a whale in its talons. The first thematic exhibit in the M C R C is on whaling, a conscious decision on the part of exhibit designers. Despite the fact that whaling has not been part of lived experience throughout most of the twentieth century, it holds a special place in Makah cultural identity.

This story, of course, does not end with the I W C decision. On 17 May 1999, the Makah whalers overcame choppy surf and persistent environmentalist protestors to successfully bring the first whale to shore.[4] I was not in Neah Bay for this event, but I glimpsed some of the excitement when I visited the reservation a month later. M C R C staff had copiously documented the activities on film and video—the four canoes pulling the whale to shore, dozens of men hauling the whale onto the beach by hand, the formal welcoming, the ceremonial blessing, and the butchering process. I also heard in great detail about the celebratory party held in the school gym which attracted over one thousand people, including Makah relatives and friends from throughout the Pacific Northwest and members of other tribes. Tribal members obtained some meat for personal use during butchering, but most of the whale was consumed at this party. When I arrived, I was unable to find even a morsel to satisfy my own culinary curiosity. The fear of some that the taste for whale meat had been lost and that it would go uneaten was apparently unfounded. Tribal members were already clamoring for more.

Nothing brought the initial excitement home to me more than an evening spent watching a portion of a ten-hour videotape of the hunt recorded live from a helicopter by Northwest Cable News. One of the three Makahs present was a good friend who also happened to be the hunter who delivered the fatal gunshots. I had been told that the entire population of Neah Bay had been "giddy" for weeks and now I saw it firsthand. While my friend had previously seen similar footage, he had not yet viewed this version. As the videotape played, I received a running commentary about the weather conditions, locations of whales and other boats outside of the viewing area, overall strategy, and most importantly, the emotions he had been experiencing at various points. He became so animated it was like reliving the event. No one who has experienced such a powerful recital by a Makah hunter can doubt what whaling means to the Makah Nation. When the fated whale finally appeared immediately next to the canoe, time seemed to stand still as it hovered on the surface. I was amazed. The whale indeed seemed to have "offered" itself to the hunters, just as Makahs believe happens when they are spiritually prepared.

Whaling is a particularly immediate means through which to draw back culture to the Makah community. Skills associated with the hunt itself, as well as the processing of the whale, returned to active use. Spiritual practices too were revived; eventually whaling gear repatriated through NAGPRA may be incorporated into these. The fact that this whale was taken off the coast of Ozette is also significant. I think tribal members fully recognized the experiential impact of reviving an ancestral tradition in the very place their ancestors practiced it. This physical connection reinforces the spiritual and historic ones.

Drawing back culture is about forging personal connections between the past, the present, and the future. On a day following the hunt, Janine's six-year-old son accompanied her to the MCRC. As he passed a turn-of-the-century photograph of Makahs butchering a whale, he observed, "That's what we did!" This young representative of the Tribe's future had perhaps for the first time recognized the past in the events of the present.

Public Law 101-601—November 16, 1990
Native American Graves Protection
and Repatriation Act

104 STAT. 3048

PUBLIC LAW 101-601--NOV. 16, 1990

Public Law 101-601
101st Congress

An Act

To provide for the protection of Native American graves, and for other purposes.

Nov. 16.
1990

[H.R. 5237]

Native
American
Graves
Protection
and
Repatriation
Act.
Hawaiian
Natives.
Historic
preservation.
25 USC 3001
note.
25 USC 3001.

*Be it enacted by the Senate and House of Representatives of the
United States of America in Congress assembled,*

SECTION 1. SHORT TITLE.

This Act may be cited as the "Native American Graves Protection and Repatriation Act".

SEC. 2. DEFINITIONS.

For purposes of this Act, the term-

(1) "burial site" means any natural or prepared physical location, whether originally below, on, or above the surface of the earth, into which as a part of the death rite or ceremony of a culture, individual human remains are deposited.

(2) "cultural affiliation" means that there is a relationship of shared group identity which can be reasonably traced historically or prehistorically between a present day Indian tribe or Native Hawaiian organization and an identifiable earlier group.

(3) "cultural items" means human remains and-

(A) "associated funerary objects" which shall mean objects that, as a part of the death rite or ceremony of a culture, are reasonably believed to have been placed with individual human remains either at the time of death or later, and both the human remains and associated funerary objects are presently in the possession or control of a Federal agency or museum, except that other items exclusively made for burial purposes or to contain human remains shall be considered as associated funerary objects.

(B) "unassociated funerary objects" which shall mean objects that, as a part of the death rite or ceremony of a culture, are reasonably believed to have been placed with individual human remains either at the time of death or later, where the remains are not in the possession or control of the Federal agency or museum and the objects can be identified by a preponderance of the evidence as related to specific individuals or families or to known human remains or, by a preponderance of the evidence, as having been removed from a specific burial site of an individual culturally affiliated with a particular Indian tribe,

(C) "sacred objects" which shall mean specific ceremonial objects which are needed by traditional Native American religious leaders for the practice of traditional Native American religions by their present day adherents, and

(D) "cultural patrimony" which shall mean an object having ongoing historical, traditional, or cultural importance central to the Native American group or culture itself, rather than property owned by an individual Native

American, and which, therefore, cannot be alienated, appropriated, or conveyed by any individual regardless of whether or not the individual is a member of the Indian tribe or Native Hawaiian organization and such object shall have been considered inalienable by such Native American group at the time the object was separated from such group.

(4) "Federal agency" means any department, agency, or instrumentality of the United States. Such term does not include the Smithsonian Institution.

(5) "Federal lands" means any land other than tribal lands which are controlled or owned by the United States, including lands selected by but not yet conveyed to Alaska Native Corporations and groups organized pursuant to the Alaska Native Claims Settlement Act of 1971.

(6) "Hui Malama I Na Kupuna O Hawai'i Nei" means the nonprofit, Native Hawaiian organization incorporated under the laws of the State of Hawaii by that name on April 17, 1989, for the purpose of providing guidance and expertise in decisions dealing with Native Hawaiian cultural issues, particularly burial issues.

(7) "Indian tribe" means any tribe, band, nation, or other organized group or community of Indians, including any Alaska Native village (as defined in, or established pursuant to, the Alaska Native Claims Settlement Act), which is recognized as eligible for the special programs and services provided by the United States to Indians because of their status as Indians.

(8) "museum" means any institution or State or local government agency (including any institution of higher learning) that receives Federal funds and has possession of, or control over, Native American cultural items. Such term does not include the Smithsonian Institution or any other Federal agency.

(9) "Native American" means of, or relating to, a tribe, people, or culture that is indigenous to the United States.

(10) "Native Hawaiian" means any individual who is a descendant of the aboriginal people who, prior to 1778, occupied and exercised sovereignty in the area that now constitutes the State of Hawaii.

(11) "Native Hawaiian organization" means any organization which--

(A) serves and represents the interests of Native Hawaiians,

(B) has as a primary and stated purpose the provision of services to Native Hawaiians, and

(C) has expertise in Native Hawaiian Affairs, and shall include the Office of Hawaiian Affairs and Hui Malama I Na Kupuna O Hawai'i Nei.

(12) "Office of Hawaiian Affairs" means the Office of Hawaiian Affairs established by the constitution of the State of Hawaii.

(13) "right of possession" means possession obtained with the voluntary consent of an individual or group that had authority of alienation. The original acquisition of a Native American unassociated funerary object, sacred object or object of cultural patrimony from an Indian tribe or Native Hawaiian organization with the voluntary consent of an individual or group with authority to alienate such object is deemed to give right of possession of that object, unless the phrase so defined would, as

applied in section 7(c), result in a Fifth Amendment taking by the United States as determined by the United States Claims Court pursuant to 28 U.S.C. 1491 in which event the "right of possession" shall be as provided under otherwise applicable property law. The original acquisition of Native American human remains and associated funerary objects which were excavated, exhumed, or otherwise obtained with full knowledge and consent of the next of kin or the official governing body of the appropriate culturally affiliated Indian tribe or Native Hawaiian organization is deemed to give right of possession to those remains.

(14) "Secretary" means the Secretary of the Interior.

(15) "tribal land" means-

(A) all lands within the exterior boundaries of any Indian reservation;

(B) all dependent Indian communities;

(C) any lands administered for the benefit of Native Hawaiians pursuant to the Hawaiian Homes Commission Act, 1920, and section 4 of Public Law 86-3.

25 USC 3002.

SEC 3. OWNERSHIP.

(a) NATIVE AMERICAN HUMAN REMAINS AND OBJECTS.--The ownership or control of Native American cultural items which are excavated or discovered on Federal or tribal lands after the date of enactment of this Act shall be (with priority given in the order listed)--

(1) in the case of Native American human remains and associated funerary objects, in the lineal descendants of the Native American; or

(2) in any case in which such lineal descendants cannot be ascertained, and in the case of unassociated funerary objects, sacred objects, and objects of cultural patrimony--

(A) in the Indian tribe or Native Hawaiian organization on whose tribal land such objects or remains were discovered;

Claims.

(B) in the Indian tribe or Native Hawaiian organization which has the closest cultural affiliation with such remains or objects and which, upon notice, states a claim for such remains or objects; or

(C) if the cultural affiliation of the objects cannot be reasonably ascertained and if the objects were discovered on Federal land that is recognized by a final judgment of the Indian Claims Commission or the United States Court of Claims as the aboriginal land of some Indian tribe--

(1) in the Indian tribe that is recognized as aboriginally occupying the area in which the objects were discovered, if upon notice, such tribe states a claim for such remains or objects, or

(2) if it can be shown by a preponderance of the evidence that a different tribe has a stronger cultural relationship with the remains or objects than the tribe or organization specified in paragraph (1), in the Indian tribe that has the strongest demonstrated relationship, if upon notice, such tribe states a claim for such remains or objects.

(b) UNCLAIMED NATIVE AMERICAN HUMAN REMAINS AND OBJECTS.--Native American cultural items not claimed under subsec-

Regulations.

tion (a) shall be disposed of in accordance., with regulations promulgated by the Secretary-in consultation with the review committee established under section 8,-Native American groups, representatives of museums and the scientific community.

(C) INTENTIONAL EXCAVATION AND REMOVAL OF NATIVE AMERICAN HUMAN REMAINS AND OBJECTS.--The intentional removal from or excavation of Native American cultural items from Federal or tribal lands for purposes of discovery, study, or removal of such items is permitted only if--

(1) such items are excavated or removed pursuant to a permit issued under section 4 of the Archaeological Resources Protection Act of 1979 (93 Stat. 721; 16 U.S.C. 470aa et seq.) which shall be consistent with this Act;

(2) such items are excavated or removed after consultation with or, in the case of tribal lands, consent of the appropriate (if any) Indian tribe or Native Hawaiian organization;

(3) the ownership and right of control of the disposition of such items shall be as provided in subsections (a) and (b); and

(4) proof of consultation or consent under paragraph (2) is shown.

(d) INADVERTENT DISCOVERY OF NATIVE AMERICAN REMAINS AND OBJECTS.--(1) Any person who knows, or has reason to know, that such person has discovered Native American cultural items on Federal or tribal lands-after the date of enactment of this Act shall notify, in writing, the Secretary of the Department, or head of any other agency or instrumentality of the United States, having primary management authority with respect to Federal lands and the appropriate Indian tribe or Native Hawaiian organization with respect to tribal lands, if known or readily ascertainable, and, in the case of lands that have been selected by an Alaska Native Corporation or group organized pursuant to the Alaska Native Claims Settlement Act of 1971, the appropriate corporation or group. If the discovery occurred in connection with an activity, including (but not limited to) construction, mining, logging, and agriculture, the person shall cease the activity in the area of the discovery, make a reasonable effort to protect the items discovered before resuming such activity, and provide notice under this subsection. Following the notification under this subsection, and upon certification by the Secretary of the department or the head of any agency or instrumentality of the United States or the appropriate Indian tribe or Native Hawaiian organization that notification has been received, the activity may resume after 30 days of such certification.

(2) The disposition of and control over any cultural items excavated or removed under this subsection shall be determined as provided for in this section.

(3) If the Secretary of the Interior consents, the responsibilities (in whole or in part) under paragraphs (1) and (2) of the Secretary of any department (other than the Department of the Interior) or the head of any other agency or instrumentality may be delegated to the Secretary with respect to any land managed by such other Secretary or agency head.

(e) RELINQUISHMENT.--Nothing in this section shall prevent the governing body of an Indian tribe or Native Hawaiian organization from expressly relinquishing control over any Native American human remains, or title to or control over any funerary object, or sacred object.

SEC. 4. ILLEGAL TRAFFICKING.

(a) ILLEGAL TRAFFICKING.--Chapter 53 of title 18, United States Code, is amended by adding at the end thereof the following new section:

"§ 1170. Illegal Trafficking in Native American Human Remains and Cultural Items

"(a) Whoever knowingly sells, purchases, uses for profit, or transports for sale or profit, the human remains of a Native American without the right of possession to those remains as provided in the Native American Graves Protection and Repatriation Act shall be fined in accordance with this title, or imprisoned not more than 12 months, or both, and in the case of a second or subsequent violation, be fined in accordance with this title, or imprisoned not more than 5 years, or both.

"(b) Whoever knowingly sells, purchases, uses for profit, or transports for sale or profit any Native American cultural items obtained in violation of the Native American Grave Protection and Repatriation Act shall be fined in accordance with this title, imprisoned not more than one year, or both, and in the case of a second or subsequent violation, be fined in accordance with this title, imprisoned not more than 5 years, or both.".

(b) TABLE OF CONTENTS.--The table of contents for chapter 53 of title 18, United States Code, is amended by adding at the end thereof the following new item:

"1170. Illegal Trafficking in Native American Human Remains and Cultural Items.".

Museums .
25 USC 3003.

SEC. 5. INVENTORY FOR HUMAN REMAINS AND ASSOCIATED FUNERARY OBJECTS.

(a) IN GENERAL.--Each Federal agency and each museum which has possession or control over holdings or collections of Native American human remains and associated funerary objects shall compile an inventory of such items and, to the extent possible based on information possessed by such museum or Federal agency, identify the geographical and cultural affiliation of such item.

(b) REQUIREMENTS.--(1) The inventories and identifications required under subsection (a) shall be--

(A) completed in consultation with tribal government and Native Hawaiian organization officials and traditional religious leaders;

(B) completed by not later than the date that is 5 years after the date of enactment of this Act, and

(C) made available both during the time they are being conducted and afterward to a review committee established under section 8.

(2) Upon request by an Indian tribe or Native Hawaiian organization which receives or should have received notice, a museum or Federal agency shall supply additional available documentation to supplement the information required by subsection (a) of this section. The term "documentation" means a summary of existing museum or Federal agency records, including inventories or catalogues, relevant studies, or other pertinent data for the limited purpose of determining the geographical origin, cultural affiliation, and basic facts surrounding acquisition and accession of Native American human remains and associated funerary objects subject to this section. Such term does not mean, and this Act shall not be

construed to be an authorization for, the initiation of new scientific studies of such remains and associated funerary objects or other means of acquiring or preserving additional scientific information from such remains and objects.

(c) EXTENSION OF TIME FOR INVENTORY.--Any museum which has made a good faith effort to carry out an inventory and identification under this section, but which has been unable to complete the process, may appeal to the Secretary for an extension of the time requirements set forth in subsection (b)(1)(B). The Secretary may extend such time requirements for any such museum upon a finding of good faith effort. An indication of good faith shall include the development of a plan to carry out the inventory and identification process.

(d) NOTIFICATION--(1) If the cultural affiliation of any particular Native American human remains or associated funerary objects is determined pursuant to this section, the Federal agency or museum concerned shall, not later than 6 months after the completion of the inventory, notify the affected Indian tribes or Native Hawaiian organizations.

(2) The notice required by paragraph (1) shall include information--

(A) which identifies each Native American human remains or associated funerary objects and the circumstances surrounding its acquisition;

(B) which lists the human remains or associated funerary objects that are clearly identifiable as to tribal origin; and

(C) which lists the Native American human remains and associated funerary objects that are not clearly identifiable as being culturally affiliated with that Indian tribe or Native Hawaiian organization, but which, given the totality of circumstances surrounding acquisition of the remains or objects, are determined by a reasonable belief to be remains or objects culturally affiliated with the Indian tribe or Native Hawaiian organization.

(3) A copy of each notice provided under paragraph (1) shall be sent to the Secretary who shall publish each notice in the Federal Register.

(e) INVENTORY.--For the purposes of this section, the term "inventory" means a simple itemized list that summarizes the information called for by this section.

SEC. 6. SUMMARY FOR UNASSOCIATED FUNERARY OBJECTS, SACRED OBJECTS, AND CULTURAL PATRIMONY.

(a) IN GENERAL.--Each Federal agency or museum which has possession or control over holdings or collections of Native American unassociated funerary objects, sacred objects, or objects of cultural patrimony shall provide a written summary of such objects based upon available information held by such agency or museum. The summary shall describe the scope of the collection, kinds of objects included, reference to geographical location, means and period of acquisition and cultural affiliation, where readily ascertainable.

(b) REQUIREMENTS.-- (1) The summary required under subsection (a) shall be--

(A) in lieu of an object-by-object inventory;

(B) followed by consultation with tribal government and Native Hawaiian organization officials and traditional religious leaders; and

(C) completed by not later than the date that is 3 years after the date of enactment of this Act.

(2) Upon request, Indian Tribes and Native Hawaiian organizations shall have access to records, catalogues, relevant studies or other pertinent data for the limited purposes of determining the geographic origin, cultural affiliation, and basic facts surrounding acquisition and accession of Native American objects subject to this section. Such information shall be provided in a reasonable manner to be agreed upon by all parties.

25 USC 3005.

SEC. 7. REPATRIATION.

(a) REPATRIATION OF NATIVE AMERICAN HUMAN REMAINS AND OBJECTS POSSESSED OR CONTROLLED BY FEDERAL AGENCIES AND MUSEUMS.--(1) If, pursuant to section 5, the cultural affiliation of Native American human remains and associated funerary objects with a particular Indian tribe or Native Hawaiian organization is established, then the Federal agency or museum, upon the request of a known lineal descendant of the Native American or of the tribe or organization and pursuant to subsections (b) and (e) of this section, shall expeditiously return such remains and associated funerary objects.

(2) If, pursuant to section 6, the cultural affiliation with a particular Indian tribe or Native Hawaiian organization is shown with respect to unassociated funerary objects, sacred objects or objects of cultural patrimony, then the Federal agency or museum, upon the request of the Indian tribe or Native Hawaiian organization and pursuant to subsections (b), (c) and (e) of this section, shall expeditiously return such objects.

(3) The return of cultural items covered by this Act shall be in consultation with the requesting lineal descendant or tribe or organization to determine the place and manner of delivery of such items.

(4) Where cultural affiliation of Native American human remains and funerary objects has not been established in an inventory prepared pursuant to section 5, or the summary pursuant to section 6, or where Native American human remains and funerary objects are not included upon any such inventory, then, upon request and pursuant to subsections (b) and (e) and, in the case of unassociated funerary objects, subsection (c), such Native American human remains and funerary objects shall be expeditiously returned where the requesting Indian tribe or Native Hawaiian organization can show cultural affiliation by a preponderance of the evidence based upon geographical, kinship, biological, archaeological, anthropological, linguistic, folkloric, oral traditional, historical, or other relevant information or expert opinion.

(5) Upon request and pursuant to subsections (b), (c) and (e), sacred objects and objects of cultural patrimony shall be expeditiously returned where--

    (A) the requesting party is the direct lineal descendant of an individual who owned the sacred object;

    (B) the requesting Indian tribe or Native Hawaiian organization can show that the object was owned or controlled by the tribe or organization; or

    (C) the requesting Indian tribe or Native Hawaiian organization can show that the sacred object was owned or controlled by a member thereof, provided that in the case where a sacred object was owned by a member thereof, there are no identifiable lineal descendants of said member or the lineal descendent, upon notice, have failed to make a claim for the object under this Act.

(b) SCIENTIFIC STUDY.--If the lineal descendant, Indian tribe, or Native Hawaiian organization requests the return of culturally affiliated Native American cultural items, the Federal agency or museum shall expeditiously return such items unless such items are indispensable for completion of a specific scientific study, the outcome of which would be of major benefit to the United States. Such items shall be returned by no later than 90 days after the date on which the scientific study is completed.

(c) STANDARD OF REPATRIATION.--If a known lineal descendant or an Indian tribe or Native Hawaiian organization requests the return of Native American unassociated funerary objects, sacred objects or objects of cultural patrimony pursuant to this Act and presents evidence which, if standing alone before the introduction of evidence to the contrary, would support a finding that the Federal agency or museum did not have the right of possession, then such agency or museum shall return such objects unless it can overcome such inference and prove that it has a right of possession to the objects.

(d) SHARING OF INFORMATION BY FEDERAL AGENCIES AND MUSEUMS.--Any Federal agency or museum shall share what information it does possess regarding the object in question with the known lineal descendant, Indian tribe, or Native Hawaiian organization to assist in making a claim under this section.

(e) COMPETING CLAIMS.--Where there are multiple requests for repatriation of any cultural item and, after complying with the requirements of this Act, the Federal agency or museum cannot clearly determine which requesting party is the most appropriate claimant, the agency or museum may retain such item until the requesting parties agree upon its disposition or the dispute is otherwise resolved pursuant to the provisions of this Act or by a court of competent jurisdiction.

(f) MUSEUM OBLIGATION.--Any museum which repatriates any item in good faith pursuant to this Act shall not be liable for claims by an aggrieved party or for claims of breach of fiduciary duty, public trust, or violations of state law that are inconsistent with the provisions of this Act.

25 USC 3006.

SEC. 8. REVIEW COMMITTEE.

(a) ESTABLISHMENT.--Within 120 days after the date of enactment of this Act, the Secretary shall establish a committee to monitor and review the implementation of the inventory and identification process and repatriation activities required under sections 5, 6 and 7.

(b) MEMBERSHIP--(1) The Committee established under subsection (a) shall be composed of 7 members,

(A) 3 of whom shall be appointed by the Secretary from nominations submitted by Indian tribes, Native Hawaiian organizations, and traditional Native American religious leaders with at least 2 of such persons being traditional Indian religious leaders;

(B) 3 of whom shall be appointed by the Secretary from nominations submitted by national museum organizations and scientific organizations; and

(C) 1 who shall be appointed by the Secretary from a list of persons developed and consented to by all of the members appointed pursuant to subparagraphs (A) and (B).

(2) The Secretary may not appoint Federal officers or employees to the committee.

(3) In the event vacancies shall occur, such vacancies shall be filled by the Secretary in the same manner as the original appointment within 90 days of the occurrence of such vacancy.

(4) Members of the committee established under subsection (a) shall serve without pay, but shall be reimbursed at a rate equal to the daily rate for GS-18 of the General Schedule for each day (including travel time) for which the member is actually engaged in committee business. Each member shall receive travel expenses, including per diem in lieu of subsistence, in accordance with sections 5702 and 5703 of title 5, United States Code.

(c) RESPONSIBILITIES.--The committee established under subsection a) shall be responsible for-

(1) designating one of the members of the committee as chairman;

(2) monitoring the inventory and identification process conducted under sections 5 and 6 to ensure a fair, objective consideration and assessment of all available relevant information and evidence;

(3) upon the request of any affected party, reviewing and making findings related to-

(A) the identity or cultural affiliation of cultural items, or

(B) the return of such items;

(4) facilitating the resolution of any disputes among Indian tribes, Native Hawaiian organizations, or lineal descendants and Federal agencies or museums relating to the return of such items including convening the parties to the dispute if deemed desirable;

(5) compiling an inventory of culturally unidentifiable human remains that are in the possession or control of each Federal agency and museum and recommending specific actions for developing a process for disposition of such remains;

(6) consulting with Indian tribes and Native Hawaiian organizations and museums on matters within the scope of the work of the committee affecting such tribes or organizations;

(7) consulting with the Secretary in the development of regulations to carry out this Act;

(8) performing such other related functions as the Secretary -may assign to the committee; and

(9) making recommendations, if appropriate, regarding future care of cultural items which are to be repatriated.

(d) Any records and findings made by the review committee pursuant to this Act relating to the identity or cultural affiliation of any cultural items and the return of such items may be admissible in any action brought under section 15 of this Act.

(e) RECOMMENDATIONS AND REPORT.--The committee shall make the recommendations under paragraph (c)(5) in consultation with Indian tribes and Native Hawaiian organizations and appropriate scientific and museum groups.

(f) ACCESS.--The Secretary shall ensure that the committee established under subsection (a) and the members of the committee have reasonable access to Native American cultural items under review and to associated scientific and historical documents.

(g) DUTIES OF SECRETARY.--The Secretary shall--

Regulations.
(1) establish such rules and regulations for the committee as may be necessary, and

(2) provide reasonable administrative and staff support necessary for the deliberations of the committee.

(h) ANNUAL REPORT.--The committee established under subsection (a) shall submit an annual report to the Congress on the progress made, and any barriers encountered, in implementing this section during the previous year.

(i) TERMINATION.--The committee established under subsection (a) shall terminate at the end of the 120-day period beginning on the day the Secretary certifies, in a report submitted to Congress, that the work of the committee has been completed.

SEC. 9. PENALTY.

Museums.
25 USC 3007

(a) PENALTY.--Any museum that fails to comply with the requirements of this Act may be assessed a civil penalty by the Secretary of the Interior pursuant to procedures established by the Secretary through regulation. A penalty assessed under this subsection shall be determined on the record after opportunity for an agency hearing. Each violation under this subsection shall be a separate offense.

(b) AMOUNT OF PENALTY.--The amount of a penalty assessed under subsection (a) shall be determined under regulations promulgated pursuant to this Act, taking into account, in addition to other factors--

(1) the archaeological, historical, or commercial value of the item involved;

(2) the damages suffered, both economic and noneconomic, by an aggrieved party, and

(3) the number of violations that have occurred.

(c) ACTIONS TO RECOVER PENALTIES.--If any museum fails to pay courts. an assessment of a civil penalty pursuant to a final order of the Secretary that has been issued under subsection (a) and not appealed or after a final judgment has been rendered on appeal of such order, the Attorney General may institute a civil action in an appropriate district court of the United States to collect the penalty. In such action, the validity and amount of such penalty shall not be subject to review.

Courts.

(d) SUBPOENAS.--In hearings held pursuant to subsection (a), subpoenas may be issued for the attendance and testimony of witnesses and the production of relevant papers, books, and documents. Witnesses so summoned shall be paid the same fees and mileage that are paid to witnesses in the courts of the United States.

SEC. 10. GRANTS.

25 USC 3008.

(a) INDIAN TRIBES AND NATIVE HAWAIIAN ORGANIZATIONS.--The Secretary is authorized to make grants to Indian tribes and Native Hawaiian organizations for the purpose of assisting such tribes and organizations in the repatriation of Native American cultural items.

(b) MUSEUMS.--The Secretary is authorized to make grants to museums for the purpose of assisting the museums in conducting the inventories and identification required under sections 5 and 6.

SEC. 11. SAVINGS PROVISIONS.

25 USC 3009.

Nothing in this Act shall be construed to--

(1) limit the authority of any Federal agency or museum to--

(A) return or repatriate Native American cultural items to Indian tribes, Native Hawaiian organizations, or individuals, and

(B) enter into any other agreement with the consent of the culturally affiliated tribe or organization as to the disposition of, or control over, items covered by this Act;

(2) delay actions on repatriation requests that are pending on the date of enactment of this Act;

(3) deny or otherwise affect access to any court;

(4) limit any procedural or substantive right which may otherwise be secured to individuals or Indian tribes or Native Hawaiian organizations; or

(5) limit the application of any State or Federal law pertaining to theft or stolen property.

25 USC 3010.

SEC. 12. SPECIAL RELATIONSHIP BETWEEN FEDERAL GOVERNMENT AND INDIAN TRIBES.

This Act reflects the unique relationship between the Federal Government and Indian tribes and Native Hawaiian organizations and should not be construed to establish a precedent with respect to any other individual, organization or foreign government.

25 USC 3011.

SEC. 13. REGULATIONS.

The Secretary shall promulgate regulations to carry out this Act within 12 months of enactment.

25 USC 3012.

SEC. 14. AUTHORIZATION OF APPROPRIATIONS.

There is authorized to be appropriated such sums as may be necessary to carry out this Act.

25 USC 3013.

Courts.

SEC. 15. ENFORCEMENT.

The United States district courts shall have jurisdiction over any action brought by any person alleging a violation of this Act and shall have the authority to issue such orders as may be necessary to enforce the provisions of this Act.

Approved November 16,1990.

LEGISLATIVE HISTORY--H.R. 5237:

· HOUSE REPORTS: No. 101-877 (Comm. on Interior and Insular Affairs).
CONGRESSIONAL RECORD, Vol. 136 (1990):
    Oct. 22, considered and passed House.
    Oct. 25, considered and passed Senate; passage vitiated.
    Oct. 26. reconsidered and passed Senate, amended.
    Oct. 27, House concurred in Senate amendment.

        o

NOTES

1. These figures for 1997 were provided by the Makah Tribal Enrollment Office.

2. These figures for 1994 were provided by the Makah Housing Authority.

3. The Coast Guard base includes about twenty houses and has approximately sixty residents.

4. Makahs generally do not use the term "tribe" to denote a *cultural* entity. When they talk about "the Tribe," they refer to the political entity as represented by the official tribal government of the Makah Indian Nation. I will use Tribe, capitalized, to mark this use. When they say that the Tribe has undertaken some initiative, such as NAGPRA implementation or whaling, they refer to activities at the government level under the direction of the Tribal Council or one of its departments. Thus, when I write that the Tribe is implementing NAGPRA, I mean that this is a tribal-wide initiative undertaken by one of its departments on behalf of the community as a whole. Perhaps the term "government" would be more accurate, but since I also refer to the United States government in the context of NAGPRA, I believe this would cause undue confusion.

5. In many cases these empty lots have been jointly inherited by numerous members of the same extended family and until contesting claims are resolved cannot be developed.

6. While on the surface it appears that there is plentiful land within the village, there has in fact been a freeze on land transactions for several years. One couple I know would like to purchase land to build a house but there is not any currently on the market.

7. There have been two or three phases of HUD housing on the reservation.

These houses are readily identifiable by their boxy shapes, small windows, uniform floor plans, and characteristic light blue, green, or beige exteriors. The majority of houses have wood stoves, which many families use as their primary source of heat, as it is cheaper than electricity. Some people have expanded their HUD homes by adding workrooms (for artists), garages, or porches. Large satellite dishes are standard since there is very little reception available without it and virtually no other sources of local entertainment.

INTRODUCTION

1. All other North American native cultures with whaling traditions are located in Canada and Alaska.

2. Particularly worth noting are special issues of the *Arizona State Law Journal* (Spring 1992) and *Federal Archaeology* (Fall/Winter 1995) which are devoted to discussions of NAGPRA by lawyers, federal agency representatives, museum personnel, and Native Americans.

3. For example, see *Museum News* (September/October 2000).

4. In general, I have tried to avoid using the term "traditional" to refer to historic Makah culture since it carries unwelcome baggage for many anthropologists. Since it is used in NAGPRA, however, it is not completely avoidable in this book.

5. "Precontact" as used in this book refers to Makah life as documented from extensive archaeological excavations at Ozette dating to approximately 1500 C.E. Material culture was little changed from this period to that recorded in early contact accounts in the late 1700s and early 1800s. Tribal members themselves tend to telescope the centuries from 1500 to 1800 into a "standardized" Makah culture (Warren 1998:30). The uniform material culture cannot be used as evidence that social structure and practice during this period were similarly unchanging. Most certainly they were not. Nevertheless, archaeological evidence does suggest some continuity. For example, a basketry hat of a type known to be worn only by high-status whalers in the nineteenth century was found at Ozette in the context of a whaler's house. Similarly, a small carved figure found inside a mussel shell seems to suggest that the Makah legend of the "Clamshell Boy" told today has been passed down through oral tradition over many centuries (Cohlene 1990).

1 / MAKAH PERSPECTIVES OF NAGPRA

1. One of the most contentious aspects of NAGPRA from the point of view of tribes is a provision for scientific study of human remains, which tribes insist panders to the scientific community. Scientists welcome the provision in a law they see as biased towards tribal interests.

2. Disputes with other tribes over objects in museum collections were less of a concern for Makah tribal members.

3. In December 1995, Richard Maniscalco of Virginia pled guilty to selling human remains and other artifacts illegally taken from federal and Indian lands in Montana. Earlier in the year, Brian and Gerald Garcia were convicted of removing kachina dolls from the Pueblo of Acoma. In each of these cases, the individuals attempted to sell the items to undercover agents of the Bureau of Land Management. In 1996, Richard Corrow was found guilty by a New Mexico court of trafficking Navajo ceremonial objects.

4. There have been fifteen NAGPRA suits filed to date (AAM 2000:48). One of the earliest concerning a cultural object was initially brought before the Review Committee, which heard testimony on two occasions from Hawaiian organizations and the city of Providence regarding a carved wooden figure. Twice the committee recommended repatriation under NAGPRA as a sacred object, which the city resisted. Legal proceedings were initiated, but eventually the case was settled out of court when the Hawaiian organizations agreed to purchase the object. The official findings of the NAGPRA Review Committee on this case can be found in the *Federal Register* 62, no. 84 (1 May 1997). The most publicized dispute regards ancient human remains unearthed near Kennewick, Washington. This case never came before the Review Committee, as scientists who wished to examine the remains immediately brought a suit in U.S. District Court against the U.S. Army Corps of Engineers, on whose land the remains were discovered. For further background on the Kennewick debate, see Downey (2000), Thomas (2000), and the National Park Service webpage at www.cr.nps.gov/aad/kennewick.

5. In fact, tribes have long accused federal agencies of having greater rates of noncompliance than do museums (see Stockes 2000). It is true that some federal agencies have yet to meet the 1995 deadline for compiling inventories.

2 / "FIVE VILLAGES, ONE HEARTBEAT"

1. For the broader context of archaeological investigations on the Northwest Coast, see the extensive and valuable overview by Ames and Maschner (1999).

2. These Nuu-chah-nulth groups are the Ahousaht, Ditidaht, Ehattesaht, Hesquiat, Ka:'yu:'k't'h/Che:k'tles'/Et'h', Mowachaht/Muchalaht, Nuchatlaht, Ohiaht, Opetchesaht, Tla-o-qui-aht, Toquaht, Tseshaht, Uchucklesaht, and the Ucluelet.

3. Makah tribal members and outside scholars alike refer to ethnomusicologist Frances Densmore's (1939) work for transcriptions of whaling songs and to T. T. Waterman's (1920) detailed technical analysis of whaling gear.

4. While tribal attitudes towards whaling gear suggest that it would best fit under

NAGPRA's definition of a sacred object, there is some indication that it could also be considered as cultural patrimony. Densmore (1939) talks about whaling floats that were displayed in a store owned by a Makah named Young Doctor, but were not for sale. Of them, she writes (1939:49): "They were considered, in a certain sense, the property of the entire village and it was said they must be ready for use at any time if a whale were sighted outside the cape."

5. However, there were many songs, such as dinner songs for feasting, which did not have accompanying dances.

6. Makah tribal members who had attended potlatches on Vancouver Island, where ceremonies have survived in more intact forms, indicated that strict seating by status is still followed by other Nuu-chah-nulth groups. I have touched here on only the most general of ceremonial privileges, which were multitudinous.

7. This legend parallels other accounts of how ceremonial privileges are obtained from supernatural beings, often animals.

8. Whistles could imitate the sounds of a variety of supernatural beings including a bear, wolf, owl, loon, eagle, thunderbird, or sandhill crane (Goodman 1991:232).

3 / MAKAH CULTURE(S) AND HISTORIES IN FLUX

1. The first recorded contact between Europeans and Makah ancestors occurred when John Meares anchored off Tatoosh Island in 1788 (Meares 1790). In 1789, Neah Bay was visited and described by a trader from Boston, Robert Haswell (Haswell 1880). A year later, the Spanish began trading in Neah Bay and established a fort there in 1792, which was abandoned after just four months. This was probably the native population's first long-term introduction to European culture. These early traders were primarily interested in sea otter pelts, which were not hunted in large numbers by Makahs prior to this time. The initial encounters were not without conflict; a Spanish commander described the local inhabitants as "warlike, treacherous and thievish" (quoted in Ruby and Brown 1986:126). Shipwrecked Russians (1809–1810) and Japanese (1833) spent time with the local population until they were rescued; some sources suggest they may have been enslaved. The wreck of another Russian vessel around 1840 apparently led to an infusion of Caucasian blood, which was later noted by early reservation employees. For early accounts of Nuu-chah-nulth cultures see Beaglehole (1967), Boit (1919), Espinosa y Tello (1930), Gunther (1972), and Jewitt (1967).

2. The Treaty of Neah Bay is the only Indian treaty with the United States government that specifies rights to whales.

3. In some cases, these allotments are now currently co-owned by as many as one hundred individuals.

4. In 1911, a treaty signed with the Makah Tribe and several others allowed limited sealing by traditional methods.

5. Deloria writes (1977:55): "The Makahs . . . had sold twenty thousand gallons of whale and fish oil for the sawmills of Olympia in 1852 and were the chief source of machine oil for the entire coast."

6. On 19 April 1884, the Canadian Parliament passed an amendment to the Indian Act taking legislative action against the potlatch, making participation a misdemeanor. The law was erratically and loosely enforced until 1921, when thirty-four participants in one of the largest potlatches ever to be held in British Columbia, by a Nimpkish named Dan Cramer, were imprisoned. A deal was offered to these individuals by the government; if they renounced the potlatch and surrendered all their regalia, they would be released. Some chose to serve time, but over 450 items passed into the collections of major North American museums. Many of these objects have now been repatriated. This incident was the single most extensive confiscation and the most vigorous suppression of the potlatch in North America and continues to represent to Northwest Coast peoples the height of government oppression of native traditions (see Clifford 1991; Cole 1985).

7. The store passed through three generations of Washburns and now operates as a fully modern grocery and hardware store under the same name.

8. Collectors discovered only later that ethnological objects were a renewable resource; ones sold were simply replaced in native ceremonies by newly made versions. As Cole (1985:301) notes: "Some items were replaceable: Kwakiutl masks, for example, might be sold and new ones made, since the prerogatives they represented were retained."

9. Detailed descriptions of the manufacture and use of these objects were recorded by Swan and published in the earliest ethnographic work on the Makah Tribe, *Indians of Cape Flattery*, which appeared in the new Smithsonian Contributions to Knowledge Series in 1870. This work is invaluable to scholars as it provides the sole systematic treatment of Makah culture when it was only just beginning to change in response to government policies.

4 / A NEW ERA

1. The picture is very similar today. In 1991, the Neah Bay economy was 36.8 percent retail and tourism, 20 percent government revenue, 14.06 percent commercial and recreational fishing, 11.4 percent miscellaneous businesses and services, and 7.9 percent timber (MEDP 1991).

2. Makah Days, which occurs in late August, is the most anticipated event of the

year. The three-day occasion attracts hundreds of tourists who peruse craft stalls, watch canoe races and dance exhibitions, and eat salmon cooked by an outdoor fire. For Makah tribal members, it is a time for family reunions and competitions against other tribes in canoe racing, slahal games, and softball tournaments. Highlights of the weekend include a parade, a talent show, and a fireworks display. Preparations consume the entire community for months prior, as traditional costumes are prepared, dance classes held, and events organized.

3. These figures were provided by the Makah Housing Authority and the Makah Social and Health Services Program.

4. Other writers view the Ozette excavation as contributing to a cultural resurgence that was already manifesting itself among Makah tribal members, rather than as the initiating factor (see Erikson 1996, 1999).

5. In archaeology, a wet-site is a waterlogged site that has preserved organic artifacts because of the anaerobic environment.

6. These archives have the most comprehensive collection of Makah documents in the world, including books, articles, slides, photographs, historical film, taped oral histories by tribal elders, and volumes of unpublished Makah research (see Oxendine 1992:119).

7. For groups with established cultural resource management programs, such as the Makah Tribe, the obligatory involvement of the official tribal government adds an unnecessary bureaucratic step. It would make more sense in this case to have the MCRC Director's signature on claims. Investing full NAGPRA authority with the MCRC would benefit the Tribe for other reasons. The MCRC staff is more stable than the council, whose composition changes every two or three years. MCRC staff is also more knowledgeable about cultural resource management issues and has a working relationship with the community on them.

8. The Assistant Interviewer was intentionally of the opposite gender than the Project Manager, so that gender-specific information could be appropriately collected.

9. The Smithsonian Institution is not subject to NAGPRA because a separate repatriation process was legislated for it in the National Museum of the American Indian Act of 1989. The NMAI funds a consultation visit for each tribe.

10. Additional museums having large Makah and/or Northwest Coast collections which are also being considered for consultation visits include: the Smithsonian's National Museum of Natural History (Washington, D.C.); Carnegie Museum of Natural History (Pittsburgh); Denver Museum of Natural History; Oregon Historical Society at the Oregon History Center (Portland); Phoebe Hearst Museum of Anthropology (Berkeley); Washington State Historical Society (Tacoma); and other local museums in Washington State.

11. This two-meeting structure was not maintained. The first community meeting was held in early February 1999.

12. I was asked as a consultant to draft these guidelines, which I did in February 1999.

13. A contrasting example is provided by a neighboring tribe divided among three reservations. Most objects in collections have only the general cultural affiliation—S'Klallam. Without more exact provenances, the three tribal councils have to jointly decide where repatriated cultural objects should go, if there should be some kind of shared facility, and if so, of what kind. Their NAGPRA coordinator was delaying the repatriation of cultural objects indefinitely until such a decision can be reached.

14. This is a temporary situation, however. I heartily agree with Suzan Harjo, who recently stated (quoted in AAM 2000:74): "As more and more Indian nations assert cultural property rights, we're going to see claims [concerning] cultural patrimony. Right now the focus is human remains and sacred objects and, to a lesser extent, cultural objects. The cultural property that belongs to the group as a whole, there's going to be huge contest for that property."

15. In July 1996, human remains were discovered in an eroded bank on the Columbia River, near Kennewick, Washington. Carbon-dated to 9,510–9,320 years ago, they are thought to be the oldest near-complete skeletal remains ever found in North America. Tribes in this region, including the Colville, Nez Perce, Yakama, Umatilla, and Wanapum, immediately claimed them for reburial under NAGPRA. The Corps of Engineers, in whose jurisdiction the discovery lay, was about to grant the tribes' request when a group of prominent scientists sued, saying the bones are too old to link to modern peoples without more study. In agreement with the tribes, nondestructive analysis of the remains was initiated in 1999 under the auspices of the Department of the Interior (DOI). Based on the results of these studies, the DOI announced in January 2000 that the remains are Native American as defined by NAGPRA. DNA testing was next attempted to determine whether Kennewick Man could be culturally affiliated with any of the contemporary tribes, but no viable DNA was successfully extracted. In late September 2000, the DOI decided that the remains should be returned to the tribes for reburial. However, debate over the ultimate disposition of Kennewick Man is likely to continue in the federal court system, as the scientists intend to reopen their lawsuit, which was put on hold pending the DOI investigation. See the NPS webpage for scientific reports, official correspondence, and DOI press releases: www.cr.nps.gov/aad/kennewick.

16. While the MCRC staff oversees official paperwork, repatriations of human remains are not handled through the facility as part of general NAGPRA duties. The most active member of the Reburial Committee, an MCRC board member, arranges

for transportation and reburial. She has been especially trained and spiritually prepared to handle ancestral remains under such circumstances. Remains have been returned from Olympic National Park, NMAI, and the Smithsonian's National Museum of Natural History.

17. NAGPRA specifically delineates the kinds of evidence that can be used in making claims of cultural affiliation. These include "geographical, kinship, biological, archaeological, anthropological, linguistic, folkloric, oral traditional, historical, or other relevant information or expert opinion." Equal weight is to be given to "scientific" and "traditional" forms of knowledge.

18. Miniatures like this, according to Greig, often had magic significance and were used in the private prayers of whalers preparing for the hunt.

19. Although neither Waterman (1924) nor Ruby and Brown (1996) mention rattles in their discussions of Shaker practice, Waterman does mention that bells were held and used like shaman's rattles. Since my interviewees were very clear that rattles played a central role in Shaker curings in Neah Bay, I would suggest that among Puget Sound tribes rattles were later replaced by bells.

5 / RECONCILING THE SPIRIT WITH THE LETTER OF THE LAW

1. Goldschmidt and Haas, writing in the 1940s, noted this for the Tlingit and Haida (1998:7): "the customs of the Tlingit and Haida with respect to property ownership are more closely akin to those of industrial society than are nearly any other aboriginal people. . . . Yet many of their customs are so foreign to American tradition that this very fact is itself generally overlooked."

2. For example, see NAGPRA *Federal Register* Notices of Intent to Repatriate by the Metropolitan Museum of Art (23 November 1994), the Indian Arts Research Center at the School of American Research (11 July 1997), and the Museum of Indian Arts and Culture/Laboratory of Anthropology, Museum of New Mexico (23 June 1998).

3. For example, see NAGPRA *Federal Register* Notices of Intent to Repatriate by Anchorage Museum of History and Art (30 June 1994 and 9 April 1999), Eiteljorg Museum of American Indians and Western Art (7 June 1996), Seattle Art Museum (14 November 1996), Denver Museum of Natural History (27 November 1996), and the American Museum of Natural History (12 July 1999).

4. Readers should recall that many Northwest Coast groups, including most Nuu-chah-nulth tribes as well as Haida and Kwakwaka'wakw groups, reside in the Canadian province of British Columbia and thus cannot participate in NAGPRA.

5. It is interesting that in addition to the special ceremony, the purchaser of family property customarily pays twice its value (Barton 1969:32). These two con-

ventions accompanying the sale of family property, absent in similar transactions of an individual's goods, serve as an indicator of the greater importance Ifugao assign to lineage property and the corresponding seriousness of its alienation.

6. See *Federal Register* 60, no. 232 (4 December 1995): 62139.

7. This possibility was also being considered by an archaeologist I spoke with who had been contracted by a Puget Sound tribe to assist with NAGPRA implementation.

7 / AFTERWORD

1. For a discussion of the MCRC's role in supporting Makah whaling, see Erikson (1999).

2. The United States government's involvement in the Makah whaling issue stems from its obligation to uphold Indian treaty rights.

3. The Makah Tribe had to provide evidence demonstrating tribal technical knowledge and expertise in using appropriate weaponry, whaling's ceremonial significance to the Tribe, the nutritional value of whale meat, and the extent of community support. The Tribe also outlined in its proposal detailed training schedules for the men who were to participate in the hunt.

4. See Sullivan (2000) for a comprehensive account of the first hunt.

AAM (American Association of Museums). 2000. "NAGPRA at 10: Examining a Decade of the Native American Graves Protection and Repatriation Act." *Museum News*, (September/October): 43–49, 67–75.

Ames, Kenneth M., and Herbert D. G. Maschner. 1999. *Peoples of the Northwest Coast: Their Archaeology and Prehistory*. London: Thames and Hudson.

Arima, Eugene, and John DeWhirst. 1990. "Nootkans of Vancouver Island." In *Handbook of North American Indians: Northwest Coast*, ed. Wayne Suttles, pp. 391–411. Washington, D.C.: Smithsonian Institution.

Arnold, Greig. 1994. *A Gift From the Past*. Produced by Robin Cutler and Dave Warren; directed by Karen Thomas. 58 min. Washington, D.C.: Media Resource Associates, Inc. Videocassette.

Bancroft-Hunt, Norman, and Werner Forman. 1988. *People of the Totem: The Indians of the Pacific Northwest*. Norman: University of Oklahoma Press.

Barton, R. F. 1969. *Ifugao Law*. Berkeley: University of California Press.

Bates, Ann Margaret. 1987. "Affiliation and Differentiation: Intertribal Interactions among the Makah and Ditidaht Indians." Ph.D. diss., Anthropology, Indiana University.

Beaglehole, J. C. 1967. *The Journals of Captain James Cook on His Voyages of Discovery*. Hakluyt Society Extra Series 36. Cambridge: Cambridge University Press.

BIA (Bureau of Indian Affairs). 1993. "Johnson-O'Malley Handbook." Office of Indian Education Programs, United States Department of the Interior.

Bitney, Raymond H. 1931. Report to Commissioner of Indian Affairs, Washington D.C. In *Annual Report of the Secretary of the Interior* (1931). Makah Archives, Makah Cultural and Research Center, Neah Bay, Washington.

———. 1933. Report to Commissioner of Indian Affairs, Washington D.C. In *Annual*

Report of the Secretary of the Interior (1933). Makah Archives, Makah Cultural and Research Center, Neah Bay, Washington.

Blinman, Eric, Elizabeth Colson, and Robert F. Heizer. 1977. "A Makah Epic Journey: Oral History and Documentary Sources." *Pacific Northwest Quarterly* 68(4): 153–63.

Boas, Franz. 1890. "The Nootka." In *Second General Report on the Indians of British Columbia*, pp. 30–52. British Association for the Advancement of Science. Committee . . . on . . . the North-western Tribes of the Dominion of Canada. Report No. 6.

Boit, John. 1919. "Log of the Columbia, 1790–1792." *Proceedings of the Massachusetts Historical Society* 53 (October 1919-June 1920).

Bray, Tamara L., and Thomas W. Killion, eds. 1994. *Reckoning With the Dead: The Larsen Bay Repatriation and the Smithsonian Institution.* Washington, D.C.: Smithsonian Institution Press.

Brown, Michael F. 1998. "Can Culture Be Copyrighted?" *Current Anthropology* 39(2): 193–222.

Broyles, Julie Anne. 1989. "The Politics of Heritage: Native American Museums and the Maintenance of Ethnic Boundaries on the Contemporary Northwest Coast." Ph.D. diss., Anthropology, University of Washington.

Byrne, Christopher S. 1993. "Chilkat Indian Tribe v. Johnson and NAGPRA: Have We Finally Recognized Communal Property Rights in Cultural Objects?" *Journal of Environmental Law and Litigation* 8: 109–31.

Clark, Earl. 1984. "Cape Alava Uncovered." *American West* 21(3): 22–31.

Clifford, James. 1988. *The Predicament of Culture: Twentieth-Century Ethnography, Literature, and Art.* Cambridge: Harvard University Press.

———. 1991. "Four Northwest Coast Museums: Travel Reflections." In *Exhibiting Cultures: The Poetics and Politics of Museum Display*, ed. Ivan Karp and Steven D. Lavine, pp. 212–54. Washington, D.C.: Smithsonian Institution Press.

———. 1997. *Routes: Travel and Translation in the Late Twentieth Century.* Cambridge: Harvard University Press.

Cohlene, Terri. 1990. *Clamshell Boy: A Makah Legend.* Watermill Press.

Cole, Douglas. 1985. *Captured Heritage: The Scramble for Northwest Coast Artifacts.* 2nd ed. Norman: University of Oklahoma Press.

Colson, Elizabeth. 1953. *The Makah Indians: A Study of an Indian Tribe in Modern American Society.* Manchester, U.K.: Manchester University Press.

Coombe, Rosemary J. 1997. "The Properties of Culture and the Possession of Identity: Postcolonial Struggle and the Legal Imagination." In *Borrowed Power: Essays on Cultural Appropriation*, ed. Bruce Ziff and Pratima V. Rao, pp. 74–96. New Brunswick, N.J.: Rutgers University Press.

Croes, Dale R. 1977. "Basketry from the Ozette Village Archaeological Site: A Technological, Functional, and Comparative Study." Ph.D. diss., Anthropology, Washington State University.

Croes, Dale R., and Eric Blinman. 1980. "Hoko River: A 2500 year old fishing camp on the Northwest Coast of North America." *Reports of Investigations*, No. 58. Pullman, Washington: Washington State University, Laboratory of Anthropology.

Dauenhauer, Nora Marks, and Richard Dauenhauer, eds., 1994. *Haa Kusteeyí, Our Culture: Tlingit Life Stories*. Volume 3, Classics of Tlingit Oral Literature. Seattle: University of Washington Press.

Daugherty, Richard D., and R. Kirk. 1976. "Ancient Indian Village Where Time Stood Still." *Smithsonian Magazine* 7(2): 68–75.

Deloria, Vine, Jr. 1977. *Indians of the Pacific Northwest: From the Coming of the White Man to the Present Day*. Garden City, New York: Doubleday and Co.

Densmore, Frances. 1939. "Nootka and Quileute Music." *Bureau of American Ethnology Bulletin* 124. Washington, D.C.

Downey, Roger. 2000. *Riddle of the Bones: Politics, Science, Race, and the Story of Kennewick Man*. New York: Copernicus, Springer-Verlag New York, Inc.

Doyle, R. L. 1868. Report to Henry A. Webster. *Annual Report of the Secretary of the Interior* (1868). Makah Archives, Makah Cultural and Research Center, Neah Bay, Washington.

Drucker, Philip. 1951. "The Northern and Central Nootkan Tribes." *Bureau of American Ethnology Bulletin* 144. Washington, D.C.: Smithsonian Institution.

———. 1963. *Indians of the Northwest Coast*. New York: The Natural History Press.

———. 1965. *Cultures of the North Pacific Coast*. San Francisco: Chandler Publishing Company.

du Boulay, Juliet. 1983. "The Meaning of Dowry: Changing Values in Rural Greece." *Journal of Modern Greek Studies* 1: 243–70.

Efrat, Barbara S., and W. J. Langlois. 1978. "Contemporary Accounts of Nootkan Culture." *Sound Heritage* 7(2): 30–65.

Erikson, Patricia Pierce. 1996. "Encounters in the Nation's Attic: Native American Community Museums/Cultural Centers, The Smithsonian Institution, and the Politics of Knowledge-Making." Ph.D. diss., Anthropology, University of California, Davis.

———. 1999. "A-Whaling We Will Go: Encounters of Knowledge and Memory at the Makah Cultural and Research Center." *Cultural Anthropology* 14(4): 556–83.

Ernst, Alice Henson. 1952. *The Wolf Ritual of the Northwest Coast*. Eugene: University of Oregon Press.

Espinosa y Tello, Joseph. 1930. *A Spanish Voyage to Vancouver and the North-West Coast of America; Being the Narrative of the Voyage Made in the Year 1792 by the*

Schooners Sutil and Mexicana to Explore the Strait of Fuca. Trans. Cecil Jane. London: The Argonaut Press.

Farrer, Claire R. 1994. "Who Owns the Words? An Anthropological Perspective on Public Law 101–601." *Journal of Arts Management, Law, and Society* 23(4): 317–26.

Fleisher, Mark S. 1984. "Acculturation and Narcissism: A Study of Culture Contact Among the Makah Indians." *Anthropos* 79: 409–31.

Friedman, Edward. 1976. "An Archaeological Survey of Makah Territory: A Study in Resource Utilization." Ph.D. diss., Anthropology, Washington State University.

Friedman, Janet P. 1975. "The Prehistoric Uses of Wood at the Ozette Archaeological Site." Ph.D. diss., Anthropology, Washington State University.

Gibbs, George. 1967. *Indian Tribes of Washington Territory*. Fairfield: Ye Galleon Press.

———. 1970. "Tribes of Western Washington and Northwestern Oregon." *Contributions of North American Ethnology* 1(2):161–241.

Gill, Steven J. 1983. "Ethnobotany of the Makah and Ozette People, Olympic Peninsula, Washington (USA)." Ph.D. diss., Anthropology, Washington State University.

Gillis, Alix Jane. 1974. "History of the Neah Bay Agency. Coast Salish and Western Washington Indians III." In *American Indian Ethnohistory: Indians of the Northwest*, pp. 91–115. New York: Garland Publishing.

Gleeson, Paul F. 1980. "Ozette Woodworking Technology." Ph.D. Diss., Anthropology, Washington State University.

Gluckman, Max. 1965. *The Ideas in Barotse Jurisprudence*. New Haven: Yale University Press.

Goldschmidt, Walter R., and Theodore H. Haas. 1998. *Haa Aaní, Our Land: Tlingit and Haida Land Rights and Use*. Seattle: University of Washington Press.

Goodman, Linda J. 1991. "Traditional Music in Makah Life." In *A Time of Gathering: Native Heritage in Washington State*, ed. Robin K. Wright, pp. 223–33. Thomas Burke Memorial Washington State Museum, Monograph 17. Seattle: University of Washington Press.

Goodenough, Ward. 1951. *Property, Kin, and Community on Truk*. 2nd ed. Hamden, Connecticut: Archon Books.

Gunther, Erna. 1942. "Reminiscences of a Whaler's Wife." *Pacific Northwest Quarterly* 33(1): 65–69.

———. 1972. *Indian Life on the Northwest Coast of North America, as Seen by the Early Explorers and Fur Traders During the Last Decades of the Eighteenth Century*. Chicago: University of Chicago Press.

Haswell, Robert. 1880. "A Voyage Round the World on Board the Ship 'Columbia Rediviva' and Sloop 'Washington' in 1787–9." In *History of the Northwest Coast, Volume I* by Hubert Howe Bancroft, pp. 703–35. New York: The Bancroft Company.

Hays, J. H. 1870. Report to Samuel Ross, Superintendent of Indian Affairs, Olympia. In *Annual Report of the Secretary of the Interior* (1870). Makah Archives, Makah Cultural and Research Center, Neah Bay, Washington.

Herzfeld, Michael. 1991. *A Place in History: Social and Monumental Time in a Cretan Town*. Princeton: Princeton University Press.

Hirschon, Renée. 1984. "Introduction: Property, Power, and Gender Relations." In *Women and Property—Women as Property*, ed. Renée Hirschon, pp. 1–22. London: Croom Helm.

Hobsbawm, Eric, and Terence Ranger. 1983. *The Invention of Tradition*. Cambridge, U.K.: Cambridge University Press.

Hooker, M. B. 1975. *Legal Pluralism: An Introduction to Colonial and Neo-colonial Laws*. Oxford: Clarendon Press.

Hoonan, Charles E. 1964. *Neah Bay, Washington: A Brief Historical Sketch*. N.p.: Crown Zellerbach.

Huelsbeck, David R. 1983. "Mammals and Fish in the Subsistence Economy of Ozette." Ph.D. diss., Anthropology, Washington State University.

———. 1987. "Whaling in the Precontact Economy of the Central Northwest Coast." *Arctic Anthropology* 25(1): 1–15.

Hughes, Helen. 1978. *A History of the Development of the MCRC, Neah Bay, WA*. M.A. thesis, Anthropology, University of Washington.

Ides, Hildred. 1994. *A Gift From the Past*. Produced by Robin Cutler and Dave Warren; directed by Karen Thomas. 58 min. Washington, D.C.: Media Resource Associates, Inc. Videocassette.

Irvine, Albert. 1921. "How the Makah Obtained Possession of Cape Flattery." Translated by Luke Markistum. *Indian Notes and Monographs* 6. Museum of the American Indian, Heye Foundation, New York.

Isaac, Barbara. 1995. "An Epimethean View of the Future at the Peabody Museum of Archaeology and Ethnology at Harvard University." *Federal Archaeology* 7(3): 18–22.

Jewitt, John. 1967. *Narrative of the Adventures and Sufferings of John R. Jewitt, Only Survivor of the Crew of the Ship Boston, During a Captivity of Nearly Three Years Among the Savages of Nootka Sound*. Fairfield, Connecticut: Ye Galleon Press.

Jonaitis, Aldona. 1999. *The Yuquot Whalers' Shrine*. Seattle: University of Washington Press.

Jonaitis, Aldona, and Richard Inglis. 1992. "Power, History, and Authenticity: The Mowachaht Whaler's Washing Shrine." *South Atlantic Quarterly* 91(1): 193–213.

Kendall, B. F. 1862. Report to Superintendent of Indian Affairs, Washington Territory. In *Annual Report of the Secretary of the Interior* (1862). Makah Archives, Makah Cultural and Research Center, Neah Bay, Washington.

Kirk, Ruth. 1974. *Hunters of the Whale.* New York: Harcourt, Brace, and Jovanovich.

———. 1980. "The Pompeii of the Northwest." *Historic Preservation* 32(2): 2–9.

———. 1986. *Tradition and Change on the Northwest Coast: The Makah, Nuu-chah-nulth, Southern Kwakiutl and Nuxalk.* Seattle: University of Washington Press.

Kirk, Ruth, and Richard D. Daugherty. 1974. "A 'Pompeii' by the Northwest Sea." *American West* 11(2): 26–37.

de Laguna, Frederica. 1990. "Tlingit." In *Handbook of North American Indians: Northwest Coast,* ed. Wayne Suttles, pp. 203–28. Washington, D.C.: Smithsonian Institution.

Lane, Barbara. 1972. "Makah Economy c. 1855 and the Makah Treaty: A Cultural Analysis." Unpublished manuscript, Makah Archives, Makah Cultural and Research Center, Neah Bay, Washington.

Lowenthal, David. 1985. *The Past is a Foreign Country.* Cambridge, U.K.: Cambridge University Press.

Macpherson, C. B. 1962. *The Political Theory of Possessive Individualism: Hobbes to Locke.* Oxford: Oxford University Press.

Makah Indian Tribe. 1937. Corporate Charter of the Makah Indian Tribe of the Makah Indian Reservation, Washington: Ratified February 27, 1937. Washington, D.C.: Government Printing Office.

Mauger, Jeffrey E. 1978. "Shed Roof Houses at the Ozette Archaeological Site: A Protohistoric Architectural System." Ph.D. diss., Anthropology, Washington State University.

McCarty, Spencer. 1994. *A Gift From the Past.* Produced by Robin Cutler and Dave Warren; directed by Karen Thomas. 58 min. Washington, D.C.: Media Resource Associates, Inc. Videocassette.

McCurdy, James C. 1981. *Indian Days at Neah Bay.* Seattle: Historical Society of Seattle and King County.

McGlinn, John P., Neah Bay, to Commissioner of Indian Affairs, Washington D.C., 1890. Published in 1890 *Annual Report of the Secretary of the Interior.* Makah Archives, Makah Cultural and Research Center, Neah Bay, Washington.

McGlinn, John P. 1891. Report to Commissioner of Indian Affairs, Washington D.C. In *Annual Report of the Secretary of the Interior* (1891). Makah Archives, Makah Cultural and Research Center, Neah Bay, Washington.

McManamon, Francis P., and Larry V. Nordby. 1992. "Implementing the Native American Graves Protection and Repatriation Act." *Arizona State Law Journal* 24(1): 217–52.

MCRC (Makah Cultural and Research Center). 1979a. Museum Exhibit Leaflet. Neah Bay, Washington: Makah Cultural and Research Center.

———. 1979b. Exhibit Text. Neah Bay, Washington: Makah Cultural and Research Center.

———. 1987. *Portrait in Time: Photographs of the Makah by Samuel G. Morse, 1896–1903*. Neah Bay, Washington: Makah Cultural and Research Center.

Meares, John. 1790. *An Introductory Voyage of the Nootka; Capt. Meares from Calcutta, to the North West Coast of America, in the Years 1786, and 1787*. London: Logographic Press.

MEDP (Makah Economic Development Program). 1991. "Report on the Impact of Sports Fishing on the Neah Bay Economy." Internal document, Makah Indian Tribe, Neah Bay, Washington.

———. 1992. "Report on Employment Status of Makah Tribal Members." Internal document, Makah Indian Tribe, Neah Bay, Washington.

———. 1994. "Report on Makah Tribal Treaty Fisheries." Internal document, Makah Indian Tribe, Neah Bay, Washington.

Merrill, William L., Edmund J. Ladd, and T. J. Ferguson. 1993. "The Return of the Ahayu:da: Lessons for Repatriation from Zuni Pueblo and the Smithsonian Institution." *Current Anthropology* 34: 523–67.

Merry, Sally Engle. 1988. "Legal Pluralism." *Law and Society Review* 22(5): 869–96.

Miller, Beatrice D. 1952. "Neah Bay: The Makah in Transition." *Pacific Northwest Quarterly* 43(4): 262–72.

Milroy, R. H. 1872. Report to Commissioner of Indian Affairs, Washington D.C. In *Annual Report of the Secretary of the Interior* (1872). Makah Archives, Makah Cultural and Research Center, Neah Bay, Washington.

Moore, Sally Falk. 1978. *Law as Process: An Anthropological Approach*. London: Routledge and Kegan Paul.

Nason, James D. 1997a. "Beyond Repatriation: Cultural Policy and Practice for the Twenty-first Century." In *Borrowed Power: Essays on Cultural Appropriation*, ed. Bruce Ziff and Pratima V. Rao, pp. 291–312. New Brunswick, N.J.: Rutgers University Press.

———. 1997b. "Native American Intellectual Property Rights: Issues in the Control of Esoteric Knowledge." In *Borrowed Power: Essays on Cultural Appropriation*, ed. Bruce Ziff and Pratima V. Rao, pp. 237–54. New Brunswick, N.J.: Rutgers University Press.

Native American Graves Protection and Repatriation Act. 25 USC § 3001–3013 (1990).

Native American Graves Protection and Repatriation Act: Final Regulations, Code of Federal Regulations, Title 43, Vol. 1, Parts 1–999.

O'Brien, Sharon. 1989. *American Indian Tribal Governments*. Norman: University of Oklahoma Press.

Oxendine, Linda Ellen. 1992. "Tribally Operated Museums: A Reinterpretation of Indigenous Collections." Ph.D. diss., American Studies, University of Minnesota.

Pascua, Maria Parker. 1991. "A Makah Village in 1491: Ozette." *National Geographic* 180(4): 38–53.

Pennoyer, Fred. [n.d.]a. "A Step into the Past: Investigations of Indian Camp Sites." Unpublished manuscript in Makah Archives, Makah Cultural and Research Center, Neah Bay, Washington.

———. [n.d.]b. "Tracing the Use of Indian Relics." Unpublished manuscript in Makah Archives, Makah Cultural and Research Center, Neah Bay, Washington.

———. [n.d.]c. "We Visit the Neah Bay Indians." Unpublished manuscript in Makah Archives, Makah Cultural and Research Center, Neah Bay, Washington.

———. [n.d.]d. Untitled. Unpublished manuscript in Makah Archives, Makah Cultural and Research Center, Neah Bay, Washington.

Pethick, Derek. 1980. *The Nootka Connection: Europe and the Northwest Coast, 1790–1795*. Vancouver, B.C.: Douglas and McIntyre.

Philp, Kenneth R. 1977. *John Collier's Crusade for Indian Reform, 1920–1954*. Tucson: University of Arizona Press.

Pratt, Mary Louis. 1992. *Imperial Eyes: Travel Writing and Transculturation*. London: Routledge.

Renker, Ann M., and Greig W. Arnold. 1988. "Exploring the Role of Education in Cultural Resource Management: The Makah Cultural and Research Center Example." *Human Organization* 47(4): 302–7.

Renker, Ann M., and Erna Gunther. 1990. "Makah." In *Handbook of North American Indians: Northwest Coast*, ed. Wayne Suttles, pp. 422–30. Washington, D.C.: Smithsonian Institution.

Ridington, Robin, and Dennis Hastings. 1997. *Blessing for a Long Time: The Sacred Pole of the Omaha Tribe*. Lincoln: University of Nebraska Press.

Riley, Carroll. 1968. "The Makah Indians: A Study of Political and Economic Organizations." *Ethnohistory* 15: 57–95.

Rosoff, Nancy B. 1998. "Integrating Native Views into Museum Procedures: Hope and Practice at the National Museum of the American Indian." *Museum Anthropology* 22(1): 33–42.

Rouland, Norbert. 1988. *Legal Pluralism*. Stanford: Stanford University Press.

Ruby, Robert H., and John A. Brown. 1986. *A Guide to the Indian Tribes of the Pacific Northwest*. Norman: University of Oklahoma Press.

———. 1996. *John Slocum and the Indian Shaker Church*. Norman: University of Oklahoma Press.

Samuels, Stephen R. 1983. "Spatial Patterns and Cultural Processes in Three Northwest Coast Longhouse Floor Middens From Ozette (Washington)." Ph.D. diss., Anthropology, Washington State University.

Samuels, Stephen R., ed. 1991. "Ozette Archaeological Project Research Reports, volume 1, House Structure and Floor Midden." *Reports of Investigation* 63. Department of Anthropology, Washington State University, Pullman, and National Park Service, Pacific Northwest Regional Office, Seattle.

Sapir, Edward. 1939. *Nootka Texts: Tales and Ethnological Narratives with Grammatical Notes and Lexical Materials.* Philadelphia: Linguistic Society of America.

———. 1978. *Native Accounts of Nootka Ethnography.* New York: ASP Press.

Seeger, Anthony. 1997. "Ethnomusicology and Music Law." In *Borrowed Power: Essays on Cultural Appropriation*, ed. Bruce Ziff and Pratima V. Rao, pp. 52–67. New Brunswick, N.J.: Rutgers University Press.

Sharma, Ursula. 1984. "Dowry in North India: Its Consequences for Women." In *Women and Property—Women as Property*, ed. Renée Hirschon, pp. 62–74. London: Croom Helm.

Stewart, Hilary. 1984. *Cedar: Tree of Life to the Northwest Coast Indians.* Vancouver, B.C.: Douglas and McIntyre.

Stockes, Brian. 2000. "Federal Agencies Seen as Number One Violators of Federal Law." *Indian Country Today* (9 August): 1(A) and 3(A).

Stoffle, Richard W., and Michael J. Evans. 1994. "To Bury the Ancestors: A View of NAGPRA." *Practicing Anthropology* 16(3): 29–32.

Sullivan, Robert. 2000. *A Whale Hunt: Two Years on the Olympic Peninsula With the Makah and Their Canoe.* New York: Scribner.

Swan, James G. Unpublished diaries, 1859–1881. Photocopies in Makah Archives, Makah Cultural and Research Center, Neah Bay, Washington.

———. 1870. *The Indians of Cape Flattery.* Smithsonian Contributions to Knowledge 220. Washington, D.C.: Smithsonian Institution Press.

Taylor, Herbert Cecil. 1974. "Anthropological Investigation of the Makah Indians." *Coast Salish and Western Washington Indians, 3.* New York: Garland Publishing.

Tedlock, Barbara. 1995. "Aesthetics and Politics: Zuni War God Repatriation and Kachina Representation." In *Looking High and Low: Art and Cultural Identity*, ed. Brenda Jo Bright and Liza Bakewell, pp. 151–72. Tucson: University of Arizona Press.

Thomas, David Hurst. 2000. *Skull Wars: Kennewick Man, Archaeology, and the Battle for Native American Identity.* New York: Basic Books.

Trope, Jack F., and Walter R. Echo-Hawk. 1992. "The Native American Graves Protection and Repatriation Act: Background and Legislative History." *Arizona State Law Journal* 24(1): 35–77.

Tweedie, Ann M. 1999. "'Drawing Back Culture': The Makah Tribe's Struggle to Implement the Native American Graves Protection and Repatriation Act." Ph.D. diss., Anthropology, Harvard University.

U.S. House 1990. Committee on Interior and Insular Affairs. *Native American Graves Protection and Repatriation Act.*, 101st Cong., 2d sess. H. Rept. 101–877.

U.S. Senate 1990. Senate Select Committee on Indian Affairs. "Report of the Panel for a National Dialogue on Museum/Native American Relations." 101st Cong., 2d sess. Reprinted as an appendix to *Arizona State Law Journal* 24(1): 499.

Warren, Kay. 1998. *Indigenous Movements and Their Critics: Pan-Maya Activism in Guatemala.* Princeton: Princeton University Press.

Waterman, T. T. 1864. "Geography of the Makah." *Bureau of American Ethnology Manuscript.* Washington, D.C.: Smithsonian Institution Press.

———. 1920. "The Whaling Equipment of the Makah Indians." *University of Washington Publications in Anthropology* 1(1): 1–67.

———. 1924. "The Shake Religion of Puget Sound." In *Smithsonian Institution Annual Report for the year ending June 30, 1922*, pp. 499–507. Washington, D.C.: Smithsonian Institution Press.

Webster, Henry A. 1865. Report to Superintendent of Indian Affairs, Washington Territory. In *Annual Report of the Secretary of the Interior* (1865). Makah Archives, Makah Cultural and Research Center, Neah Bay, Washington.

Wessen, Gary C. 1982. "Shell Middens as Cultural Deposits: A Case Study from Ozette (Washington)." Ph.D. diss., Anthropology, Washington State University.

Willoughby, Charles. 1882. Report to Commissioner of Indian Affairs, Washington, D.C. In *Annual Report of the Secretary of the Interior* (1882). Makah Archives, Makah Cultural and Research Center, Neah Bay, Washington.

Whitner, Robert. 1981. "Makah Commercial Sealing 186?-1897: A Study in Acculturation and Conflict." Manuscript on file in Makah Archives, Makah Cultural and Research Center, Neah Bay, Washington.

Wike, Joyce. 1958. "Social Stratification Among the Nootka." *Ethnohistory* 5: 219–41.

Wray, Jacilee. 1997. *Olympic National Park: Ethnographic Overview and Assessment.* Port Angeles, Washington: Olympic National Park, National Park Service, United States Department of the Interior.

Wright, Robin K. 1991. *A Time of Gathering: Native Heritage in Washington State.* Seattle: University of Washington Press.

INDEX